# cured

## THE TALE OF TWO
## IMAGINARY BOYS

# Lol Tolhurst

# Quercus

First published in Great Britain in 2016 Quercus Editions.
This paperback edition published in 2017 by

Quercus Editions Ltd
Carmelite House
50 Victoria Embankment
London EC4Y 0DZ

An Hachette UK company
Copyright © 2016 Laurence A. Tolhurst

Artwork courtesy of Pearl Thompson, © 2016

All photos are the author's own, except for:
Page 2, image 3: Barbara Rich
Page 4, image 1: Lydie Goubard
Page 4, images 2, 3: Richard Bellia
Page 5, images 1, 2, 3: Richard Bellia
Page 6, images 1, 2: Richard Bellia
Page 6, image 3: Andy Linden
Page 7, images 1, 3: Martin Judd
Page 8, image 3: Jane Granby

A CIP catalogue record for this book is available
from the British Library

PB ISBN 978 1 78429 337 6
EBOOK ISBN 978 1 78429 336 9

10 9 8 7 6 5 4 3 2 1

Typeset by CC Book Production

Printed and bound in Great Britain by Clays Ltd, St Ives Plc

For Cindy and Gray.

# CONTENTS

## PART 3
## (WHAT IT'S LIKE NOW)

# AUTHOR'S NOTE

There's a difference between memoir and autobiography.

They might seem the same but they're very different beasts.

You may have heard that some of the events described here happened otherwise or went down a different way. Well, this is my version – how I remember things, my truth.

The conversations are as close to verbatim as I could manage and honestly presented. A name or two has been changed to protect the innocent.

Mostly this is a record of the things that have kept me awake at 4 a.m., the precious flowers of the past blooming in the dark corners of memory. I have tried my best to capture whatever that light shone on. I hope it illuminates events for you as much as it has for me.

Love, Lol
Los Angeles, California
February 2016

'Wisdom is knowing I am nothing, Love is knowing I am everything, and between the two my life moves.'

– Nisargadatta Maharaj

# PART 1
# (WHAT IT WAS LIKE)

# Prologue:

# THE FIRST PUNKS IN CRAWLEY

Most people don't associate The Cure with punk, but Robert and I were the very first punks in Crawley.

Crawley is just twenty miles south of London but it might as well be another planet. It is a town with no centre and no end, just endless rows of suburban bleakness that blurs into the dark, dank countryside. Crawley is a place where it's always raining and a slate grey sky hangs over everything. It is where The Cure was born and always struggled to leave, the place we were never quite able to put behind us.

Crawley was one of the handful of 'new towns' that popped up around London after the Second World War. A suburban swamp built around shops, schools and factories: the Holy Trinity of English post-war 'progress.' They were towns with no future and no hope. The late 1970s was a terrible time to grow up in England. It was a troubled era marked by a flagging economy, rampant inflation, political unrest, and no reason to think it was going to get better anytime soon. There were no jobs and everyone was on the dole. Even electricity was being rationed. While other places around the world were thriving, we were stuck in the shadow of austerity.

The boredom in our little town was palpable. It seemed like most of the people we knew were treading water and content to do so. As bad as things were, serious changes were rumbling through the wires. We could hear the call ringing out from London.

It was a time of protest and discontent that gave birth to punk music, punk fashion, punk rebellion. Robert and I swapped precious details about the latest punk songs we'd heard on John Peel's radio show, or seen in the record shop in Horley where we hung out on Saturday afternoons. We didn't have to go to London to see punk gigs. Punk came to us.

Robert and I were both students at Crawley Technical College, whose dull, unimaginative campus could have been dreamed up by Joseph Stalin. It was a place where you could study English literature or learn how to mend cars. A mix of the high and the low. A vocational school putting on airs. I was learning to be a chemist: a blend of personal and professional interests. Robert studied literature, of course.

Many big London bands came to Crawley and played in the strangely named 'leisure centre' or at our little school. In the years 1977–78 that meant bands like The Clash, The Jam and The Stranglers. Robert and I went to every gig and we paid very close attention not only to the way these bands sounded, but to the way they looked as well. We were drawn to the spectacle – a lot of people were – but what made the biggest impression on us was their attitude, and we were quick to copy it.

It didn't take much to stand out in Crawley in those days. Conformity was the rule. To be different was to declare oneself as exceptional and that was an affront to English manners. To the Neanderthal-like kids in Sussex, anything they couldn't understand was a perversion of normality. To them we were 'poofs.'

We didn't care. We didn't believe in stereotypes. When I was told that an earring in my right ear was the equivalent of declaring to the world that I was gay, which I wasn't, I promptly had it pierced twice. The time for being polite was over. We were confrontational because we had to be.

On 3 February 1977, I went out to celebrate my eighteenth birthday with my three best friends – Robert, Michael Dempsey and Porl Thompson, all fledgling musicians. We had started to morph from Malice, the band we'd formed in secondary school, to Easy Cure, a name that I came up with and was quite proud of, to simply The Cure. We were still finding our way musically, figuring out what we liked and throwing out the rest.

For my birthday, I went all out in putting together my outfit for the evening. I wore a hand-dyed orange jacket with 'NO CHANGE' stencilled on the back. I'd made buttons from photos cut out of porno magazines – just the performers' ecstatic heads, mind you, none of the offending body parts. Very subversive. I had on a pair of straight-leg trousers and winkle-picker shoes from Brighton. For good measure, I stuck safety pins here and there to complete the outfit.

Robert's get-up was more subdued. He wore brothel creepers and the dark full-length raincoat that he wore everywhere in those days. The only time he took it off was to put on the leather jacket that each member of our band took turns wearing.

Our destination that night was the Rocket, the hangout for Crawley's disaffected locals. These consisted of three groups: hippie burnouts stuck in the 1960s, working-class skinheads and us. We were like a secret society, neither with one faction nor another. We had our own passwords, our own lore. We were our own cult and our bond was a deep-seated longing for something, anything other than *this*.

Although Robert and I were close to the same age, we had been drinking in the Rocket for a year, which wasn't unusual in 1970s England. Back then most people over sixteen could get served alcohol in the pubs, a government ploy to sedate the natives in that cold, grey, miserable climate. Easier to control if they're all drunk, you see.

Like most English pubs back then the Rocket was an unappealing mix of browns and beiges with a multicoloured carpet designed to hide the cigarette burns and vomit stains. Fred, the Rocket's usually taciturn landlord, took note of the large number of drinks being ordered and wanted to know why we were celebrating.

'My birthday,' I told him. Fred wisely didn't ask which birthday that might be. See no evil, hear no evil. Less than a year later, Fred would offer us our first real gig as a band that would eventually take us away from Crawley and on to bigger and better stages. But we couldn't see so far into the future. On this particular evening we were content to drink and enjoy one another's company. We were young, exuberant, and didn't give a toss what others thought about us.

That attitude, as well as our flamboyant dress, attracted the attention of the skinheads in the bar. They were sullen, working-class kids who aped the diatribes they heard at home from their uneducated parents. They made their intolerance known by joining extreme right-wing groups like the National Front. Where we could hear the revolution coming, these yobs tried to drown out the sound with bigotry, prejudice and hate. Just as we could feel the anarchistic pull of punk, they tried to hold on to their old fears masquerading as values. We all got very, very drunk.

The pub called last orders at 10.30 p.m. It was thirty years after the war and pubs in England were still obliged to close early, a practice that had been devised to ensure that its citizens would not be too drunk to make it to the factory the next day, manufacturing guns and bombs for the war effort. In the car park at the back of the pub, Robert suggested we go to his house and continue to celebrate with some of his father's lethal home brew. It was a Thursday night and I didn't have any lectures the next day. I told Robert I was game and we decided to catch a train to his house. As we crossed the old, wooden footbridge to the station, I heard the words behind us:

'Bloody poofs!'

Turning slightly, we caught sight of three large skinheads in National Front T-shirts just thirty yards behind us and closing fast.

This was nothing new. For as long as I've known Robert people have been out to get him. On stage, in the pubs, or on the street, he's always been a target. I've never seen Robert instigate a fight, yet there's something about him that provokes people.

On one hand, Robert is the dark, brooding, creative, melancholic sort. It's obvious from the way he carries himself that his head is somewhere in the clouds. It's always been part of his persona: the tortured artist, the all-seeing poet, the messenger with news from the other side. He's also quite normal, someone who enjoys sitting down with a pint and watching football. People sense this dichotomy about him and it doesn't add up. He's part of the world but also not part of it. Here and not here. Matter and anti-matter. People don't like that. They want you to be one thing or another. If you don't fit into a neat little box, they get upset. Pretty soon they're demanding to know, 'Who do you bloody well think you are?' and the fists start flying. If I've seen it once, I've seen it a hundred times.

There was a time when I had a reputation as a hard man. I had to be because Robert was always getting into fights. I can't tell you how many times a pint glass would come flying out of the audience and hit one of us. We'd set down our instruments and leap into the crowd to settle the matter.

This probably clashes with many people's idea of The Cure, but that's how it was. We had to fight to be heard, fight for our place on the stage, fight to be taken seriously. We weren't loud rock or fast punk. We were something else, something new, and people didn't know what to make of us. If we hadn't stood up for ourselves in those early days, we wouldn't have been able to weather the storms to come. Robert was in the eye of most of them.

On this particular night, however, it isn't fair to blame Robert. The way I was dressed with my bright orange jacket was like a neon sign that read 'Beat me', and those National Front thugs with their shaved heads and Doctor Martens boots were all too happy to oblige.

I stole a glance at Robert to see what he wanted to do but he'd already stopped and turned to face the skinheads. That's when I noticed the glass in his hand. A thick, proper English pint pot with real heft and weight. He'd seen this coming. In a flash, he hurled it across the bridge. I could see its arc flashing past me in the cloudy moonlight before the glass smashed against the iron-work and exploded in a million shattered stars at the skinheads' feet. They were as stunned by this turn of events as I was, but their shock and surprise quickly turned to anger.

'You wankers!' they shouted. 'We'll fackin' kill you!'

Discretion being the better part of valour, we legged it across the bridge and down the street, past the station doors and con-tinued to our old primary school where we'd been classmates, eerily lit up on this cold February night. There would be no train for us. We were on our own. Once we put those fat, fascist fuckers behind us, we collapsed on the grass at the edge of a park, laughing uncontrollably.

I was eighteen years old. We were making our own rules. It felt like my life was about to begin.

# 1

# THE DAY THE MUSIC DIED

How did it all begin? I mean *really* begin?

I came into this world the day the music died. I was born on 3 February 1959, the day that Buddy Holly's plane crashed in a tangled metal heap in a cold, snowy field in South Dakota. The music had died in Horley, the town where I was born, long before that. Horley is a forgotten outpost in the urban hinterland of south London that has struggled for its identity against the capital to the north and the burgeoning new town of Crawley to the immediate south, schizophrenically being neither town nor country.

My early years were filled with that bland greyness so drearily familiar to anyone who has had the misfortune to grow up in England in the 1960s and 70s. Iron-grey skies and unrelenting rain were the backdrops to the post-war austerity that had infiltrated the British psyche. My daily routine as a small boy revolved around three things: family, school and church. Especially church.

My mother, a devout Catholic convert, had recently made the acquaintance of a new Catholic family who had just moved to our town. In fact they lived a couple of doors down from my grandmother on Vicarage Lane. The Smiths hailed from the even grimmer and greyer north of England and had several children. Richard and Margaret were around the same age as my brothers, but their youngest son, Robert, was the same age as me.

The only Catholic primary school in our region was in Crawley, five miles to the south. In the late 1950s, hastily built housing estates were thrown together in small forgotten villages on the edge of the capital. They were the government's attempt to relocate families from London's bombed-out city centre after the Second World War. They were drab and utilitarian and were only slightly less dreary than the tower blocks of Eastern Europe. An eccentric combination of estate housing with clumps of genteel country living. Very proper and very English.

On a damp September morning in 1964 my mother threw Robert Smith and me together. A bus had been arranged to take children from the outlying areas to St Francis of Assisi School in Crawley. On our first day of school, Robert and I stood at the designated stop at Hevers Avenue with our mothers, and that's when we met for the very first time. We were five years old.

Up until then my world was microscopically small and insular. I was a late baby, born when my parents were both in their forties. They should have been taking it easy, not raising a baby, especially since they had already raised three other children who had left home. Strangely, my parents didn't have any pictures of my siblings in the house. The only indication that other children had once lived there was a cupboard in the kitchen in which my mother kept an endless supply of well-worn shoes, which I had to wear as I grew into them.

I think my older siblings left the house to get away from our father. William George Edward Tolhurst joined the navy at a young age and found himself on the Yangtze River in China as an engineer on a British naval gunboat when he was only eighteen years old. My father arrived around the time of the Rape of Nanking and saw severed heads and other body parts floating down the river. By all accounts, he returned from the Second World War a changed man. He did the only logically English thing he could do to block out the horrid memories: he drank. A lot. He wasn't an easy person to be around. He was either a virtual recluse who barely spoke to me, or an angry alcoholic who was prone to loud bouts of shouting.

Although my father was a difficult man to know or understand, much less love, he passed down the musical genes in the family. When he was in his cups he would pound out drunken sea shanties on the upright piano in our living room in a way that would make Tom Waits jealous. He was a gruff man who was full of dark secrets and wild emotions that he kept under lock and key, but when he played the piano, a little bit of light from that locked room slipped underneath the door. I like to think that light is in me, too.

My father and I didn't have any common ground. A knack for music was his only gift to me. He didn't know me and I didn't want to be around him. We were bound by blood and obligation, but I had no way of breaking through to him, and he was too caught up in his own silent world.

It wasn't just that England in the 1970s was austere; my whole life was bleak, especially around my dad.

Something in the Second World War had beaten any ambition

out of my father. I remember finding his naval journal in the back of a dark cupboard one rainy afternoon when I was home sick from school. I read it avidly, as it was full of exciting things he had seen and places he had been. This clashed tremendously with the version of the man I knew as my father. To be honest, I hardly felt I had a father at all.

He seldom shared anything with us except his small house and bad moods. He never took us anywhere. In fact, I can only ever recall one family holiday.

I was about eight or nine, I think. We were staying in a small wooden hut on a forgotten beach on Hayling Island on the south coast of England. I have a gossamer-thin remembrance, of tar-paper mixed with the acrid smell of a chemical toilet. It was like a smuggler's hideaway on the shore. Looking at the walls, you would see small translucent cracks between the boards, hastily papered over with felt.

My mother was there, seemingly more or less worn out, as was my Aunty Molly in her flowery summery dress, and my grandmother, known as 'Nanny' to me.

This hardly ever happened. My relatives were never in the same room together if they could help it. Weddings or funerals were about it. No elaborate family get-togethers for the Tolhursts. They could stand to be together on a one-to-one basis. Only then could they be civil to each other. We were not like other families. I remember, as I got older and started to hang out more at my friends' houses, being baffled by the levity and love between the parents to their children, and not just on special occasions but during the course of daily life.

The Smiths were like that. Whenever I went to their house

Robert's father, Alex, always seemed to be joking and laughing. To be sure, there were some more intense moments like the ones I was used to. I recall Robert getting a clip around the ear from Smith Senior for swearing in his mother's presence, but these occurrences were few and far between, not a daily tribulation like in my house.

The main difference, of course, was my dad. Father was never included in family life because his temperament meant he would probably upset someone or something. Depending which way the drink had sent his psyche that day, he could be either garrulous or grotesque. This was something most of the family wanted to avoid, so they instinctively limited their contact with 'Sailor Bill' (as his drinking buddies at the Chequers pub knew him).

The hut was painted eggshell white and it blended into near invisibility with the wash of grey-blue sky that passed for summer in England. The white noise of the sea and shingle being perpetually sucked up and down along the coast was pierced only by the occasional shriek of a seagull.

The striking thing to me, when I recall this scenario now, is that it's like a dream of a favourite painting or photo. The scenery is there but somehow the people are missing from the image, like someone stole them from the foreground and only the background remains. I cannot recall any of my brothers or older siblings; to be sure, my little baby sister was there, but she's an almost ghostly shadow of something not real. I hear in my mind the sounds of my mother, my aunt, and my grandmother talking. Family stuff mostly, but occasionally I felt the unmistakable sympathy of a mother's love enter the conversation.

My mother Daphne, unbeknownst to me, was working up to full-blown lung cancer, but in those days her slightly breathless whisper of a voice was the one solace in my young life.

'Laurence, don't go far, and please mind the tar on the beach. Don't get it on your nice new summer clothes now!'

'Okay, Mum! Don't worry, I'll be really, really careful,' I said with that mixture of childish irritation and loving awe I reserved for mother.

As I got older she would become more three-dimensional, but during that summer at Hayling Island my love was unequivocal.

I don't recall any laughter during our holiday, just the forms of the women moving about the cramped hut. I don't remember where I slept or how it looked through the windows. I barely remember my father being there at all.

If he was, which I doubt, he probably didn't talk to me much. I can't recall a single walk along the sand with him or even a kick-about game of football on the beach. No loving connections between father and son to bond over.

I don't remember any other children playing on the windswept shore, just me scuffing along the pebbled beach in my brown summer sandals with the white crepe soles, short white socks, navy-blue cotton shorts, and a blue and white striped flannel T-shirt.

With my ever-present magnifying glass in hand, a present for being in my cousin's wedding party, I looked at anything I found on the beach, trying to discern what was under the surface of it all. Even in this empty world, I still had a child's natural curiosity. I was excited about things in the way only a small boy can be. I'm sure I found a piece of driftwood or two and imagined they were swords or telescopes that could be used to scout and defend the seashore. After clearing out the old beer bottles, rusted tin cans, and clothes left behind by tramps, I took over the old decaying Second World War hexagonal pillbox guard post by the golf course as a fort. From there I'd keep watch over the shore and look out across the beach to the grey sea and try to figure out what was missing.

Walking along the beach, grains of sand would sting my face as the wind came up off Selsey Bill or Portsea Island to the other side. I'm sure I imagined that there were pirate treasures to be had if only I had a map – an adventure I might share with another boy if he had been there – but these things never appeared. No canvas piece torn from a sail with an 'x' to mark the spot. No escapade to be had. I yearned for excitement, but as our holiday drew to a close, I realized that if it was an adventure I was after, I would have to seek it out on my own.

Almost by design then, I was a lonely boy.

When I was seven or eight, Robert's family moved to Crawley, where his father, Alex, had taken a job as head of Upjohn Pharmaceutical. That meant I now took the bus from Horley to Crawley alone. I didn't really know the local kids in Horley and seldom saw my friends from Crawley outside of school. Robert and I did not have much contact besides the occasional birthday party. The long days of school holidays were the worst. My mother brought books into the house, and they were my closest companions until I was old enough to venture to the local library on my own.

In the summer of 1970, I obtained the keys to unlock the prison of my perpetual boredom. The library allowed members to check out books *and* records. Soon I was taking home as many as nine LPs a week. I spent the summer listening to blues, folk music, anything I could get my hands on. My curiosity had been sparked, and when I exhausted the library's collection I went on forays to Horley's only shopping street, where, for some bizarre reason, the local tobacconist kept a bargain bin of records for ten shillings apiece.

The Fugs' *It Crawled into My Hand, Honest* was my first selection. Songs with titles like 'Johnny Pissoff Meets the Red Angel' and 'We're Both Dead Now, Alice' spoke to my preadolescent imagination. I hurried home, clutching the record in its brown paper bag like some kind of contraband. I loved The Fugs and the anarchic spirit of those proto-punk songs inspired me to seek out more American artists, like Steppenwolf and The Jimi Hendrix Experience. Nearly fifty years later, I can still remember every lyric on every track on *Axis: Bold as Love*.

That autumn I went to a new school, an experimental Catholic middle school called Notre Dame that had been started by a social reformer named Lord Longford. The kids from all the Catholic primary schools in the area ended up at Notre Dame and I struck up a friendship with a boy named Michael Dempsey. By now my hair was nearly as long as that of my rock and roll heroes, and Michael figured anyone with hair as long as mine must be okay. My freak flag was flying and we connected over our love of music.

Notre Dame was everything St Francis was not: liberal and forward thinking. The pupils were given more freedom, and lessons were presented in a radically different manner. Subjects were bundled together as 'integrated studies', and instead of teachers lecturing in front of a blackboard, we worked together in groups on various projects. We were given an extraordinary amount of freedom, and students who showed extra promise were permitted to work on their own. I usually found myself in the library with Michael and Robert. It's true: we were all excellent students.

One day Robert cornered me in the library and whispered, 'You like Jimi Hendrix?'

'Hendrix? I love Jimi Hendrix! I've got a huge poster of him on my wall!' I told him that I was also a member of his UK fan club.

Robert's eyes sparkled with recognition. 'Me too!'

'You know, I bet nobody else in the school has even heard of him!' I said.

'Well, my older brother has some Hendrix stuff. *Are You Experienced?* is bloody great, actually!' Robert enthused.

'Yeah? I bought *Axis: Bold as Love* for a pound in Radio Rentals!' and with that our bond was reignited.

During lunch, we were allowed to use the art room to play records on the old turntable there and I became the unofficial DJ. I played LPs that people brought to school, but of course I had my favourites. My old friend Robert and new pal Michael were usually there to listen and offer their choices for me to play. Pretty soon it transpired that not only did Robert and Michael listen to cool music, they were trying to learn how to play it, too. Once a week they were allowed to go into the music room and use the instruments. They also had a stereo system, and Robert would plug in his electric guitar and play through the speakers.

'Do you play anything, Lol?' said Robert.

'Yes,' I lied. 'The drums?'

'So maybe you want to join us the next time Michael and I get to use the music room?' Robert asked. 'I think they have a drum kit there. Pretty certain I saw it in the back of a cupboard last time we were there.'

'Um, okay, all right. I'll be there!'

I rushed to the library that day and checked out Buddy Rich's book of snare drum rudiments. Back at home in my bedroom I pulled out the drumsticks my elder brother had left me before emigrating to Australia. I read the book and banged away on my pillow. The next day we returned to the music room together, where I dug out the old drum kit they had at the school. It was a start.

When people ask me when The Cure began, I often point to that day in 1972 at Notre Dame when Robert, Michael and I jammed for the first time – the very same line-up that recorded our first single, 'Killing an Arab'. In fact, the cymbal I used on that song was stolen from the old school kit!

But in my mind The Cure began much earlier than that, on a gloomy rainy day in 1964 with the mists swirling all around. It began the moment the school bus pulled up to the stop at the top of Hevers Avenue and the doors swung open with a hiss. Neither Robert nor I wanted to get on that bus. We didn't want to leave our mums and go to a strange school in another town where we wouldn't know a soul. I probably would have started crying if Robert hadn't been there. I can hear my mother's voice even now, gently urging me along. 'Hold Robert's hand now and look after each other.'

Robert took me by the hand and led me onto the bus. It was the first of many journeys together. If only in my imagination, we are still those boys.

## 2

# THIRTEEN

I turned thirteen the winter of 1972. Who knows anything at thirteen? I certainly didn't. All I was aware of was my burgeoning hormones and a lack of any decent outlet for them. I spent long afternoons and evenings in my bedroom, which I had painted bright orange with white doors and lit with a single red light bulb – a sort of psychedelic den, or what I imagined one would look like. Listening to my records was the pinnacle of each day. I minutely analyzed every record cover, reading all the notes inside the sleeve and looking for clues I could use to get out of this world, escape my humdrum existence.

Robert's older brother Richard, or 'The Guru' as he became known to us because of his counterculture appearance, had an extensive record collection and knowledge of music. He grew up in the 1960s and went to school with my older brother John, so we knew each other fairly well. One spring Notre Dame asked volunteers to help dig the new swimming pool they wanted to install. Apparently the Catholics had no problem with child labour. My brother Roger picked me up in his VW Beetle and dropped me off for a day of digging at the large hole that was appearing in the school grounds. Being older and more responsible, The Guru had been assigned to supervise the unfortunate diggers. In rain and mud we toiled. During our digging we would chat, and I mined The Guru's extensive knowledge of music for some hints as to what I should buy to get my collection started.

'Two albums you should get,' he said, '*The Age of Atlantic* and *Nice Enough to Eat*. They're both samplers, one on the Atlantic label and one on Island Records.'

'Samplers?' I asked.

'Yes, *Nice Enough to Eat* has a sampling of songs from English acts for half the price of a normal album. There are tracks by Nick Drake and King Crimson, amongst others. They're pretty good, you know.'

'Oh,' I said, completely not knowing.

The Guru rambled on that '*The Age of Atlantic* is a similarly budget-priced sampler album with mostly American underground acts such as MC5 and Vanilla Fudge. So for a couple of pounds, Lol, you can pretty much hear all the good music from both sides of the pond.' The Guru considered this for a moment while stroking his beard.

'Yeah, just two pounds for a lot of good music,' he said, staring into the middle distance. 'Some good shit.'

One thing for sure, The Guru did indeed know his shit. I ordered them both from Radio Rentals the very next week.

In order to fund my expanding record collection I had a part-time job at the local newsagent's delivering newspapers on my old blue and red bicycle. I did this come rain or shine. However, the crème de la crème of jobs was marking up of the papers at the newsagent's. It meant I could stay dry in the warm shop and had access to the magazines and other papers, specifically the music papers, of which there were three back then: *New Musical Express*, *Sounds*, and *Melody Maker*.

I avidly read them all while marking the top pages with an address on the piles of newspapers, ready to be picked up by the boys and girls coming each morning to do their rounds. These newspapers gave me a view into a different world, one that I could barely imagine. After reading the music weeklies, I shared stories with my friends, specifically Michael and Robert. They seemed the most interested in music and musicians and what we took to be their glamorous world. They shared my fascination with the goings-on in this strange other existence that seemed so remote from us at the time. Remember that the predominant music scene of the early seventies was either disco or horribly overblown progressive rock. Neither genre resonated with us, three white boys from the suburban edge of south London.

In any era there are always artists who make their presence felt by not being part of the mainstream, and those were specifically the types of musicians we were drawn to. Among them was David Bowie who, in the summer of 1972, made such an impression on my teen self that he became an influence on my whole psyche. I'm pretty certain he had the same effect on Robert.

Bowie's performance of 'Starman' on BBC TV's *Top of the Pops* that July changed everything for me. It was as if suddenly a being from another world had landed at the television centre. Bowie and his band, The Spiders from Mars, just looked and sounded so different from the other acts we saw. His whole demeanour shouted that here was someone we could trust to show us the way to a different world than the dull one we normally inhabited.

He had an androgynous sexuality and strangeness that immediately entranced me. If you look now, all these years later, at the clip of that performance, it's amazing at just how completely different from the everyday he was.

Looking behind the stage of *TOTP* (as it was known to all and sundry), you can catch a glimpse of an audience member in the standard teen get-up for the time: a jumper with no arms and a teardrop collar shirt. You realize immediately that this man on stage was doing something completely different.

I remember sitting on my couch at home with my mother, Daphne, watching this spectacle unfold, and at the point where Bowie sang the line 'I had to phone someone so I picked on you' he pointed directly at the camera and I knew he was singing that line to me and everyone like me. It was a call to arms that put me on the path that I would soon follow.

I went to school the next day and exploded with excitement to my friends about it.

'Did you see him?'

'Who?'

'Bowie on *Top of The Pops*, of course.'

'Yeah,' said Robert, 'he was *bad*!'

Way, way before Michael Jackson misappropriated the phrase, we had taken to calling anything that was really, really, great, bad. It just fit in with our view of the world, looking through the other end of the telescope at everything.

That summer I tried to understand as much as I could about how things worked in this strange new world. I spent a great deal

of time reading about all kinds of music people, and I was baffled
by some references. After all, sex, drugs and rock and roll were
hardly on my radar yet. Especially drugs and alcohol, of which I
had no personal experience.

That was about to change.

'Lol, you want to come DJ the party?'

My brother Roger was asking if I would bring my record collection, which by now was much bigger than his, to the party he
was throwing for my other brother, John, who was emigrating
to Australia.

'Yeah, absolutely, I'd love to play my records! I can play them
louder than Mum lets me, right?' I asked.

'Of course! Turn up the volume, brother!' Roger was getting
a kick out of seeing his little brother so excited.

It was the first adult party I had ever been invited to and I
was to go unchaperoned by my mother. However, I had no real
experience with adults and what they liked to do at parties. It
wasn't that long ago that the parties I attended had jelly and ice
cream, like the one I recall on Robert's seventh birthday at his
new family house in Crawley.

My carefree young life was changing and I was about to be
introduced to the real world. Perhaps a little too early, but it was
coming at me like a freight train, and there was no avoiding the
circumstances that were about to unfold.

I had always viewed drinking alcohol as something my father
did which made him either very happy or inhospitable. It didn't
really seem that appealing to me. However, when my mother would
send me down to the Chequers to collect my father, I caught a

whiff of a certain bonhomie and joyous good time that seemed to lie inside the old oak doors of the pub. Even the normally dour townsfolk seemed happier inside the Chequers.

So, despite my misgivings, it seemed like it might be worth investigating one day. I, of course, had no idea that it would be at my brother's going-away party that I would be introduced to the demon alcohol.

My brother Roger arrived in the late afternoon to take me to his house in Crawley and set up my stuff for the evening's festivities. I had brought my treasured purple satin shirt to wear, the one I had bought at Whitworth's, the small clothing shop at the top of my street. I loved going into Mr Whitworth's: I never knew what sartorial secret he might impart to me.

'Men with short legs should wear wide Oxford trousers to look more impressive,' was one gem I never forgot.

The small bell attached to the door rang as I walked into the musty little clothing shop.

'Ah, young Mr Tolhurst, what are you seeking today?'

'I saw that purple shirt in the window?' I said.

The real reason I went in was to seek out the one or two trendsetting items that stood out in his otherwise drab menswear section. He usually priced these to sell to a teenager with very limited income; in other words, yours truly.

'Ah yes, the one with the *modern* collar.' Mr Whitworth looked like it hurt his lips to say the word.

'Yes, that's it. The one with the teardrop collar.'

He pulled it out of the window display and handed it to me.

It had a £5 price tag, much more than I could afford. He saw my glum expression as I noticed the price.

'How much do you have, Mr Tolhurst?'

'A pound?' I said hopefully.

Mr Whitworth looked out over the top of his glasses and tugged on the tape measure he always carried around his neck.

'All right, £1 it is, but do *not* tell anyone else that I gave you such a bargain, otherwise they'll all want one. Do I have your word?'

'Yes, of course! Thank you, Mr Whitworth!'

I walked back to our house clutching the shirt, thankful for the old tailor's generosity.

So it was that at the age of thirteen, and living in a small town on the edge of the bustling metropolis, I was already something of a fashion trendsetter. For the party, I matched the purple satin shirt with a pair of Lybro Sea Dogs, or blue jeans by a plainer name.

I set up my turntable in the corner and started to assemble a rough playlist for the night. By this time, some of my brother's friends had arrived for his farewell party. Then I saw them out of the corner of my eye: the bottles of wine in my brother's kitchen. It never occurred to me that anybody drank at home. I viewed drinking as an activity exclusively to be done at the pub at night. My life until then had revolved around a very few outside activities, mostly church and school. This was a totally new experience for me, and as such quite exhilarating.

Roger rounded the door, 'Like a drink, Lol?'

I had never thought that I would partake in this ritual. That's how naive I was.

'Sure,' I answered, my voice just a little stronger than the pubescent croak which had appeared at the same time hair began growing in strange, unaccustomed places.

I grasped the proffered glass of red liquid, taking what I supposed looked like a confident gulp. My first impression was how much it stung my throat on contact, but it was the second sensation that really caught my attention, so much so that I can instantly recall it, forty-three years later. It was a subtle but definite feeling at the same time, mysterious and malevolent in equal measure. Bad with goodness mixed in. It felt bloody wonderful!

Although I have a better understanding of it now, this sensation and instantaneous craving is still baffling to me.

I walked into the next room; it was still early so it was empty. I marvelled at just how free and great I felt! Like a poet, I could easily summon up the words that my normally tongue-tied teenage self couldn't. I had never experienced such a feeling before. The hues and colours in the room seemed changed but still familiar, perhaps just a little more vibrant and beautiful, or maybe I just imagined this. It didn't seem to matter at that moment, to be perfectly honest. I had a strong sense that everything was okay, and suddenly the burden of just *being me* seemed to evaporate. It was as if time, space and normality had been shifted by a few degrees to the left, and given an extra frisson of excitement for good measure.

The addition of this new substance to my system also made music more exciting to me. I seemed to understand it more, and appreciate just what it was these musicians were trying to convey with sounds and rhythms.

I had a vague inkling that this was maybe what people wanted from being 'stoned' or 'loaded', but I had never felt it before so I hadn't really had anything to base my assumptions on. Now I did.

The year before, Michael and I had been to our first concert proper with his sister and her boyfriend. They took us to Hyde Park to see a free gig. At one point we were standing by a soft drink vendor at the edge of the park when a very dishevelled young woman came by and lurched jerkily towards us.

'Have you got the time?' she said.

'About a quarter to three,' I replied, glancing at my watch. She shook her head furiously.

'No. Have you got the time, man? I mean, really have you got the time?'

I looked uncomprehendingly at Michael. We were just twelve years old, after all, and extremely baffled by this.

The Greek drink vendor said, 'She's stoned, boys,' by way of explanation, as he could see our confused faces. That was the only clue I had so far.

Was this that? Was I stoned? Never mind. The fact it felt good was all I knew or needed to know.

I sought out my eldest brother and asked if I could have some more. I figured that if one was good, more would be better. He filled my glass and I wandered back to my records and turntables. Now the party was in full swing, with people talking and starting to dance.

Soon my brother John appeared at my side. 'Fancy a breath of fresh air, Lol?'

I said I did, and we made our way out through the crowd into the night air. It was cold and chilly as we walked briskly down the dark street. 'I thought I would get you a present before I left for Australia. Anything you would like?' he asked.

I thought hard as the night air's crisp slap had sobered me up a little and my thoughts became a little less grandiose.

'I think I'd like something to do with drums,' I said. I was listening to songs with greater clarity now and I had started to discern the separate elements. I could make out the bass, guitar and vocals, but what intrigued me the most (besides the words) was the rhythmic thump of the drums. It seemed to me that this was what created the dynamic impulse in the songs, lending them excitement and power. It made me want to move, to dance, to be joyous! I thought I could do something with that. It felt like something was drawing me to the drums and the power they contained. Even then I found myself split between the profane and the sacred. I loved the physicality of drums but I also found words and what they could express, with a deft couplet or turn of phrase, beguiling and attractive. I knew I wanted to combine both sides somehow. Drums looked hard to play, but with my new friend alcohol I felt I should be able to do anything.

Right at that moment the ground fell away from my feet, or so it seemed, as I tumbled feet first into a large trench dug in the road and lit by a very dim warning light.

'Ah, shit!' I shouted as I fell into a pool of soft mud at the bottom. Then I saw John's face peering over the side of the trench to look at me. He laughed a little, then remembered to be concerned at his now drunk little brother.

'Here, give me your hand,' he said more solemnly, and proffered his right hand for me to hold on to and use to haul myself out of the soggy bottom of the trench.

'Didn't see that,' I said. It felt like my mouth was full of cotton wool. When I tried another phrase, it came out just as mangled as the first. This was too much for John; he could barely contain his mirth.

'You're drunk, Lol!'

We walked back towards my other brother's house. I was peering intently at the ground trying not to attract any other large holes towards my clumsy feet, while trying to stay upright. This didn't feel quite as wonderful as the first minutes of being drunk, but I presumed it would pass. I thought I probably needed to drink more to get back to that original state.

I walked up to the door of what I thought was Roger's house. I rang the doorbell and started shouting for him to come and answer the door. Unfortunately, it wasn't his house. John dragged me up the road to the actual door. My head by now was not feeling so good, so I walked into the kitchen and grabbed another glass of red wine and knocked that back. Surprisingly, to me at least, it didn't seem to improve matters, and soon my head was swimming.

As for the rest of the party, I remember the following: a white bathroom and the shiny surface of the toilet bowl as I knelt over it and vomited. The concerned face of my sister-in-law as she tried to help me from falling down on the stairs. The anxious faces as I turned and spiralled down the staircase again, ending in a heap.

That's all I could remember.

The next day I awoke with the parched, awful taste that was to become part of my life for the next seventeen or so years. My tongue stuck to the roof of my mouth. I lifted my head and immediately wished I hadn't as the dull low throb of my first hangover came marching in with full force. I lay back on the pillow and wondered how I had got there, as I couldn't recall much of the last part of the evening. This pattern would become a constant part of my life over the coming years.

Blackout is how doctors refer to it. When you can't recall what happened the night before, or sometimes even whole days before. It took me many years to understand that this wasn't how normal people felt or reacted when they drank. They might get an occasional fuzzy recall, but in general, they got a little tipsy then backed off and went to sleep without forgetting what had occurred. They didn't lose control.

This was not how it worked for me. From the very beginning I was a blackout drinker. When I didn't have enough money to drink to my heart's content I would have a few beers, go home, go to sleep and remember everything about the previous day. But from that day on, if I had the funds, I drank to get drunk, and when I got drunk I blacked out.

I blacked out quite a bit.

# 3

# THE BRIDGE

I then really started to embrace rock and roll, so the sex and drugs part started to factor into the equation pretty quickly.

Like most teenage boys, I hadn't really been aware of girls until I put together the basic facts and biological imperatives. While at Notre Dame I had had a bit of a disagreement with a young Italian chap who decided to take a well-aimed kick at my midriff, which ended with me spending a few days in hospital having a hernia stitched up. The teen ward was a veritable gold mine of information about what happened when boys and girls 'did it'. Of course, I would find out later that pretty much all of it was completely erroneous.

It didn't take long to walk from my house into Horley High Street proper, where I received much of my rock and roll education. I used to go to see what records the tobacconist had in his bargain bin that week, or listen to what was available at the library.

Horley High Street combined family-owned businesses like Bunkell's the butchers with national chains like Boots the chemist and Woolworths, where Michael and I both worked during our teen years. An old haberdashery stood alongside Collingwood's department store opposite Radio Rentals. This was where Simon Gallup's brother Ric worked in the little record department at the back of the shop, which was a treasure trove for us.

This comprised our territory for quite a few years, and we knew all the hidden little paths and vantage points. We could cross town virtually invisible to any adult who might know our parents and report on our whereabouts.

The old single-screen cinema had yet to be converted to a night-club, and so occasional visits were arranged – Saturday morning pictures with a B movie before the main feature, and a two-level balcony where you could smoke if you wanted, which we did.

There was one building in Horley with mock Gothic red brick and flat white stone arches that hinted at a semblance of sanctity. However, within lay a rather different type of ecstatic experience than the founders of Horley Methodist Church first envisaged. I forget who it was that imparted the vital piece of information to us about what went on inside the church hall on Saturday nights, but whoever it was set the scene for our future adult lives without even being aware of it.

And so it was that one spring evening Michael, Robert and I lined up around the edges of the carefully trimmed rose beds that surrounded the Methodist church hall. The water pooling in drops on the dark green leaves of the rose bushes from a late afternoon shower reflected our youthful faces spoon-like in the fading daylight. Above the door at the side of the hall was the glow of a single light bulb illuminating the entrance. Unbeknown to us, herein lay the pathway to teen nirvana.

At fifteen we had already started to change our attire to dis-
tinguish ourselves from our fellow teens. In fact, way before
we became famous for our all-black attire, we wore all white!
Both Michael and I had white hipster flares called 'loons', with
matching white shirts. We topped off the effect of all this plain
white with scuffed white plimsolls, giving us a less angelic look.
Robert had on similar trousers, perhaps the darker ones with
ties around the bottom, which his mother had attached for
him at his request. (He had a pair of white high-waisted jeans
that he also liked.) It certainly made us look different. Over
this, Robert wore a long fur coat and a long scarf around his
neck. We looked like a strange cult, with Michael and myself
as white-robed acolytes to our floppy fringed, fur coat-wearing
leader.

We did indeed behave like a cult, as we had our own language
and way of being that excluded outsiders. There were other members of our clan, including early Malice guitarist Marc Ceccagno,
but the trio of myself, Robert and Michael was the nucleus.

Inside, things were heating up. Around the edge of the hall sat
girls: strange creatures that we had never really considered before,
but now felt inextricably drawn to. They fascinated us in a way
we couldn't explain, making us uncomfortable in a way that we
really quite liked.

Boys clumped together in small groups at the side, as if there
was some kind of bottomless pit that we had to avoid in the middle
of the room, with a swirling vortex that might drag us down into
the bowels of hell if we crossed the centre. We weren't going to
go over there and talk to the girls just yet, but we wanted to. The

music became the lingua franca, a bridge to the interaction we secretly sought.

T. Rex, The Sweet and Slade were the flavour of the times and the Methodists had thoughtfully supplied a couple of decks to play such songs at a reasonable and respectful volume. If you brought a record along, they had one of the older boys play it on the turntable. If it was the sad, slow song of the time, Terry Jacks's 'Seasons in the Sun,' you might ask a girl to dance. Or maybe not, if either one of you thought that was perhaps a little too forward!

It was dark in the recesses of the room and that meant you might be able to sneak a kiss, or maybe more, from one of the more forward girls. The room filled with the smell of teen lust and cheap perfume intoxicating us all, and like bees to the honeypot, we were drawn. The lights suddenly went on in the wooden hall. Our blinking eyes tried to focus and squinted at the minister in the middle of the room.

'Ah, boys and girls, now we come to the best part of the evening . . . prayer time!'

We were agog – prayers? After the minister had chanted a few sentences, and we mumbled in reply the call and response, thankfully the lights dimmed and we went back to our furtive fumbling at the room's periphery.

Out in the church car park, more discoveries awaited.

'I've got a bottle of Dad's home brew,' Robert said. He produced a screw-top glass bottle from inside his voluminous fur coat and we scooted around the corner at the back of the youth club to look at the brown fermented liquid.

'What's it taste like?' I asked.

'Bloody brilliant,' said Robert with a big grin, before offering me a slug. I knocked some back and it hit me again, that wonderful feeling I had first experienced at my brother's house. I still liked it.

We decided to walk down the street towards the town centre. After the shops had shut this was really a ghost town. There were a couple of restaurants: one Indian and one Chinese takeaway. Many years later I wondered how the proprietors of these places avoided jail time, having dealt with the drunken youth of Horley after the pubs had shut. Their patience must have been extremely tested.

The soft glow from the cinema beckoned in the distance, the light filtering through the twin distorters of alcohol and a steady drizzle that was coming down. We stumbled up to the front of the cinema and saw the night's offering. We decided against going in and turned back to the youth club. It was just finishing up, and outside a gaggle of boys and girls (as well as a few parents) warily eyed Robert, Michael and me as we swayed a little in front of the door. In the distance, I heard 10cc's 'I'm Not in Love' for the first time and my heart broke. Robert had already met Mary Poole, the great love of his life, but for me love's path was to be far more torturous.

Her name was Sarah and we met at the Methodist.

I had noticed her one Saturday night, with her long hair and petite figure, and got talking to her. She lived about three miles from me in the countryside with her mother, stepfather and younger brother.

She went to school in Horley with Simon Gallup, a kid I vaguely knew around town. Years later Simon told me that once Sarah and I started going out she had embellished my reputation as a hard man at his school, so much so that when he saw me in town he would cross over to the other side of the street! I'm surprised I didn't get in more fights after that.

We had been going out a few weeks when her parents saw me with her outside the Methodist when they came to pick her up one Saturday. They then decided, based solely on my appearance, that I was obviously not the right sort to be squiring their young daughter about. They had also seen the company I kept – that strange boy with the long fur coat and his friend with the motorbike and long hair. We were obviously bad news.

I called her the next day at her house. Her stepfather picked up the phone, and when I identified myself, he warned me in no uncertain terms to stay away from her. I realized it was going to be tough seeing her again. It didn't stop us, of course. Teen love is never thwarted for long.

Michael had a small motorbike, a Fantic Caballero, a strange Italian moped that looked quite a bit mightier than its 50cc engine would have led you to expect. No matter. It would suffice.

We concocted a daring plan: Michael would take me to Sarah's house in the nearby countryside and under cover of darkness he would drop me off. I would hide in the bushes until a suitable moment arose, when I would sneak up to her bedroom window on the ground floor and make my presence known by tapping gently on the window, at which point she would leave her parents' house and we would be united in love.

Of course, as in the best-laid plans of mice and men, it didn't turn out to be quite as straightforward as that.

The first time Michael dropped me off, her mother appeared

silhouetted against the front door of the house as the light from the hallway shone out across the vast front lawn. Beside her, a large German shepherd sniffed the air suspiciously in my direction. It was enough for me to postpone my amorous adventure that night.

A couple of days later Michael dropped me off at Sarah's home again, and this time I figured the coast was clear, as the house was in darkness. I slid on my belly on the grass across the lawn up to the window frame and furtively tapped on the leaded window. No Sarah, no sounds, nothing. A couple of minutes later I tried again, and this time I was a little more insistent, but still no answer.

In the pale moonlight illuminating this midnight scene, I saw the solution. The top window of the bathroom was open a little, and there was a flat roof directly below that. I would vault onto the roof and crawl through the window, then once in the bathroom I could find my way down to my beloved's room. Perfect!

It was only once I was halfway through the small bathroom window that it occurred to me that several unpleasant things might happen now: her dad, or worse, the large German shepherd, could intercept me. Neither seemed a particularly wonderful way to end the day.

Somehow, I managed to make it through the small aperture and into the bathroom with one leg in the toilet bowl and the other on the pale pink furry bath rug. Pulling my foot from the bowl, I shook the drops of water off. In the dark, I could just about make out the door to the landing. I tiptoed out and started gingerly down the stairs. The moonlight filtered in through the windows, casting a ghastly shadow of my creeping form on the wall.

Once at the bottom of the stairs I froze. The large black dog was right in front of me. I braced myself for the inevitable biting and howling, but nothing happened. I glanced down at the large black form and noticed its tail wagging. Thank God for that! I patted it on the head and carried on, now accompanied by my canine companion. I pushed open Sarah's door and walked inside. Shaking her gently awake she gasped when she saw me at her bedside.

'What are you doing here, Lol?'

'I thought I'd come see you for a stroll in the moonlight!' I said, trying to cloak my burglary with amorous bravado.

'Okay, sure. Why not?' I was gratified to see she was smiling now. She was game for an adventure, it seemed.

Sarah got up, dressed quickly and we let ourselves out via her bedroom window. We wafted along in the yellow moonlight across the large lawn at the front of the house and into the muddy country lane at the bottom. We walked across a couple of fields and into the woods until we reached our destination: the pillbox on the edge of the woods. Once inside we were shielded from the elements. It was a little off the beaten track to be noticeable from the road. It had not been infiltrated and there were no signs of creatures or other midnight revellers.

And so it was on a cool October night, in a pillbox on a bed of autumn leaves, that Sarah and I finally did what all young people in love eventually do. In case you were wondering, that's where the 'Pillbox Tales' song title originated as well.

Although the Rocket in Crawley was the pub where the seeds that became The Cure were planted, there was another pub that we used to hang out in before that: the Cambridge in Horley.

The Cambridge epitomized teenage rebellion of the late 1970s more than anything in our heads. I still look at it as the place where I came of age.

We graduated from the Methodist church youth club once we started seriously thinking about drinking, music and girls. Sex and drugs and rock and roll were better suited to pubs than dances at the church. The pub was little more than an annexe to a rather seedy-looking hotel on the outskirts of Horley town, but it was the place where I started to discover the darker, secret side of the world.

Inside, the Cambridge bore a resemblance to one of those terrible Spanish/British bars on the Costa Brava: all horse brasses and stuffed donkeys with sombreros. Tasteless doesn't begin to describe it, but most importantly no adult would dare go there, especially none of our parents or parents' friends. For them it was to be avoided at all costs. The occasional out-of-towner driving down to Brighton from London might make the quite easy mistake of thinking it was a normal pub, but once inside they realized their mistake and beat a hasty retreat. The ones that didn't were usually up to no good, looking for jailbait and such.

I came to realize much later that there was a strict demarcation inside the pub which was very similar to the kind of groups found in American high schools. You only sat at the table that represented your particular subgroup. There were 'the smoothies' or 'casuals'. The nearest American counterpart would be 'jocks': people who dressed in designer logos but were unintelligent, loud, and prone to vomiting over their fairly vacuous-looking girlfriends. Now, I believe, in the UK at least, they are called 'chavs'; back then they hadn't been given that name yet, but the behaviour was the same. They generally didn't talk to or mix with us in any way, which I think suited everyone. We sat at our own table with what I would term 'the outsiders'.

The Cambridge had a Pong machine and the occasional DJ amongst its attractions, but most of all it had beer and girls, which was why we went. Michael would turn up on his motorbike, Robert would occasionally drive over in his grey Mini, which was his first car. It had been some other colour, I seem to recall, but on a whim he had decided to paint it grey. Unfortunately, when it was first sprayed the paint had not dried before he took it for a spin to show it off to his girlfriend Mary, his secondary school sweetheart whom he'd been going out with since he was just fourteen. Being autumn, the leaves on the trees that were blowing around stuck to the wet paint. Pretty soon it looked like he was driving a small hedge down the road.

It was actually at the Cambridge that the mysterious leather jacket we all wore in The Cure's early photos first appeared. It belonged to a rather damaged biker called Arthur who felt comfortable enough to sit with us at our table. One day he gave me his leather jacket (for reasons I don't recall), but we knew that a black leather jacket was not just a coat, but also a flag, and so Robert and I took turns wearing it. We knew the power it possessed.

This being the late 1970s, what with the deprivation and unrest in England, there was always an undercurrent of violence at the pub. Add hormones and alcohol to the mix, and fights frequently erupted, turning the Cambridge into a cauldron of pain. Mostly the fights took place outside in front of the faux-leaded glass windows with faces pressed against the glass, anxious to have the outcome be in their group's favour.

These events always ended the same, with the combatants

fleeing once they heard the police car's siren coming up the driveway, into the caravan park behind the pub and onwards to freedom. Or so they thought. Many of them made the mistake of returning a little while later when they thought the coast was clear. Some even tried to disguise themselves by changing their blood-soaked shirts. The police would be hiding amongst the trees, waiting for the guilty parties to return. It was almost as much fun watching that scenario play out as anything else.

However, there was still the overwhelming sense that nothing was really going to change unless we were prepared to change it ourselves.

Michael and Robert and another kid I knew, Marc, had been playing music in St Edward's church hall for a few weeks and invited me to come see them one night. There was no audience. They were just jamming and seeing what they could come up with. They already had a drummer. His name was Graham, and he was a nice enough person and a reasonable drummer, it seemed to me. Nevertheless, I knew I had to be the one. These were my friends, we grew up together, and we hung out together. *I* should be the drummer in the band. Thankfully, it felt right to Robert and Michael, too. Graham was such a mild-mannered person that he made no objection when I asked him if I could sit behind the kit.

I had 'borrowed' a snare drum from school and was doing the exercises in Buddy Rich's book in my bedroom. I also took drum lessons on Saturdays from a guy named Andy who played in bands on cruise ships like the QE2. I could already handle some simple beats.

I sat down and played with Robert, Michael and Marc. It felt right straight away. I played the drums in a style that was stripped down and simple, but with passion.

Marc wanted more complexity, like his jazz-rock heroes, so I don't think I was his cup of tea. Soon enough he would form his own band called Amulet.

That left Robert and Michael and me. The three of us melded in a way that hadn't been obvious in the ensembles we attempted in the music room at Notre Dame or our other attempts in the band room at St Wilfrid's, our secondary school. Now we felt that we had something going here, and started to work in earnest on what would become The Cure.

I had persuaded my mother to accompany me to the local music shop, which was called Down Under, as it was in a basement, to purchase my first drum kit. It was covered in a hideous brownish-gold sparkly finish. A basic four-piece with spindly cymbal stands that had a nasty habit of collapsing when the cymbals were hit. It would do for now. My mother had to act as my guarantor and the kit was overpriced, but I didn't care. I would have spent all I had to get the drums I loved back then.

We established a pattern of practicing our instruments at Roberts parents' house three nights a week. When they had company, we relocated to the church hall at St Eddie's. Father forgive me for I have sinned, and these are my sins. While at the church hall we noticed that they had a bar. Unfortunately for us, they also had it all locked up with a screen across the bottles of spirits that were suspended upside down with spouts you had to push to get a measure.

Being teens, an ingenious solution presented itself. We got a long stick to manoeuvre one of the glasses underneath the spout and pushed the spout through the screen. Then, by fashioning a long straw made up of several interlocking straws joined together, we were able to drink for free. We liked rehearsing at St Eddie's.

# 4

# THE LOST BOYS OF SUBURBIA

The Smiths' house in Crawley was tucked away down a leafy cul-de-sac that dripped suburbia. They had moved from my grandmother's street in Horley a few years back and now lived in one of the nicer areas in Crawley. That's a bit of an oxymoron, but they had managed to find a pleasant refuge amidst the general blandness of the new town.

Their house was hidden behind a screen of tall trees on a big plot. This meant, luckily for us, that they would be able to extend, should they wish, which indeed they did in the late seventies. For once it seems we had come of age at exactly the right time to make use of the extra room that was being added to the Smith residence. I still believe that Robert's mum and dad, Rita and Alex, planned it that way, saw the writing on the wall, and with great foresight gave us our place, our woodshed that enabled us to become a proper band.

The summer of 1976 was extremely hot. Way before anyone was thinking about global warming, we had the hottest summer of the twentieth century in London and the UK.

Almost a decade after the hippies we had our own 'summer of

love'. We learnt how to love what we did and formulate a plan to get out of dullsville. Most of that hot summer I rode pillion on Michael's new Honda motorcycle, grateful for the cooling breeze that it brought while speeding down narrow roads to one of the many small country pubs that surrounded us in the outlying districts of Horley and Crawley. In hindsight, these were rural rooms full of bitterness and bile. However, we spent most of our time at the Smith house, plotting our next move.

If you looked around teenage Robert's bedroom, you would have seen, amongst all the usual objects, the signs of future greatness.

A tiny black 30-watt Watkins Electric Music guitar amp sat next to his bed, doing double duty as his bedside table. It was very small and very discreet but precisely what he needed to learn to play the Woolworths Top 20 guitar he had saved up for and bought for £20.

The most telling items in the room sat in a neat row on the shelf above his bed. Next to the existential tomes of Camus and Sartre, he'd assembled an unusual collection of every kind of tin can you could imagine. What seemed plain and ordinary in the corner shop had been cleaned, emptied and elevated into punk art on Robert's bedroom shelf. A minimalist show of everyday ordinariness that spoke to the greater longing for escape from suburbia, where commonplace items could stand symbolically for our teenage angst and as an absurdist counterpoint to the innate, inexplicable violence waiting on every corner for us in Crawley new town. Life here was rendered meaningless by default, and the teenage Robert knew that instinctively.

*

We would practise our songs and our cover versions at the Smiths' and try to come up with new ones three times a week. Rita and Alex were blessed with great patience, as it must have felt like they were living next door to a little girl learning to play the violin. Except louder, much louder, especially after Robert became the proud owner of a black Marshall stack!

Those were a strange couple of years for us. I had left school at sixteen to work at Hellermann Deutsch (known as Hellermann's to the locals) in East Grinstead, ostensibly to be trained as a chemist for their laboratory, which allowed me to study at Crawley College. I found out later they were much more than an electronics firm: they were a defence contractor that made missile parts. If only I'd known then what I know now.

Both Robert and Michael elected to stay on in the six form until eighteen, but then left school to join me at Crawley College. We were not quite on career paths and were making do with a kind of halfway existence between teendom and adulthood, but out of that strange no man's land came The Cure.

That long hot summer I helped both Porl and Michael obtain employment at Hellermann's factory with me. I thought it would be better for us if we were all together. I had met Porl through his sister Carol, whom I had gone out with. I still recall our first conversation at his house where I was visiting his sister, and desperately tried to ingratiate myself with her older brother. It went something like this:

Me: 'Would you like a cup of tea, I'm just making one?'

Porl: 'Not if it's anything like your taste in shirts, mate!'

Of course, we became friends immediately. In fact, we were so engrossed in talking about music that summer that it wasn't very long before Carol dumped me, as I was paying her too little attention and Porl far too much! At that point, I discovered he was a really good guitarist and hatched a plan to get him in our band.

As usual, Robert was way ahead of me and was already aware of Porl, as he'd met him in Crawley's only decent record shop – Cloake's, just off Queen's Square, the banal 1950s pedestrian plaza in the middle of Crawley. Years later we would play on the tiny bandstand in the middle of Queen's Square on the fast track out of there.

Porl and Robert had bonded over a recording of whale songs, of all things, and mutual admiration of The Sensational Alex Harvey Band (remember their guitarist Zal Cleminson and his crazy clown face in 'Delilah'?). Pretty soon Porl made his way over to the Smiths' house and we started playing together.

There was another enticement for Porl: Robert's younger sister Janet. It wasn't long before they became a couple. The plot was thickening . . .

For Porl, Michael and myself the Felbridge pub next to Hellermann's was our comfort and respite from the heat in the air-conditionless factory. We would be served by our friend Quincy's beautiful older sister, who worked at the pub. We all sat adoringly at her feet, watching her pour foaming pints of solace. The pub was dark and brown and rumoured to be run by the Scientologists, whose headquarters were not far away in Saint Hill. The sullen but exquisite factory girls would distract us occasionally, but we were much too weird and young for them, so they mostly left us to our own devices.

After a typical English winter of rain and cold, it felt liberating to bask in the near-constant sunshine of the highly unusual summer of 1976. Growing up as we did in near perpetual drizzle and gloom, I've always loved the sun, and I believe that particular year provided us with the energy we needed to create and be free in a way that might not have happened had it been a typical English summer. There was more than heat in the air.

Although the political climate was dire and we stood very little chance against our preordained future, this extra burst of life force charged us up. It made us believe we could dream, and if we could dream, we could escape. Anything was possible. One of the central ideas for us was not to have to live a normal life and not to go to a normal job. We were determined not to be 'wage slaves'. We wanted to create our own future. Robert, especially, was dead set against anything that would set him on the path to a boring life.

When the career adviser at our secondary school, St Wilfrid's, asked him what profession he was considering, he had the effrontery to say 'pop star'. But I knew he meant it and the smirk would one day come off the adviser's face. Michael also wanted to study to be a writer and was told, 'Not many openings in journalism. Try business studies.' In other words, forget your dreams. It's not going to happen for you and your ilk, the lost boys of suburbia.

Back in the Felbridge, I was sitting at the bar in my torn Levi's that had once been flared, but now, thanks to my mother's dexterity with needle and thread, were punky skintight drainpipes. I was tapping idly against the barstool rail with my new black brothel creepers when I heard a noise coming from the back room of the pub. It seemed quite familiar, but at the same time oddly different. Music like we made at the Smiths' house, but more muscular and polished in a way that I had never really heard before. Sure, we were regular attendees at the south London Greyhound Ballroom on a Sunday, seeing such disparate bands as Thin Lizzy, Can and Stray, but I hadn't heard something like this sound at such close quarters. The band, whoever it was behind the noise, were rehearsing, because they were stopping and starting to improve pieces of the music. There, in the middle of the pub on a weekday afternoon, I was hearing modern music being deconstructed in a way I hadn't personally experienced before.

The drums in particular were of interest to me. The drummer soloed from time to time, and between songs I could hear him make fills and beats I had only ever heard before in conjunction with other musicians' efforts. The mystique of making rock music was being unravelled before my very ears.

I drank the cold brew in sips and listened intently to the thumping tones coming from behind the bar, which eventually stopped when the door opened to reveal the perpetrators of this lovely noise. As the guys trooped out into the bar, I recognized one of them straight away: Woody Woodmansey! Was this, then, The Spiders from Mars, David Bowie's famous band? Were The Spiders rehearsing in our local pub? Maybe Bowie himself was there too?

It turned out that it was Woody's new band, U-boat, rehearsing. Nevertheless, I felt like I had been blessed by rock royalty to be given a backstage pass to hear how it was done for real.

The passing of the torch, you might say, even though he never said a word to the group of dumbstruck teens sitting in the Felbridge that sunny afternoon. Woody looked regal in his full-length fur coat and various glam accoutrements as he swept through the door of the pub.

'Bloody hell, Porl. Did you see who that was?' I asked, wide-eyed.

Porl grinned back at me. 'Woody bloody Woodmansey, I believe, Lol!'

However implausible it seemed, we took Woody's presence in our midst to mean that we were on the right track. It had to mean *something*. It was a sign from the gods, surely?

Continuous sun in England is as much of an anomaly as regular rain in the Sahara. But the summer of 1976 was just like that, an anomaly. We were teenagers just starting to consider life as adults. It was a summer I would never ever forget. For one thing, we finally had our own room to practise, despite the many attempts by the Smiths' neighbours to shut us down.

One day the doorbell rang and there stood a portly, red-faced, middle-aged man. 'Your son and his friends are making that noise, yes?'

'If you mean their band rehearsal, then, yes, that's them,' Robert's mother replied.

'Well, whatever it's called it's got to stop. They're disturbing the community. I can't hear myself think with that bloody racket going on!'

Rita considered this for about a millisecond,

'Well, I'll tell them to stop playing when you tell your dog to stop pooing on my lawn!'

And with that, she firmly closed the door on the matter and The Cure had in Rita Smith our first champion. Of course, the neighbour was quite right: we were disturbing the community, but that had been our intention all along.

\*

In the middle of that road-melting summer, Alex and Rita Smith decided to go on holiday, leaving Robert in charge of the house and environs. A little unwise, on reflection.

We were delighted by this development and immediately sprang into action. We knew exactly what was going to happen now: band camp!

College was on holiday, and I had accrued a few days off from Hellermann's, so with some careful planning we could play at the house for at least a week. A week or more of non-stop bliss for us.

Outside the thermometer was creeping towards 90 degrees – an unheard-of temperature in England. We had abandoned the stuffy annexe to take up residence in the Smiths' dining room because there was a smidgen of air blowing through the house that we could trap there and use to cool the practice sessions. Many cables snaked across the dining-room floor, as we wired up everything we owned to make as much noise as possible. Connecting all of our instruments together took a while, but the resulting cacophony was surely worth it. We had bought a green Roland echo box, which we could feed all the vocals through to give us what we felt was a very professional sound.

The heat was intense, so I stripped to my shorts and a T-shirt for banging the drums. We found the heat also required that we drink copious amounts of liquid to keep hydrated. Of course, this also meant that we had to make frequent forays to the local pub during breaks in our band practice.

The Grey Fox pub had an atmosphere familiar to any inhabitant of late-1970s England. Just having the temerity to walk into the pub was enough to enrage one of the local drunks. They were mostly bleary-eyed, middle-aged men whose light had been extinguished years before, and now sought to intimidate and bully those who crossed their path. This usually meant anyone coming into the pub that they didn't know personally. These guys didn't have a lot of friends.

A loud, red-faced man playing a harmonica very badly dropped the instrument from his lips as soon as we entered. He swivelled his head around, and with one squinty eye scouted out anyone that might be offended by his ineptitude on the instrument.

'What youse fucking looking at?' he slurred.

Once he caught your gaze, he would violently hurl his glass on the ground, or – more spectacularly – at the mirrored back of the bar, and start to fight anyone who came into range. We steered clear. He was like a captive monkey, playing to the crowd that was entirely inside his head. Yes, we had plenty of examples of the types of people we definitely didn't want to become in Crawley pubs in the summer of 1976.

I walked across the carpeted room and out onto the patio beyond. It had been so hot for so long we had almost forgotten what England was normally like.

This was a country woefully underprepared for a summer like the one of 1976. There was no air conditioning to speak of and precious few ice-making facilities. We sweated it out night after night and day after day.

The tar on the streets resembled a molten black river. Kids sneaked eggs out of the fridge to throw on the ground and watch them fry in the sun.

We were gawky adolescents just getting used to our not-quite adult bodies and minds and, like many teens, we were trying to find our way through the jungle of such conflicting information.

We spent a long time that summer on the Smiths' patio looking out over The Guru's chickens, clucking away at the back of the garden. Most of time we played records from his collection outside on a little portable, from which we would glean various truths of rock and roll history and try on different styles. This was where certain elements of what was to become The Cure's signature sound came from. And some of it will surprise people. For instance, one LP on steady rotation that summer was Mahavishnu Orchestra's second album *Birds of Fire*. Other contenders included Nils Lofgren's *Cry Tough* and the usual Brit rock stalwarts like Pink Floyd, The Beatles and The Stones. We all had our personal favourites. I recall Robert particularly liked Captain Beefheart's *Trout Mask Replica*. We were devoted acolytes of much that had come before, plundering The Guru's precious back catalogue of rock and roll history.

More than anything we were united in our general dislike of most of the overblown pap that masqueraded as 'progressive' music, plus the fact that it all seemed so far removed from our own experience growing up in Crawley. I couldn't imagine The Moody Blues having a running battle with racist skinheads in their hometown streets. Then again, they came from Birmingham, so who knows . . .

As the Smiths' holiday wore on, we spent more and more time bashing out our sound in their dining room. I had the Pearl Maxwin kit, my first, and I loved it. Besides the aforementioned Marshall, Robert had added a brown Gibson Explorer guitar – a copy, I hasten to add, as none of us could afford the real thing at that point. British amplification and American guitar; the archetypal rock and roll set-up. Michael completed his array with a brown Guild bass, and Porl with his black Les Paul copy. We were ready to make a lot of noise, and we did. In between songs, we drank the Smiths' home brew and sometimes smoked Gitanes in their beautiful blue box. When hungry, a trip to the fish and chip shop sufficed.

It was a beautiful time, without artifice or pretence. We were discovering our art. Life was very simple and pure.

Robert and I got ready for rehearsal by sneaking into The Guru's room when he wasn't about and playing a couple of tracks.

Robert was flipping through the albums on the shelf when he asked me if I'd heard Ray Charles's 'Hit the Road Jack.'

'No, I don't think so.'

He put it on The Guru's expensive turntable. We listened intently for a couple of minutes.

'Pretty bloody great, right?' he said, grinning.

'It's brilliant!' I agreed.

We were in awe of the power of that piano riff. Total genius.

You have to remember that in the late 1970s, there was no Internet to inform us how to become a band. Nor were there any helpful TV shows to show the way. We didn't grow up in a big city where we could follow the example of others. We were on our own. This proved to be a blessing. We were allowed to flower on our own with fewer outside influences than most bands of our time. If we had been in the centre of London, for instance, I feel certain we would have turned out very differently.

Where we grew up was as much a factor as anything else that influenced The Cure's sound. For a start, there was the uniformly drab nature of the new towns after the Second World War, which had the overflow from bombed-out London mixed in with the more rural folks of Surrey and Sussex. Then there were the asylums.

Many mental hospitals operated in our area, mainly because we were close to a large population that would need their services. These institutions were tucked away in the pleasant southern English countryside where there would be more space for them.

Although there were high-security facilities like Cane Hill (where David Bowie's half-brother was a patient for a while before he escaped and committed suicide), there were also more benign facilities, like Netherne, where, back in 1948, Eleanor Roosevelt had visited and proclaimed, 'The United States has much to learn from a hospital like Netherne.' It was the first hospital to offer art therapy for its patients, which was a radical departure in an era that generally only offered a routine of heavy sedation or lobotomy for any extreme mental problems the patients might have.

On any given Saturday some of the less disturbed patients might be allowed to get on a bus and come into our town, where we would occasionally encounter them. They were strange, lost-looking people. Men mostly, some of whom wore their jackets up over their heads as if to protect themselves from the outside world. They wandered the streets like ghosts, or sat hunched all afternoon over a single cold cup in the local tea shop. I suspect many of them were what we would now call post-traumatic stress disorder casualties from the Second World War, but back then there was no real treatment other than permanent institutional-ization. However, our connection to this strange world got a bit stronger when Michael got a job at Netherne as a porter.

Although we were certainly old enough to go to London by ourselves and wander the streets of the capital, it was still a dif-ficult twenty-five-mile drive with no motorway. A trip would take two hours or more through many small towns on the A23, which was invariably congested and slow as sludge. Sometimes we might go up on the train, but mostly I rode on the back of Michael's bike, which meant more often than not we just stayed in our local area and contented ourselves with the usual run of pubs before heading back to the sanctuary of the Smiths' house and our musical discoveries.

One night we decided to go to the rolling lush lawns of Neth-erne for a party. It promised a diversion from our normal Saturday night routine at the Cambridge. We all piled into Robert's latest vehicle, a small blue Vauxhall Chevette, named perhaps after the American car of the same name, though it hardly resembled its stateside counterpart. It was a small engine hatchback that four people could barely squeeze into.

Robert had access to several cars growing up, mainly because of his father's job. There were always cars being retired from Upjohn's representatives' fleet. They were quite worn out, having been driven the length and breadth of the country several hun-dred times by the pharmaceutical company reps, but for young teens, they were just the ticket to take us out of our humdrum hometown.

The party was being held in one of the nurse's residences, inside the actual grounds of the asylum. A little daunting under normal circumstances, but there was the lure of excitement and diversion from our normal activity.

We drove the seventeen or so miles north to Netherne Hospital. It was also closer to London, so we naturally associated it with excitement and action, as we did with most everything coming from the capital. We were suburban middle-class boys and the city held the promise of the new world we were anxious to partake in. Even an old Gothic asylum on the edge of town would do.

The party was unremarkable and not in the slightest bit memorable. It was a dull affair with lots of drinking and little talking going on. We didn't really know anybody, and our appearance, with our punky outfits, was at odds with the general attire of the other partygoers. They were still trapped in dismal disco culture, while we wore strange trousers we had found at village jumble sales, and mohair jumpers we had persuaded our mothers to knit. I had a black one with large holes in it and the aforementioned jumble sale trousers. This was looked on with a kind of apathetic anger by the locals, who avoided talking to us for most of the evening. I say most of the evening because occasionally they might attempt to interact with us, although you could hardly call it friendly.

'What do you call that get-up?' one of the smirking yobs would shout to much chuckling from his mates. 'You look a proper dog's dinner, you do! Are you poofs or what?'

Most of the time we tried to avoid replying to the unpleasant jibes. Not because we didn't want to tell them to fuck off, you understand, but we knew instinctively that this line of questioning was usually the precursor to having a punch-up if you engaged with them in any way. Also, our being outnumbered meant it was not likely to go in our favour. So we decided to bite our tongues and ignore the ignorant baiting.

'You must be on drugs to dress like that, mate!' This was usually the end to the reasoning process for them. If you didn't look like them, you must be either homosexual or on drugs or both. Stupid wankers.

Strangely, we were probably only slightly aware of what drugs were or even what they represented. We were babies, really. Everyone at the party got very drunk, including us. It's been said that around 80 per cent of the population in England drink, and I can attest to that statistic based on this one night.

Robert, Michael and I stumbled out to the waiting baby-blue Chevette. Through the haze of alcohol-impaired thinking the conversation went something like this:

'I don't think I should drive right away. I'm feeling more than a bit pissed!'

Michael said he didn't think he could drive either. I didn't know how to drive, something I would not learn to do for many years. As the only two licensed drivers amongst us couldn't function properly, we were at a little bit of a loss as to how to get home that night. Nobody was going to let me drive even if I could have done it. I hadn't passed my test yet, and we were (at the core of our beings) still nice, law-abiding, middle-class boys.

'So shuuul we sleep ittoff on the grass?' I slurred.

Someone suggested we should sleep it off in the car. Looking at the small confines of the Chevette, it seemed a little uncomfortable as a solution, but we didn't have much choice. We had no money for a taxi or a hotel, so unless we wanted an encounter with the local constabulary our only alternative was to stay put until we sobered up enough to drive. We'd had our share of run-ins with the police, as we lived right next to London's second airport, Gatwick. There were many more policeman on the local streets than would be usual for a small suburban town like ours. As they had nothing to do, they spent a lot of time harassing the local teens, or so it seemed to us.

Michael then came up with a solution. As he worked at the hospital, he knew of a safe place for us to hide out until we sobered up.

'The home farm!' he exclaimed. 'It's very quiet and nobody goes there at night. We can park next to the runner beans until we can drive home.'

I looked a little unsure about staying overnight at a psychiatric hospital. 'Um, everyone's locked up for the night, right?'

Michael assured me it would be fine, and so Robert and I grabbed a few last bottles of beer from the party and we quietly drove over to the home farm, basically a really large vegetable garden where the hospital's inmates could help grow some of the food needed on a daily basis for the patients and staff alike.

We sat on the side of the Brussels sprouts, talking and drinking a little more, until we crawled into the seats of the hatchback, the wan moon glinting slightly through the clouds off the dusty windscreen. We attempted to get comfortable in the confines of the Chevette. It was a little like one of those old contests you see where thirty people get inside a Volkswagen Beetle, except it was just three drunk Imaginary Boys. Eventually sleep came, or rather a kind of sedation, brought on by the booze.

I think my foot went to sleep first, because it was wedged under the front seat and pinned down by a metal rod. I felt the unbearable tingle of pins and needles, so moved it slightly to get relief. That's the last thing I recall.

The interior of the car had that pale morning glow familiar to any stop-outs or all-night revellers. That point where you're not sure if the morning is coming, yet in fact you can't quite believe it actually is. The windows were misted with our combined breath, so I rubbed a small patch clear on the glass and noticed that we were tucked under the hanging branches of a tree drooping with early morning drizzle.

Another day. I could start to feel my limbs now in the cold car interior as I attempted to stretch out a little straighter. Robert was sprawled across the front seats with an almost beatific look on his sleeping face, while Michael was stuffed deep into his jacket across from me. The atmosphere of a thousand teenage Sunday mornings – stale beer fumes mixed with tobacco – wafted in the old car as we all gradually came to.

At first I thought a falling branch from the overhanging tree had struck us. The sound was loud and startling. Looking up, I saw that it was in fact a large flat hand pressed against the window. Followed very shortly by another hand, then another and another. Suddenly there were at least six separate hands on the windows of the car, slapping against the glass. Wiping the misty windows, we peered out into the early morning gloom. Faces! Then a low guttural grunting sound as the hands continued to slap on the glass.

It was the first shift of inmates who had noticed the rather churned up tyre tracks leading directly under the tree. Yes, we had been quiet coming in last night to the home farm, but hadn't noticed the muddy conditions under foot. It probably looked to all intents and purposes that we had just slid off the hospital driveway in the rain and crashed into the tree at the side of the churned-up rows of cabbages and sprouts.

We quickly cleared parts of the misted windows to look out. This meant the patients could see that there were occupants in the car, which surprised them and made them feel anxious. This was something different and disturbing to them. Then one picked up a large cabbage and threw it in the direction of the Chevette.

At that precise moment Robert's voice croaked into life.

'Shit! Let's get the hell out of here!'

He slid over into the driver's seat and turned the key of the Chevette. It sprang into life, which surprised me for such an old car. The immediate effect of this was startling to the inmates who now started to back away from the vehicle. Robert, sensing our chances of escape were thin, gunned the engine.

'Crap!' he shouted. 'The wheels are spinning in the mud!'

It seemed to us we might be stuck here with the angry inmates of the hospital about to cabbage us to death for disturbing the delicate equilibrium of their morning. Right then the wheels spun free and we lurched forward to freedom. The car got a little more purchase on the sodden ground, and then we were bumping along the rutted track up to the home farm gate and out of the vegetable patch at last. We held our breath until we passed the guard hut at the front entrance, and drove out onto the A23 and back into civilization.

'So we weren't in any real danger back there?' I asked Michael after we had put a couple of early morning miles between us and the farm.

'No, they're not like the lot at Cane Hill, Lol. These are just depressed or confused people, mainly sent here to recover in the bucolic English countryside.'

I heaved a sigh of relief and settled down into the back seat of the Chevette. In the rear-view mirror I caught a glance of Robert's grinning face and we started to laugh.

'Bloody hell, you couldn't write this stuff!' I exclaimed, and then the car was filled with our teenage laughter and the boyish excitement that we had somehow managed to find in this very bland and boring place we lived in.

Robert's parents had been away a few weeks when it occurred to us that they might come home soon. So, we decided to have a bit of a party and figured we could tidy up the next day. For some reason I still can't fathom, I elected to sleep in the nude under the Persian rug in the Smiths' living room.

It was hot. I was drunk. The most absurd notions always seem like a good idea when you're a drunk teenager.

Light was just starting to come through the curtains of the living room, and as it was summer, there was a warm tinge to the light. The summer had outstripped all expectations and many originally porcelain-pale limbs were gradually turning brown in this most unaccustomed sun and heat. Shorts and T-shirts were the order of the day – except when I stripped down to sleep under a rug apparently. Just as I was coming to and considering my position on the floor, I heard it:

'This place smells like a dirty lavatory!'

It was the unmistakable voice of Rita Smith that reached around the door and slapped me firmly about the head with her disgust. I don't think I have ever moved so fast either before or since.

Getting up from the floor, and into my shorts was accomplished in barely a wink of the eye, and then it was a few short steps to the partially open French doors in the dining room where I escaped into the back yard and hid behind The Guru's chickens, clucking and scratching in gay abandon in the early morning light.

I realized at this point that I had no shoes or T-shirt on, and they must be lying on the couch or under the rug as a makeshift pillow. Oh my God, Rita will see them and put two and two together, surely? I could not flee any further, stuck as I was on the edge of the property. I sat there catching my breath and heard the sounds of . . . laughter!

Looking from my vantage point behind the chicken house, I slowly ventured out to see Robert holding my T-shirt and shoes in his hand by the French doors. He motioned to me and I gratefully took the clothing from him.

'How are they?' I hissed under my breath.

'It's probably better we don't practise today, but I'm sure it'll blow over.'

As parents, the Smiths never ceased to amaze me. If my parents had stumbled upon the mess we'd left all hell would have broken loose, but Alex and Rita weren't my parents and Robert was right: the incident was never mentioned again.

The life-changing summer of 1976 wore on and soon enough autumn was around the corner. Shortly we would be forced back into the routine of normality that we were trying so hard to escape. Back to work for me and Porl, back to college for Michael and Robert. It was not something that we relished.

'I mean, it's just not what I want to do with my life, you know?'
Robert said.

We were sitting in Milton Mount Gardens, a small park near
the Smith house. Just Robert and I. It was late at night. We had
decided, on a whim, to come and sit in the park with a couple of
bottles of his dad's home brew – the totally inebriating concoction
that Alex Smith had perfected over many years of experimental
brewing. We just wanted to enjoy these last summer days as long
as we could before horrid reality intruded again.

'It seems really worthless to slave at some job for the rest of
your life and then just die,' I said.

I had seen it with my own father. He didn't really seem to be
alive to me, just an eating and sleeping machine that didn't have
much purpose in his life apart from going to work and the pub.
It was not a future I wanted for myself. It seemed like he wasn't
living, just existing.

It was warm still. The dark gardens were completely empty
except for the two of us and the birds that made their home in
the reeds of the small lake. Aware of our presence, they made
suspicious bird noises to ward us off.

We had brought a guitar and a pair of bongos with us, so we
sat on the grass cross-legged, Robert with the acoustic guitar
across his lap and me with the bongos in front of me. T. Rex live
at the BBC. Sort of.

We both took long draughts from the bottle of home brew
and Robert gently started to strum the nylon strings. I listened
intently to the cadence of the chords Robert was playing. I got
the rhythm and started to play along with him, and together we
got a kind of rudimentary musical mantra going out there in the

park, late at night. I was entranced by the music; the warmth and the home brew helped with that. I felt as if we should sit out here for ever playing in the balmy night air. Robert started to sing quietly, words or maybe they were just word sounds as we sat in the gloomy park. It didn't seem to matter much. After a while we stopped, and both of us just lay back on the soft earth looking up at the starry night sky glimpsed over the dark treetops. I don't recall anything being said by either of us. There was no need. We knew what we wanted.

# 5

# THE ROCKET

Personally, I consider the first gig we did as the band that became The Cure was on 20 December 1976, the Malice gig at our old secondary school, St Wilfrid's. True, we had done a gig of sorts a couple of days earlier in the minstrels' gallery at Worth Abbey for Upjohn's Christmas party, and a rather strange 'performance' in 1973 as The Obelisk, but this was our first full-blown *concert*.

We had settled on a most unlikely character named Martin Creasy as a singer. He worked as a journalist for the local paper, so we thought he might be able to get us a review. I don't know if he ever did. I do remember he did a great David Cassidy impersonation.

I had persuaded my mother to purchase a full-length black studded catsuit for me to play in that night. I had seen pictures of drummers and that looked like what you wore. I was going to top off the look with Alice Cooper-style black mascara eye make-up. I loved Alice.

Sitting in the small dressing room area at the school, I had on the black studded catsuit. I had a black mascara stick in my hand, but no matter how I tried I couldn't get the right effect; this rock and roll stuff was harder than it looked.

Robert's girlfriend Mary was there. I knew Mary well, as we were all in the same class in school, so I asked her to help me apply the black lines for the desired effect, which she did. I'm sure it looked wonderful and exactly what I wanted, but I'm glad there are no photographs of that get-up.

We started off the gig with our friends Steve Forrester and Peter Doherty (no, not *that* Peter Doherty) slowly opening the curtains and bringing up the stage lights. We opened with 'Jailbreak' by Thin Lizzy, and then Martin Creasy appeared at the side of the stage in a brown three-piece suit! Not very rock and roll. He didn't last as our singer for long. A nice guy, but not right for us.

It was a suitably awful concert for our first proper gig. We had a couple of 'triple songs'. At the time we liked to write songs as triptychs for some reason. I sang my party piece 'Wild Thing'. It was a disaster, really, and I thought, 'Well that's that, then!' But it wasn't.

One night that winter at band practice, Michael, Robert and I were all sitting around the kitchen table. Porl was up in Janet's room.

I was idly looking through *Melody Maker* sipping a cup of Rita Smith's best tea. ('No sugar, Laurence, it's bad for you.')

We had reached a kind of impasse with our songs. We were unsure quite where to go with them, but open enough to want to explore the new stuff that was coming out of punk. We were a little restless.

I saw an advert for The Stranglers playing at a club near us, the Red Deer in Croydon, south London.

'Why don't we go see this?' I said.

Robert looked up from the book he was reading. 'See what, Lol?'

'The Stranglers are playing tonight. At the Red Deer. We should go. Better than just sitting around here. I'll get us in if one of you drives.'

I had a job, I could buy the tickets.

'All right, so why don't I drive up and Michael drive back?' said Robert, suddenly perking up a little at the thought of having a few drinks and watching The Stranglers. Michael agreed to drive home afterwards. He was not as keen on drinking during the week as Robert and I were.

I think the gig at the Red Deer was the first punk gig we all went to together. Mary came with us, too. Porl demurred and stayed at the Smiths' with Janet. Punk wasn't really Porl's thing anyway.

When we got there, it was full of all the London punks we had heard about and seen on TV and in the newspapers but never in the flesh. Spiked-up hairdos and safety pins everywhere!

Robert and I pushed our way through the assorted punky types to the front. We watched and danced for the whole gig. Michael sensibly stayed away from the bar. He was driving us home, so he couldn't get as happily drunk and deranged as Robert and me.

I saw the look of wonder on Robert's face. 'This is more like it!' I shouted over the loud music. We had found a place to start from. We could see a way to get out of the drab environs of Crawley and make real music that was exciting and alive, right here, right now.

A month or so later The Stranglers played at our college, and I got up on stage and danced with J.J. Burnel, the Stranglers' bassist.

I went home minus one shoe as the result of being somewhat inebriated. I had a new-found alcohol supply (200 proof) from the
laboratory at work. I would bring a small bottle with me to gigs
and pour it into a pint of beer, which now alcoholically resembled
a pint of whisky. People were totally aghast at how drunk I was
after one beer. If only they knew. I would have been just as wild
and enthusiastic even if I wasn't drinking. I was in love with the
energy and sheer exhilaration of the new punk sound. It had lit
a fire underneath me and I identified with the stuff they were
singing about, the alienation, and the desire to change things.
Something better change! This I understood. It spoke to me as
eloquently as anything I had ever read. Somehow I just knew it
would propel me out of this place. I knew it would be the key
to a more exciting and meaningful life. I also knew that I had
nothing to lose by following this path. I could see that staying
in Crawley would mean I would die there, and probably sooner
rather than later. My life had to mean something more than that,
didn't it?

I started to buy the 45s that Ric Gallup brought down from
London to his shop in Horley and snatched up the new punk
records that came out every week. I changed my clothes to fit
in with the scene. Straight-leg, jumble-sale trousers and pointy
boots. I wanted the world to know that I had found the way, that
I was a true believer.

After a couple of aborted attempts at finding a suitable singer (Gary
X, anyone?) we eventually co-opted our mate Peter O'Toole (no,
not *that* Peter O'Toole) as our vocalist. He was a Bowie fan and a
really good footballer. Both suitable qualifications to be our singer.

Robert had seen an advert in *Melody Maker* from Hansa, a German record company looking for English groups. We sent them a tape and a photo and they invited us to Morgan Studios in London to audition for them.

When we got to the studio they said, 'Just stand by the instruments and play your songs, boys. We are going to film you now, okay?'

That sounded strange to us – didn't they want to record our songs, too? Never mind, we did as asked and went through two or three songs while they got all the footage of us that they wanted. We didn't really know what to expect and it was exciting to think we might get a break here to make a record.

Out of the darkness at the back of the studio, an American voice said, 'Okay, that's great, boys. Just one more set of shots for us under these lights over here please.'

It was Steve Rowland, Hansa's A & R head. We went home slightly mystified by the whole process, but as total neophytes we had no reason to think that this was not the normal process for 'getting a record deal'.

A few days later, we got a call. 'Congratulations! We have decided to sign you to our label!'

Well, that was surprise! We didn't expect it to be quite so fast. Apparently we, along with David Sylvian's Japan, were signed from these auditions. We felt quite amazed.

If our audition was weird, things soon got even stranger. They sent us lots of old songs to cover, like 'The Great Airplane Strike' and 'I Fought the Law' and then booked a studio for us with a 'big name' producer. It didn't make sense to us that we were recording other people's songs. We sent them cassette tapes of our songs, which they ignored. That seemed odd, too. Didn't they like our music? It was an ominous sign, as we would soon find out.

We finally got a gig at the Rocket in May of 1977.

We were now all eighteen, so Fred, the Rocket's landlord, wouldn't fall foul of the child work laws or something. Clever old Fred.

He actually didn't ask us outright anyway. Rather, our friend's band Amulet, fronted by ex-Malice guitarist Marc Ceccagno, couldn't do the gig they had been booked for at the Rocket, so, sensing an opportunity to actually get us out there in front of real people, I called Fred.

'Er, yes . . . the Rocket public house?'

The phone was answered by Fred himself in the voice I presumed he usually reserved for outstanding creditors.

'Yes, hello, Fred? I heard that Amulet can't play the pub this week. They all have bad colds, they asked us to fill in for them?'

Fred sounded a little suspicious, 'And what are you lot called, then?'

'Easy Cure.'

We had literally pulled the new name for the band out of a hat. After our disastrous gig at St Wilfrid's it seemed like a wise idea to change the name, but we couldn't agree on one. Robert hit on a solution. He had seen something about Bowie or William Burroughs cutting up phrases from their writings into strips and reassembling them into new prose or song lyrics. So we cut all our own lyrics up and put them into a hat. The first fragment we pulled out would be the name of the band. It seemed both democratic and punky all at the same time.

We sat in the small hallway of the Smiths' house, by the harmonium we sometimes utilized for the triptych songs we were currently making.

'So the first bit of lyric we pull out of the hat will be our new band name, right?' Robert asked.

'Sounds good to me,' I said.

Robert reached in and pulled out a small, white, screwed-up scrap.

'What's it say?' Michael and I asked.

'Easy Cure,' said Robert, who looked a little crestfallen that one of his word fragments wasn't the plum pulled from the pudding. 'Easy Cure' was from a lyric that I had partially written.

'Anyway, fair's fair, so Easy Cure it is!' I thought out loud.

However, Robert got his way later on, because we changed it to The Cure, which he thought sounded much more punky and *now* than Easy Cure, which sounded more hippiefied.

I couldn't really argue with that. I wanted us to be more punk anyway.

'So what kind of music do Easy Cure play?' asked Fred.

I panicked slightly. I hadn't really thought about that one. We just wrote songs from our own experiences and thoughts. I don't think we thought about labels, although we were certainly influenced by the current rash of punk bands we were now seeing whenever we could. In addition to The Stranglers at the Red Deer and Crawley College we saw Buzzcocks at the Lyceum.

'Um, well, we do some of our own stuff and a few popular covers,' I offered hopefully.

'Yeah, well, they like to hear something they know, so play something they know,' said Fred, hammering his point home. 'Be here at 6 p.m., start playing at 6 30–7 p.m. You play two sets and you have to finish before last orders at 10.30 p.m.'

To this day I've no idea what they paid us. I probably didn't take it in, as I was just so happy to get our first proper paying gig!

And so it started. Paying our dues in the Rocket at first to the regulars, and gradually, over the next year or so, to increasingly varied audiences from the area as word spread.

Of course, we had to play some covers, as Fred had predicted. 'Locomotive Breath' by Jethro Tull, made completely punky by leaving out the long piano intro and flute(!), was one I recall that was particularly liked by the Rocket's older patrons.

Gradually we honed our set to include more of our own material, crammed together on that tiny stage in the corner of the pub, and learnt what every band must learn if they hope to establish themselves as a real band.

We perfected the subtle signals between us all to enable the songs to come out sounding right and keep the show rolling along with intensity and power. We learnt our stagecraft on that small stage all through the year, in between seeing some of the best bands of the punk revolution.

We played about thirteen gigs at the Rocket. It felt like we were there so often we were practically the house band. At every gig there were more people, and we grew in confidence as we honed our sound.

In the autumn of 1977, Peter left the band. We had played a gig at the Rocket on 11 September and after the gig he told us it was his last.

'Hey, chaps, I think I have a different calling. I'm, um, off to a kibbutz in Israel.'

'Really?' I asked him somewhat incredulously. 'That's what you want to do?'

'Yeah, Lol, that's the plan.'

I was a little stunned. After all, we were just getting properly started. In retrospect it had been obvious the last few months that his heart wasn't in it anymore. We wished him luck and looked around for another singer to replace him. It was frustrating, to say the least. We were starting to express our own ideas, finding our own raison d'être, and now we were in desperate need of a good front man to convey that to audiences who didn't know us at all.

Then Robert did something that really changed the whole course of The Cure. Up until then I don't think Robert had thought about being the guitarist *and* the singer, but I think he realized right then, when Peter left, that if he was going to make a difference in this world, if he was going to be able to get across what he wanted to say, he would have to be the front man, he would have to take that on.

I have a theory. There comes a day when every single one of us is confronted with the abyss. Sometimes it's a heart-wrenching break up. Sometimes it's the loss of a loved one. Some have it early and some people get it late, but we all have that moment when we look down and there's nothing fucking there. People want their rock stars to go further out on the edge and hang out there for a bit, take a good long look at that abyss, and then transmit what they find there through their art.

Ian Curtis did it. Kurt Cobain did it. So did Robert Smith, except he didn't just look at the abyss, he was on intimate terms with it. He had things he had to say about the darkest parts of the human experience, and people were either attracted to that or repulsed by it. He's been like that for as long as I've known him. Even at the very start, he had stuff he needed to say. He tried to fight it. I think that's why he picked up the guitar, so he'd have something to put between himself and the abyss. In the beginning, he tried to hide behind it. He was *just* the guitar player. When Peter left and the band wasn't working right and the music we were playing didn't match the vision he had for it, he assumed the duties of the vocalist. We were still teenagers, but even then he knew what it meant, what he was getting into. It's one of the bravest things I've ever seen anyone do.

The Rocket was where Robert taught himself how to front a band, how to be in the centre of the storm and love being there.

In that dismal little room in deepest Sussex, a whole new future was started.

It seemed like a good idea at the time. After trying to get going for most of 1977 as Easy Cure, we were looking to expand a little beyond Crawley and environs. While we had played some other gigs besides the Rocket, it was nothing too exciting. I mean, where the 'eff' was Effingham Park?

Michael's brother-in-law Richard, newly married to his older sister and no doubt wishing to ingratiate himself into the Dempsey clan, had hurriedly hatched an idea to get us gigs further afield.

One day he came round to rehearsal with Michael and cornered us.

'Every band has a manager, right?'

'Er, yes, I suppose so,' we said.

'Look at these, then!' And out of his pocket he triumphantly pulled a wad of business cards.

On inspection, it had his name and, in large letters, 'Manager of Easy Cure'.

Then, much to our chagrin, in even larger letters, 'Available for weddings, parties and all your entertainment needs.'

He looked expectantly at our faces.

'Well, what do you think, lads?'

'They're business cards,' said Robert diplomatically. I knew what he meant; we were not really in the business of anything at that point.

'Oh, and I've got us our first engagement,' he said, positively beaming at this point. 'Orpington General Hospital!' You could have knocked us down with a feather at that moment. I couldn't have imagined a less rock and roll venue than a general hospital.

'Yes, the annual hospital staff dance on New Year's Eve!'

That sounded ominous. 'Playing to a lot of pissed-up hospital porters!'

'It's okay,' he protested. 'I told them you play some of your own stuff and do covers of popular songs.' That last bit fell with a loud thud into the room.

It's true we could play a few covers, we did so at our gigs at the Rocket, but I doubted we had enough for a dinner dance at the hospital or if any of them were even suitable. Then he dropped the decider.

'They'll pay us £100! And all the beer we want!'

The money was a much more abstract concept to us, but free beer was extremely enticing.

'Okay, how long do we have to play for?'

'We only have to do two sets of an hour each.'

Hmm. We were lucky if we could play for forty-five minutes

at the most, so to do that twice? Would we be able to just swap things around a little and play a sort of combination of songs so the audience wouldn't notice that we were playing the same tunes again?

The day of the gig duly arrived and we drove with Michael's Woolworths van to Orpington General Hospital in the south-east corner of Greater London. The hospital was originally built by the Canadian government at the turn of the twentieth century. It saw a lot of action in the First World War treating Canadian and Allied troops, and became central to the town's life thereafter.

By now many of the original Victorian buildings had been replaced by the faceless 1970s architecture so common around the south of England: lots of brick and glass in the blandest possible combinations. A minimalism without charm or thought. Just plain dull. No wonder we wanted to escape. Even though we had grown up in this area, the small portion of Surrey/Sussex that we inhabited had many more intriguing facets than this. It was such a forgotten area. There was very little in the way of true progress; rather, a sort of Band-Aid approach that prevented everything from falling into ruin that kept the locals at least marginally interested in living life and not starting a revolution. We had other ideas about that.

Richard met us at the entrance to the hospital to ensure that the security guard at his little hut would actually let us in without calling the police.

He had dressed up a little for the occasion in what he took for rock manager's attire with a silk bomber jacket and a chain with a large medallion on it hanging rather incongruously over his nice sweater – knitted by mother, perhaps? A bizarre combination.

'Okay, lads. You should *definitely* play a few songs they know just to keep them happy.'

And suddenly it dawned on us that this might not turn out quite as we had intended.

Taking the gear out of the van we trooped into the empty dining hall where we were to perform in a couple of hours. Tables were set up for dinner, which we were assured would be removed 'for dancing' later on. Dancing? We weren't sure we had anything that would accommodate dancing. A rough pogo up and down or a lurch to the left or right maybe, but actual dancing? No, not really.

I had set up the Maxwin kit (finished in a lovely Naugahyde sparkle) and started to tune the drums when I noticed Richard running across the dining room floor, medallion akimbo.

''Ere, Lol! You'll have to keep the noise down. It's disturbing some of the punters ... er ... patients!'

Good lord. How did they expect us to play later on? He read my thoughts.

'In a couple of hours they'll all have had their meds and will be out for the night so it won't be a problem then, but right now some of the them might get a little agitated, if you know what I mean!'

*One Flew Over the Cuckoo's Nest* came to mind, and I had visions of the Chief running through the dining room and throwing a water fountain through my precious Maxwin kit.

We finished setting up in silence and adjourned to the little side room they had set aside for us to use as a dressing room.

'I've drawn up a rough set list,' Robert said.

Robert has always handwritten The Cure's set lists ever since I can remember. He tends to find a method he likes for most things and sticks with that. He has that self-sufficient punk ethos. Even now.

The set list was probably in his neo-child's script. People ask me if that's always how he's written and I can sincerely tell you that even when he wrote what I consider his first lyric back in Notre Dame middle school (an ode to footballer Rodney Marsh), his penmanship looked the same. There is no artifice with Robert. What you see is what you get, that's who he is. Some find this disturbing, but I always found it comforting.

I looked it over – a few cover songs, but mostly our own fledgling material. 'Killing an Arab' and '10:15 Saturday Night'. Nothing really suitable for a dinner and dance.

I wondered how the audience would take to us. There were nurses, porters, some clerical staff, and assorted balding, middle-aged men. They definitely did not seem like the sort of punky young people that would appreciate our particular noise.

How right I was.

We were required, it turned out, not only to play two sets, but to start off with some 'light instrumental music' to accompany dinner.

So I pulled out my felt beaters and Robert, Porl and Michael gently riffed and noodled away in what we thought was an approximation of 'light instrumental dinner music'. When I looked out into the audience I saw the sort of expressions I imagine greeted John Cage at the premier of 4´33´´, his avant-garde silent 'piano' piece, which he debuted in Woodstock in 1952. That should have been our first clue. A sneering disbelief that would eventually manifest as anger.

Dinner over, we turned our attention to performing 'properly' and playing 'songs for dancing'. About fifteen minutes into our set, I realized something was not quite right and the night might not be the easy money we had first envisioned.

Michael's brother-in-law was standing at the side of the stage, twitching. At first I thought it was a sort of understated pogo, the type a hip young manager might be expected to perform at the side of the stage, perhaps in Madison Square Garden or CBGBs. But no. It was his way of trying to get our attention without being too obvious, which of course made him seem just plain mental.

Porl sidled over to his side of the stage to get whatever news it was Richard wanted to impart to us, nodding as he spoke to him. It didn't look good. There wasn't much dancing happening on the dance floor they had made by clearing the dinner tables away, with many couples choosing to sit around the edges of the room in their party dresses and such, trying to ignore the din coming from the stage. Mercifully our set break came.

'So, yes, ladies and gents,' Richard broke in. 'Easy Cure have to take a break now.'

I turned round to see Richard clutching a microphone in one hand and gesticulating wildly to us with his free hand to get off the stage.

'They will be back in a while with more super hits for you to dance to all night,' he said, an air of desperate hopefulness in his voice.

We convened in the little side room and, as he closed the door behind us, we sat on the small couch while he perched on a wobbly fold-out metal chair.

'Well, I thought they might be a little more receptive to you, lads, but the general consensus is that they want something more along the lines of Tony Orlando and Dawn – you know, "Tie A Yellow Ribbon"?'

We all looked at each other, bewildered. We vaguely knew of the song but I don't think any of us knew how it went or how to play it. Big problem. Then Porl spoke up.

'Hmm, yes, well, I used to play that in my cabaret days.'

I did not know Porl had had any cabaret days!

'Anyway, you have fifteen minutes before the next set so work something out to keep the natives happy, all right?' Richard pleaded.

All eyes turned to Porl. Robert spoke first.

'So teach us "Tie A Yellow Ribbon", then.'

There followed the fastest learning of any song in the history of music. The only problem being that Porl couldn't remember a part of the song, probably one of the most important parts: the second verse! Undaunted, we went back onto the stage, slightly glowering faces surrounding us.

''Kay, well, now we are going to play a song you all know and love.' We started into the song led by Porl's gestures to change chords here and there. Then it happened. Just as people were starting to like us a little. I could see them mouthing the words silently as they danced, but the chorus just carried on and on with no second verse. Like one gigantic moment of *coitus interruptus*. I could see the audience's nervous faces unsure of quite what was wrong or what they were hearing. It must have felt like a record stuck in a groove permanently going round and round on the chorus.

Eventually we had to admit defeat and stop. We all looked at each other with uncertain faces and just bashed on with the rest of our set. Nobody danced anymore. I could hear the grumbling over the sound of our guitars.

'Call that bloody music?'

'Just sounds like noise to me!'

It was going to be a long night. Eventually we got to the end of our second and last set. I think someone chucked a bottle at us. We packed away our gear. Robert had driven up behind the van with Mary, in the hedge Mini, and went out to the car park with her just after the gig, followed by several disgruntled patrons. They pursued them to their car and provoked a fight with Robert. Nothing new there, then.

I don't think we even stopped to collect the money. Just high-tailed it out of there fast. Not a very auspicious start to Richard's hopes for us as the new cabaret sensation of the south coast.

# 6

# FICTION

Steve Rowland, Hansa's A & R man, who we were supposed to 'liaise' with, called us on the phone.

'Come and meet me in my London office, boys. We gotta have a talk.'

We went to see him at some swanky place in Mayfair, and as we entered his office he swung round in a big brown leather executive-type chair with 'Steve' in big gold letters above the headrest.

He had been apprised of our last abortive session with a 'name producer'. The one where I got hit on the head by a London bus on the way to the studio so we went to a pub to get a brandy for the shock and a nice old Rastafarian gentleman had given me a plaster for my bleeding skull. That session had not got off to a good start. Despite the bleeding there was the name producer's version of witty repartee to deal with, too.

Being a young, inexperienced drummer, I still had difficulty with what is known as 'four-limb independence'. Basically this is a difficult skill you have to learn because most drummers' lead hand and foot are on the same side of the body, and playing different patterns between them is the first big hurdle beginner drummers typically encounter.

Robert had spent endless hours in rehearsal at his house playing along with me while I learnt to play different patterns with my right foot and right hand at the same time. A good song to practise this, and another reason why Charlie Watts is a godlike drummer, is 'Honky Tonk Women'. Once you can play that properly, you've got it. Especially as there are two people playing it on the studio version: Jimmie Miller on cowbell and Charlie Watts on the drums.

During this particular session I was still having difficulty with the technique. The name producer ran the tape a bunch of times and couldn't resist putting his oar in from the control room.

'Lol?'

'Yes, Name Producer, sir?'

'Do you think you can play a straight four on the kick with a different pattern on the hi-hat? Maybe eights or something? At the moment you're playing the same pattern on both, mate!'

'Yeah, I'm having a little trouble today but I'm getting it, don't worry!'

'Lol?'

'Yes?'

'So when you're wanking does your foot move up and down at the same time, mate?'

I could hear stifled guffaws in my headphones and looked up to see the name producer and recording engineer with their 1970s moustaches cracking up behind the mixing desk in the studio control room. Ha, bloody ha. Stupid tossers! This would never do.

'So,' said Steve Rowland, bringing me back to his office as I snapped out of that last 'hilarious' studio memory. 'It seems that

Trudy and Peter Mitsel, the label owners, have heard your last efforts in the studio and aren't very happy that you recorded some of your own material besides the songs they wanted you to do. Their exact words were, *Even people in prison wouldn't like these songs!*

We didn't quite know what to say to that. Richard hadn't booked us any prison gigs – at least, none that we knew about.

'You know,' he continued, 'I was pulling for you guys, but I don't think I can help you here anymore.'

We had recorded 'Killing an Arab', and they in their wisdom had decided they couldn't release it. Prison material.

Robert's next move was brilliant.

'Okay, well, drop us from our contract if you want,' he said, 'but can we have the rights back to the songs we signed over to you? You know, the ones you don't like?'

The American looked a little surprised at that. I think he expected us to capitulate and beg to do some more songs we hated for them, just to have a record deal.

'Um, well, I'll see what they say. Okay, guys?'

Eventually they agreed to let us have our 'prison songs' back. I suspect they now wished they hadn't.

We spent a little while trying to regroup from our first contact with the horrible side of the music business. It wasn't that we were sad at leaving Hansa – quite the contrary, actually. We felt liberated. In the way of most young men, we had some bravado, but not too much certainty about our next course of action. I think we all would have felt better if it had been us asking to leave and not the other way around.

We did know that a change was needed, and it came in the form of Porl leaving the band. Now it would just be Robert, Michael and me.

In the greenhouse at the back of the Smiths' house where The Guru used to grow his organic vegetables, Robert, Michael and I convened one horribly hot afternoon after rehearsal. Porl's decision was doubly hard for Robert, as Porl and Robert's sister Janet had become boyfriend and girlfriend. This meant a great deal of Porl's time at the Smiths' house was spent in Janet's room.

It's kind of an unspoken law in most bands that the band comes first when it's time for band things. Just think John and Yoko. Robert generally tended to avoid direct confrontation unless he had to. In the greenhouse we discussed why Porl wouldn't work in the current version of the band.

'I'm not being funny, but I'm not sure Porl's style works with the new songs,' Robert said. 'He's going off to art college in Worthing soon, which means he won't be able to play any more gigs with us anyway.'

The music was getting more minimal, and Porl's flamboyant playing style was at odds with that. I think it also irked Robert that some people in Crawley knew Porl as the local 'guitar hero' and therefore any band he might be in would be 'Porl's band' by default. That kind of old-school rockist thinking had to go! We weren't like that. For now at least, we were more a democratic collective.

I don't remember Robert being particularly vindictive or upset about Porl. He's not like that. He doesn't harbour grudges. He can usually think things through in a startlingly logical fashion – albeit his own logic.

*

We were still going to the record shop in Horley where Simon's brother Ric worked on Saturdays. Ric Gallup was as eccentric as they come, although he would probably shudder to hear himself described as such. He had half a moustache on one side of his face and half a small beard on the opposite side and one sideburn. It was kind of like looking at a living cubist painting. His attire was also generally quite unusual too, involving fluorescent dresses with colourful boots to match. Of course, we adored him. He really understood what we were trying to do and he helped lift us out of the doldrums we were experiencing.

'Why don't you go record a demo of your songs on your own? I'll give you £50 for the studio time. Better than sitting moping around here, right?'

That perked us up. 'Really, Ric?' I said. 'You would do that for us?'

'Yes, just go do something, you know?'

He was absolutely right. We had to do something.

We booked some time at Chestnut Studios in Haslemere, West Sussex. In very little time we had a demo tape of 'Boys Don't Cry', 'It's Not You', '10:15 Saturday Night' and 'Fire in Cairo'. We made up a bunch of cassettes and stuffed a short letter and a photo taken by Robert's brother-in-law, John Taw, in some envelopes and mailed them off to every record label we could think of.

We waited, and then we waited some more.

The rejection letters trickled in one by one. Every label turned us down. Then we got one from Chris Parry, head of A & R at Polydor. He liked what he heard and wanted to meet us!

We arranged to see him in London at Polydor's offices in Stratford Place, just off Oxford Street. At first, the security guard was quite suspicious when we turned up at the rather grand address.

''Ow do I know you are supposed to meet Mr Parry here like you say, then, lads?'

At that moment, we saw Parry rushing past and he recognized us from our photo. 'It's okay, Chas. They're with me.' Turning to us, he said, 'Fancy a pint?'

We liked him immediately. Off we went to the Lamb and Flag on the corner of St Christopher's Place and James Street.

It turned out that Parry really liked our music and was interested in signing us to his own label that he was setting up, as he was leaving Polydor. We were a little disappointed with that. We were still under the impression that bigger was better as far as record companies were concerned. Never mind. It was the only offer we had at that point so we were game. He wanted to come and see us play.

'You have any gigs in London coming up?' he asked.

'Not at the moment, but why don't you come see us at the Laker's in Redhill?' Robert said

'We play there quite a bit,' I added.

Redhill was a few miles further north from Crawley towards London. We had snagged a gig there ourselves. It was run by old hippies who had their favourite band, The Hotpoints, play all the time. Occasionally we could get a gig with some other up-and-coming acts, like The Vapors, who were following behind local favourites The Jam. It was almost, but only almost, a happening kind of place.

'Yeah, perhaps I should see you in your own environment?' Parry mused absentmindedly while slopping Directors best bitter over his Italian loafers, which he habitually wore sans socks.

'That would be really the best way to see us,' said Robert.

Robert has always been very particular about how The Cure are presented, so it was important that the first time Parry came to see us it should be in front of our own crowd, on our own turf.

Parry came down to Redhill a couple of months before Christmas in 1978. It wasn't an elaborate affair. There wasn't a stage so we just played on the floor, but it was where we were comfortable, which helped us as we got through our set.

Afterwards we went over to the Home Cottage, a pub with ridiculously strong beer, and got drunk with him as he explained his idea for what was to become Fiction Records. By this time we had decided that we would probably be much happier on an independent label than with a big company. We had, after all, had the very difficult and demoralising experience with Hansa. Now we were keen on having a say on the type of music that we recorded. So that's how we got to know Chris Parry and how our true professional lives started. Making life-changing decisions while drinking strong beer!

The next couple of months Parry, who had by now assumed the nickname Bill (it's a long story) and some managerial duties, decided we needed 'toughening up' by playing some gigs around London.

One of the first gigs he got us was supporting Wire at Kent University in the campus dining hall. We figured that we would need a better vehicle to get as far as Canterbury so we enlisted one of my brother's friends, the strangely named Jim Crow. He was the only one of my brother's acquaintances that my mother banned from our house, because he insisted on wearing a white uncured cowhide jacket, which stank to high heaven. Anyway, Jim had a truck, and was willing to drive us to the Wire gig and back for a few pounds. We figured it would be fine.

We arrived at Kent University, and as we were walking backstage I encountered Lewis, Wire's bass player, in the hallway. The thing that struck me immediately was that he had a very, very normal short haircut until you saw the back of his head, which had one long rat tail hanging down the back. That freaked me out: the appearance of normality subtly subverted. I never forgot what it said to me about challenging people's perceptions about what's normal or not.

The Wire gig was a revelation to all of us in many respects. They seemed so much further along the path of their creativity than we were feeling. That point wasn't lost on Robert. I feel that day was when the germ for the minimal sound that came to fruition over the next few years was planted in our psyches. Not as a slavish copycat sound, but rather just the idea that we could deviate from the straight-ahead rock and roll standards and utilize a different set of rules to describe our musical journey. That definitely interested us. After all, wasn't that what punk was about – a call to revolution, a changing of the old guard?

I remember watching Wire play, all monochromatic attire with Colin Newman, Wire's vocalist, holding a black Synare synth drum in his hand and occasionally hitting it with a single drumstick. They had just released their second album, *Chairs Missing*, which was a lusher version of their debut, *Pink Flag*. The simplistic arrangements with the icy-sounding synthesizer were very enticing. We took note. Our performance was strong, but we knew now there was more to do. It was a revelation to us, especially Robert and myself.

As incredible as the gig had been, we nearly didn't get home alive that night. Jim had decided to put the truck's very large spare tyre unsecured on a little shelf above the passenger compartment. A sharp turn on the way home dislodged the tyre and, but for the grace of the universe, The Cure story might have ended that night, as the huge lump of rubber missed our necks by inches.

We were due to support Wire again at the next gig they had in London. We decided we should go in something else rather than the murderous Crow-mobile and got another friend to drive us to London. Unfortunately, his van broke down and we missed playing the gig entirely.

Parry was furious, and told us in no uncertain terms that 'You have to be more professional.'

We countered with the fact that it was very hard to be fully committed as we were all still having to hold down jobs and attend classes, and that we would love to have the wherewithal to 'go professional' and be able to be musicians full-time. We just put it out there and hoped that Parry would hear what we were asking of him. The night dissolved into more talk and beers and at one point I thought maybe, just maybe, I heard Parry say yes . . .

The next day my phone rang. It was Robert, 'So it seems that Bill is making good on his word. He's going to advance us some money so you don't have to go to your job anymore, Lol!'

We had discussed what we would do if we actually got signed again after the Hansa debacle. I never gave up on hoping we would do something, but Robert was certain of it. He saw no other way but for us to continue and keep the band alive. He was determined to prove everyone wrong, determined to show the world what we could be.

'We should probably divide it up over the course of a year to give ourselves some money every week, right?'

Robert was talking about the contract that had arrived from Parry, and in it the advance for the first year. Although it was not a fortune, it would enable us all to take out £25 a week to live on, and the rest we would put towards some new gear to play with. That was just like Robert. Pragmatic and selfless. Although he had gradually become our leader, he didn't want to take all the credit or all the money. First and foremost, he wanted the band to succeed, and so he put forward the most logical plan to keep the band alive and keep us all going.

He knew that I wasn't in the best situation to support myself without a job, so he made sure we all got enough to survive. My mother received the news less enthusiastically, reasoning that my income from my job was £50 a week, so this was a substantial drop. In the end, though, she saw the look in my eyes and knew this was really what I wanted to do, more than anything in the world. Ultimately, she relented and gave me her support.

'I expect to be sitting in a grand box when you play the Albert Hall!' she said.

If I have one regret in my life it's that she didn't live long enough to see that happen.

I was walking down Albert Road in Horley in the middle of the afternoon. A Tuesday, perhaps? What was surprising to me, as I had always been at college or work on weekdays, was how quiet everything was. Nothing and nobody about. A movement behind a curtain here and there signifying a disgruntled dog or pensioner, but that was it. I was doing the right thing by getting out of there. Although £25 a week wasn't much, I was being paid for playing music! For doing what I loved! It was a very strange feeling, like a frozen ocean beginning to melt with the spring thaw. Suddenly I could see that all we were led to believe about the world was only one way of looking at it. You could actually follow your instincts and do something boldly creative, and still be able to exist! It was a very alien concept to me, as I had always felt that artists existed in another world, one that I loved but was only able to view from the outside like a fairy tale – slightly surreal and not quite whole.

Even though Parry had booked us some time in a studio in London and we had recorded a double A-side single 'Killing an Arab' and '10:15 Saturday Night', we'd had to record it at night while I was still working. To make our first single seemed like an impossible dream to me, but it had happened, and now I could play music full time.

Gradually, very gradually, it was dawning on me that you could be anything you wanted to be if you really wanted it badly enough. If you were prepared to go the extra mile and forgo other so-called 'pleasures'. We had been rehearsing three times a week every week for three years in Robert's house. It didn't seem like a chore because we loved what we were doing. Now it seemed to be paying off a little.

I continued down Albert Road and into the equally deserted high street. No, I wouldn't be sad to get out of here. I could feel the pull of the unknown.

*

The white van was piled high with our gear and off we drove to Morgan Studios in Willesden, north London. It was where we auditioned for Hansa, but now we returned to make our first album! It felt magical and real all at the same time. We had been in studios before, but this was different. Real bands recorded here, real bands with records out and a history that we knew. The places we had been in before were more like hobbyist versions of studios with spare rooms used as drum booths and walls covered in old bits of carpet. Good enough for demos, but something a little more professional was needed for our first album.

Parry had a small office in the studio building out of which he was intending to run his new independent label. He had one person working with him. Indeed, she worked with him until the end – Ita Martin, a transplant from his days at Polydor. I always liked Ita, she had to handle many different personalities over the years, and she was a good match for Parry, too.

We had arrived in the early evening; apparently some other band was recoding during the day, so we had the night shift. This was a studio where bands like Yes and The Who had recorded. In fact, their recordings were in the tape library.

Walking into the main room of Studio 2, I was struck by all the shag carpeting, even over some of the equipment. The pervasive smell of incense and weed hung in the air. Still, the gear all looked top-notch – not that we had any idea what most of it did. The 24-track recorder was probably the only thing we had half a clue about and, as to the rest, well, it all looked very complicated.

Over the next year we would become educated in the technology of the studio and become more involved in the recording process, especially Robert, but for now we were content to trust

Parry as producer and the young engineer he had hired, Mike Hedges.

Hedges was a tall, imposing man with a shock of red hair, but most importantly, he liked us and understood what we wanted from the beginning. Sometimes the studio can be a fraught place where the interaction between the engineer/producer and the band becomes a minefield of conflicting ideas and needs, but I always felt we worked well with Hedges.

We set up our equipment more or less like we had while working out the songs in Robert's house, with me in the middle of the room and Robert to one side and Michael to the other. It's funny because I feel I have always been the go-between for Robert and Michael, and even to this day I facilitate communication between the two of them. Some things never change.

I was lucky enough to have Rick Buckler from The Jam's kit, which Parry had somehow finagled for a few days as he deemed my new blue Premier kit 'not really up to the job'. I had acquiesced without much fuss, as Rick's was a nice new black Yamaha kit. It sounded great. Parry, however, having been a drummer in his day while growing up in New Zealand, always wanted to fiddle with the drum sound and so started a regular recording ritual until we were able to take over and do it ourselves. We tuned and tried out many different snares. I think Robert and Michael both showed immense patience as this process went on and on and on. Nine times out of ten, we ended up using the first version we had tried.

It didn't take long for us to record the basic versions of the songs for *Three Imaginary Boys*. After all, we had played and rehearsed them so many times before we went into the studio. With the exception of 'So What', we had all of the lyrics worked out before we got to the studio. For that song Robert just had a sugar bag and read off the back of that, along with a sheet of lyrics I had given him. Very Dadaesque, I thought.

Mainly it was just a case of getting the best version down on tape. There was no cutting and pasting digitally back then, only the most basic form of tape editing, which involved immense skill in judging just where to cut the tape and glue it back together. Hedges was young and aware of new studio techniques, but also old school enough to be able to splice tape together properly. After the initial instrument tracks were recorded, we listened to them and then Robert sang over them. The idea of overdubs, that is, re-recording over existing tracks, was fairly alien to us, but we experimented on a couple of tracks and added over-dubs in the form of an extra guitar here and additional backing vocal there.

Then that was that! We had no idea of how to mix on such a complicated desk so we pretty much let Parry and Hedges get on with it for the first tracks. I think this is why Robert doesn't rate *Three Imaginary Boys* as a 'good' album by The Cure. We were left out of the mixing process so I understand why he feels that way about it. I still love the songs and I know he loves some of them, too. Otherwise he wouldn't play them still.

We spent most of the time when we weren't playing either at the back of the room drinking beer or in the little café at Morgan Studios, which was like a small, exclusive club for musicians, with people like Gary Moore and Iron Maiden hanging about. Being the new wave we generally kept ourselves to ourselves and avoided the large Marshall cabinets lurking in the hallways of the studio, which were liable to shriek uncontrollably if you got too close. Apparently, the best place to record metal mayhem was in the hallway. Who knew?

We slept at Parry's house, given that we didn't have an awful lot of money for a hotel. He had one room with two beds for us so we slept two to one bed, and the other bed was for the lucky one that got his own space. No glamour in rock and roll, kids.

We tried to add our two cents' worth to the sessions, especially Robert, who reasoned – not unreasonably – that Chris had signed us based on the demo we had made. We were ignored, as we were his new signing and he was running the show. He had just signed The Jam, who had some success, so his views prevailed. He couldn't have been much older than his late twenties, but to us he came across as adult. He was certainly more worldly, so we acquiesced.

We were new to this and we didn't really know where we stood, so we took a more passive role. We watched and waited. We were determined to learn the ropes so that the next time we recorded an album it would be different. That freedom was coming, even though we didn't know it yet. Still, it finally felt like we were on our way, getting somewhere at last.

Wherever that might be . . .

# PART 2
# (WHAT HAPPENED)

# 7

# GEN X

Things changed dramatically for The Cure the moment we signed the record contract with Chris Parry's label in 1978. Up until that point, we had been totally a law unto ourselves. Granted, we hadn't moved very far into the crazy world of rock and roll, but anything we had done prior to signing with Fiction Records emanated out of us and our own thoughts and ideas. Now, because we were funded by someone else, we had to take their wants and ideas into consideration. We tried to minimize the influence from outside but found that difficult to achieve.

I think it all started the day Parry presented us with the cover for *Three Imaginary Boys*. I say 'presented' because we didn't have any say in what the cover would be like. The same thing had happened for our first single, 'Killing an Arab'/'10:15 Saturday Night'. We were just presented with the artwork, a fait accompli.

It seems impossible to me now that we would have accepted that state of affairs. In our defence, we were really quite young, and we assumed that this was how it was done, and because Parry was bankrolling us we had to go along with his ideas. To be fair to him, I think his heart was in the right place and he genuinely thought this was a good way to represent the band. However I now understand why Robert has such antipathy towards the album and artwork. It's part of us but at the same time not part of us. I mean a fridge, a standard lamp and a vacuum cleaner? When journalists asked us about it, we had to make up stories about who was what on the cover. Nobody ever wanted to be the fridge, trust me.

There's another more serious side to the change that occurred. It was really the first time we realized we would have to negotiate with other people outside of our own immediate circle. We were going to have to leave the safety of our home area and everything that was familiar to us. We would have to go from being big fish in a small pond to being small fish in a large ocean. Initially that worked out in our favour. We were such a close unit that nobody could really get inside and divide us. At least for a little while.

We had been playing some London gigs that Parry had arranged for us, supporting various bands. Charlie Harper's UK Subs was one of them. I'd met Charlie previously at a club I used to go to in Croydon, the Greyhound, where he had asked me to become a member of the Subs. I declined, of course. People were starting to take us seriously, I could feel it, and I didn't want to disrupt that. At the Moonlight Club in West Hampstead, where we were supporting the Subs, a United Artists scout turned up and tried to poach us from Fiction. He was too late: we had already inked a six-month deal with Parry in September.

The first tour in which we played gigs outside of London and environs, just fresh from the pub and village hall circuit, was with Generation X, Billy Idol's first band. As a sort of pop-punk band, they had had a couple of hits, so were playing to larger audiences than we could reasonably expect to pull in on our own.

The first gig was in High Wycombe, a large market town just west of London. The venue was the town hall: an old Georgian red brick and white stone façade building. A little different from the downtrodden pubs and clubs we had been used to so far.

Inside we could see the stage had been set for Generation X, with many large amps and a huge silver drum kit with double bass drums. The big time beckoned enticingly. Alas, it was not to be the glamorous affair it seemed from the outset.

We were approached by a large, brutish-looking man and informed fairly quickly of the harsh realities of touring as an opening act.

'You're going to use the lights and PA, right?' the large man asked us.

'Er, yes,' Robert replied.

'Okay, £25 then,' said the large man, who by now had introduced himself as the tour manager.

'Is that all?' Robert asked. He, like Michael and myself, who had been following this conversation, had assumed the tour manager meant £25 was all he was going to be paying us if we used the PA and lights. Suddenly a look of understanding crossed Robert's face as he realized the large chap wanted to charge us £25 for the privilege.

'We haven't got the money for that,' Robert said. 'We only have enough for petrol to get home.'

The tour manager then pulled out what he thought was his ace card. 'No £25, no lights or PA!'

We had heard of this type of rock and roll chicanery, and as flag bearers of the new reality were having none of it. So the look on his face was priceless when Robert replied to his ultimatum.

'Right then, we won't use them!' Robert turned and motioned to me and Michael to go back and start pulling our gear out of the van. 'We'll use our own PA!'

We wheeled our small club PA system onto the large town hall stage and stuck a couple of floor lamps we used in pubs on either side of us. Punk self-sufficiency.

I don't know how much that endeared us to the tour manager, but it certainly interested the lighting guy, Angus 'Mac' MacPhail, because he is still the lighting director for The Cure today. I think because he felt sorry for us being bullied by the tour manager, Mac put up a couple of channels on the desk – lighting director speak for giving us a couple of lights to see by/be seen on stage – for which we were grateful.

The doors opened and we were ushered on stage almost immediately 'to warm the punters up', as the tour manager informed us. I'm sure Robert gave him a disdainful look as we marched on stage. We were not the same as these old hippies running the show. That much was obvious to all. However, we welcomed the opportunity to play, even if it meant we had to deal with the predictably capitalistic remnants of the counterculture from time to time.

Mostly people ordered drinks at the bar when the opening act was on, or arrived halfway through the set. That happened for the first gig or so on the Gen X tour, but pretty soon people were staying out of the bar and watching us play. Our conviction in what we were doing was obvious to everyone. We played for about thirty minutes and then removed all our own gear. No roadies for us!

The Gen X show was quite a spectacle of punk rock. As the opening number, 'Ready, Steady Go', started, Billy Idol, resplendent in a red leather jump suit, strode to the front of the stage and then, almost on cue, a thousand gobs of spit came arching over the stage front like arrows shot from longbows into the spotlight towards Billy. To our amazement he didn't recoil from this assault of phlegm but positively revelled in the ghastly gobbing frenzy. Suddenly, the purpose of the red leather suit became shockingly clear. It was the only suitable material for such an onslaught, especially considering this same scene was repeated every night of the tour. We watched from the side of the stage for a few more minutes, transfixed by the spectacle of Mr Idol being drenched with sputum. I think we were all secretly glad that the audience had decided we weren't worthy of their shower of spittle.

As we adjusted to the feeling of actually being on the road for the first time, we made a startling discovery. Generation X's dressing room had a lot of beer in it and it was apparently free!

After that we made sure that every night, as Billy and Co. went onstage, we paid a visit to the free beer room and grabbed a couple of cans to drink while either watching the gig or talking to the new fans we were making. Little by little, we seemed to be getting across to people who actually watched the opening act.

It was there I think I noticed for the first time Robert's wonderful ability to talk to each fan of the band. People lit up as he talked to them, and he had that charismatic way of making each one feel as though they were the only fan that mattered. He still has that ability today. I always thought it was a great quality to have. People responded to it in a very positive way. We were just starting to find out how The Cure seemed to make people feel like they belonged, even if they were outsiders like us. In fact, it was probably because they saw that we were outside the normal rock and roll channels that they felt that kinship.

And they still do.

The Generation X tour rolled on full steam after that inauspicious start. The tour manager avoided us as we set up our equipment but we gradually got acquainted with Nigel who ran the PA system for Generation X. He liked us, and we felt that he might be a good choice for mixing our sound at our own gigs after the tour. We were getting better offers now, and we would need to ramp the show up a bit from our old club PA and floor lamps! Perhaps we could persuade Mac to come 'run a few channels' for us, too?

We played the Croydon Greyhound, a south London ballroom, opening for Generation X at a club which we had often been to as paying customers. This was where for the first time the supposed 'glamour' of rock and roll was destroyed before my eyes.

At the side of the stage two large swinging doors provided access to the backstage area. As an audience member, I had often seen bands came through these doors to get on stage. In my adolescent fantasy I had thought that behind these doors lay a very exciting dressing-room scene complete with all the trappings of rock and roll mythology.

On entering the Greyhound as a performer, my first order of business was to find out exactly what lay behind those mysterious doors. I rushed headlong through only to discover . . . the fire escape stairs. There was no dressing room. The bands came up from the street directly onto the stage. The glamorous stories exploded right there for me. It was as I had feared all along: smoke and mirrors (or staircases). Nothing solid.

At Aston University a week later several large bikers loomed up at the front of the stage, took one look at us, and screamed, 'Play "Paranoid", by Black Sabbath. We decided that it was a reasonable request and at the end of our set we did just that. Actually, we could only play what we knew of the song, but it seemed to satisfy them, as afterwards their large leader, in studs and leather, approached us in the student bar.

'You're all right, youse are,' he said in a broad Midlands accent, pointing a skull ringed finger at us.

Robert looked at him and said, 'Thanks. I'm glad you liked it,' or words to that effect. This seemed to mollify the other bikers lurking behind their leader, and they skulked off back into the bar. As much as Robert could be a lightning conductor for violence, he could also be a soothing panacea to some of the more outré elements of society. I think they were just appreciative of the fact that someone would acknowledge their existence. I think that's true of most us, really.

Two nights later the highlight of the tour occurred. I was searching desperately for the Gents to relieve myself of several pints of free Gen X lager consumed after the Bristol gig at the Locarno, a throwback 1960s Mecca ballroom complete with sparkly curtains and glitter balls. It was the kind of place that was more accustomed to hosting beauty contestants in bikinis and grass skirts than punk gigs.

I finally spied the men's toilet and burst into the room, unzipping my flies as I entered to save precious time, as the pressure had built up substantially. As I rushed towards the urinal I saw, out of the corner of my eye, Billy Idol perched somewhat precariously in the next stall with a young lady clasped to his bosom (or maybe he was clasping her bosom, time distorts such distinctions).

A guttural sound passed from my throat, which might have been recognized as 'Hello, Billy' were I in a more sober mood, but it just sounded like a low grunt after that much alcohol.

The young lady looked somewhat startled by the fact that there was another musician in the vicinity of their love nest, so the ever chivalrous Mr Idol tried to calm her down with a valiant, 'Don't be nervous, love,' or something to that effect, while she anxiously eyed the toilet door.

Unfortunately, by this time I had reached the point of no return and a stream of urine shot outwards to the porcelain bowl next to Billy. Regrettably for me (as well as Billy and his date), my aim was not improved terribly with the consumption of so much cheap lager and, as I looked down towards where I assumed the urinal was, I realized that I was in fact urinating on Billy's leg. Pissing on the Idol!

He gave me one of his trademark sneers and I hastily zipped up and hightailed it out of there in a flurry of drunken apologies. On the drive home, as I sobered up, I had already perceived that this event might not be seen in the 'jolly japes, all lads together' kind of way one might hope. However, I thought, not unreasonably, that someone who was bathed in spittle every night wouldn't find much wrong with a little urine on his strides as he was caught *in flagrante delicto* with a local lass. It might even be seen as 'punk camaraderie' of sorts. Right? How wrong I was on that count.

The next gig was two days later at the California Ballroom in Dunstable. I cannot, especially as I now live in Los Angeles, conceive of a place more unlike California than Dunstable. (Although the Palm Cove in Bradford, which was decorated with a pathetically hopeful mural of a beach and palm trees, came close. If you squinted your eyes hard enough you could almost suspend belief that you were looking at peeling paint. Almost.)

As we pulled into Dunstable and the California Ballroom, known as 'the Cali' to the locals, we noticed our van had a slow puncture. Not a great start to our night. We started to set up the gear. Then I saw him, the tour manager, red-faced and striding purposefully towards us.

'Last show for you chaps after that stupid prank!'

We gave each other knowing looks. Apparently my accident in the Gents was not appreciated by the headliners. Or was it perhaps that our set was enticing too many of their fans that finally upset the apple cart?

That last night we trooped on stage to an audience made up mostly of snarling skinheads intent on mayhem. This was, after all, where most English bands will tell you the real trouble went down, not in the capital but the satellite towns. These were the chicken-wired stages, the Blues Brothers type gigs of the UK.

We played our allotted time, while the skins lunged onto the stage to dismantle anything they could lay their hands on. Using my hickory drumsticks I smacked a couple of probing fingers that I caught trying to remove my drum mics. We exited stage right before they finally overpowered the black-suited bouncers in bow ties lined across the stage front.

Billy and Gen X came on and the place erupted into a sort of war zone that may be familiar to those who attended the earlier punk gigs in the UK. We sat backstage and contemplated whether we were being chucked off the tour because of the reaction to our songs or the actions of my penis (not the first time it got me in some trouble). We were quietly absorbing this sorry state of affairs, after having spent much of Gen X's gig fixing the tyre of our van in the rain, when suddenly the dressing-room door burst open and several fierce-looking skins more or less fell into the room.

'Where is 'e?! Where's Billy'?

The looks on their faces indicated they didn't wish to have a polite conversation with Mr Idol about the state of British punk music. Rather, they wanted to dismember someone with a peroxide haircut. In a flash of inspiration it occurred to us that we could redeem ourselves and save our own skins (pun intended) in one fell swoop.

We pointed the Neanderthal-looking youths in the totally opposite direction of Gen X's dressing room, and they hurtled around the corner into the arms of several of those mean-looking bastardy bouncers they had chased away from the stage front. The bouncers chortled with glee when they realized heads would indeed be bashed in after all!

We quickly made our escape out the backstage door and into our van, which was now ready to go, and shot across the dismal car park of the California Ballroom. A few miles down the motorway we felt we had escaped both the skins and the tyrannical tour manager.

However, ten miles down the road we realized that while fixing the rear tyre we had inadvertently put the car jack through the petrol tank of the van, and now, because of a massive leak, we had to fill up every twenty miles in order to get home. Dunstable to Crawley – so, 76.8 miles on four tanks of petrol! Jesus wept! Goodbye gig money, hello rock and roll reality!

There is a sequel to this tale. A few years later I found myself in a club in New York City when one of my companions asked, 'Hey, Lol, do you know Billy?'

I swung around sharply to face Mr Idol again in the flesh! I fearfully stammered my hellos and we chatted haltingly for a few minutes. Billy made no mention of my previous indiscretion. Perhaps I had judged him too harshly, as he acted like the epitome of punk brotherly love, friendly and charming in the extreme. Or maybe no words were needed to convey what had happened between two young men that cold December night, backstage in the tinselly disco of a dismal English market town?

# 8

# THE HOLY TRINITY

Every band has their share of ups and downs, moments in time when it feels as if either the stars are aligned in your favour or you've been cursed for ever by fate. Good or bad it always comes down to a handful of events that make or break a band. For The Cure that time was the winter of 1979.

To support the release of our single 'Killing an Arab' backed with '10:15 Saturday Night', Parry had booked us for a solid month of gigs, including dates at the Nashville Room, the Hope and Anchor, and the Marquee. This was the holy trinity of London's constellation of clubs, of which the Marquee was its brightest star.

The Nashville Room was a grim little place that reeked of stale beer and cigarettes. Despite its respectable neo-Gothic red brick Victorian façade, the Nashville Room was punk rock central. At any time during the day you could find lads with spiked-up hair decked out in drab-looking raincoats drinking at the long, mahogany bar, tracing anarchy symbols with their boots on the sawdust-covered floor.

It's a good thing it was just three of us, because the stage was unbelievably small. At the back of the stage, a small door led to a dressing room that looked like a holding cell in a police station. A single bare bulb illuminated a small stained sink and not much else. This is where we hid until it was time for us to go on. Lined up along the chipped mahogany bar was a crowd of surly-looking skinheads, stamping their feet and pawing the floor with their boots. They looked more like a herd of bulls than boys.

This was exactly what we were afraid of.

'Killing an Arab' was inspired by the novel *The Stranger* (*L'Étranger*), written by the French existentialist writer Albert Camus. In the novel, the protagonist, for reasons he doesn't understand and cannot explain, shoots an Arab on the beach. Although the song is a treatise on existential angst and has nothing to do with racism, or indeed killing, it can attract the wrong type of 'seeker'.

That's what happened at our gig at the Nashville Room. A bunch of National Front skinheads had turned up, hell-bent on making trouble. Underneath their tough veneer they were disaffected young punks like us, but instead of making a go of it they blamed others for their troubles: namely, foreigners. They were anti-anything that wasn't a hundred per cent white Protestant British. With a song like 'Killing an Arab' these blokes were probably expecting to see a kind of Nazi skinhead band. They were as disappointed to see us as we were to see them. These were exactly the kind of small-minded yobs we'd fled Crawley to get away from.

We piled onto the stage and eyed one another suspiciously. Our punk outfits had evolved somewhat since the early days. Robert still wore a full-length grey raincoat and big blue brothel creepers, and his hair was cut in a kind of floppy Tom Verlaine fringe. I'd traded my wannabe Afro for a sort of scruffy shag, and I wore a white shirt with black drainpipes and a skinny tie. Michael wore a striped T-shirt and jeans with Converse trainers. The overall effect was somewhere between old rock and new wave, and decidedly un-punk. We were changing both the look and the music at the same time.

This didn't sit well with the skins, and their fears were realized when we started up our set with 'Boys Don't Cry'.

We braced ourselves for the worst as the expressions on the skinheads' faces turned from confusion to anger to hate. *Here comes the ultra-violence*, I thought. This was nothing new, after all. Looking like we did, we never backed down from a fight, and Robert took the brunt of it. We were always coming to his rescue. I don't mean to suggest that he wasn't capable of defending himself, because he was. There was a part of Robert that was almost dreamlike in the way he seemed to have his head in the clouds. But Robert wasn't from cloudland: he was from Crawley, and if you messed with him he wasn't going to back down. If you messed with me or Michael he always, always had our backs.

As the skinheads prepared their assault on the stage they were held back by a bare-chested skinhead with an enormous tattoo of a gleaming eagle on his sweat-covered chest. He moved towards the stage, clapping his calloused hands together and smiling from ear to ear. Bloody hell! He liked us!

His companions were a little dumbfounded by this development. Did their leader, the biggest and most intimidating member of their tribe, really like this poofy-looking band from bloody Crawley?

He did, and his enthusiasm proved to be infectious. Soon *all* the skinheads were dancing to 'Boys Don't Cry'. Robert looked around at me and grinned broadly. Breathing a sigh of relief, I let the elation I felt at this moment take me higher. We'd won the first battle and no bones had been broken, but the war was far from over.

Number 90 Wardour Street was easy to miss. Soho. The heart of London's sex trade. Depravity central. The only clue as to its importance was a small pale neon sign that jutted out across the pavement in the fog: the Marquee. To those in the know, its light shone out like a beacon. The Marquee wasn't just any old place. It was perhaps the most important venue in the history of European rock and roll music. From the street you had to go down a long corridor lined with old yellowing posters of everyone that had ever played there. That gave us the chills.

The Who. Jimi Hendrix. The Rolling Stones. David Bowie. The Clash. To us it was a kind of temple, the inner sanctum of English music, and we were about to make our mark with a month-long residency: every Sunday night in March. The actual club, however, was dark and dismal-looking. Enormous black bass cabinets on either side of the stage took up most of the space. Like the Nashville Room, the only entrance to the dressing room was through a door at the back of the stage.

Once inside we were confronted with the sheer awfulness of the facilities. The walls were as damp as a cellar and covered in graffiti from other bands. At the far end of the sloping- ceilinged room was a famously vile bathroom where the glamour of rock and roll went to die. It felt like you could catch hepatitis just by breathing in the air.

Despite the depressing accommodations we were agog with

excitement. Nothing could dampen our enthusiasm. We were playing a residency at the Marquee! We even got to hand-pick the opening acts for each gig. We selected up-and-comers like ourselves who didn't fit into other scenes, so projected the right tone. The bands were The Scars, Fashion, and Local Operator, but on that first night none other than Joy Division opened up for us. Despite this it was a disappointing opening. We played our hearts out to a half-empty room.

Between Marquee gigs Parry had us playing gigs all over England, usually on the venue's 'punk night'. The first of these was the Lafayette Club in Wolverhampton, run by a large and gregarious character named Vernon who was always dressed in an impeccable tuxedo. He treated us like royalty and so we thanked him on the sleeve of our first album.

Our performance at Bournemouth Town Hall made the local news: 'Girl Bites off Boyfriend's Ear at Punk Show' was the headline the following morning. At Isleworth Poly, the skinhead with the eagle tattoo and his band of jolly skins turned up and served as our protectors from other not-so-jolly racist thugs who were intent on making trouble. When a huge brawl broke out, our ally 'calmed' things down by whirling a wooden crutch he'd liberated from some guy with a broken leg, clearing a space between the skins and the stage. As local security had fled at the first sign of trouble, we were grateful for Eagle's presence. Robert invited our protector to come to the rest of our gigs at the Marquee, and he did, joining the swelling crowds that grew larger and larger for each gig. I think he took a fancy to Robert. Many people did. People were captivated by him. Charmed, in the literal sense of the word.

At Kingston Poly, the student union informed us that we

couldn't perform our single 'Killing an Arab'. We got permission to play it after Robert calmly took several of the students aside and explained the song's literary origins. They were embarrassed, but grateful for the explanation. It wasn't just the skinheads who thought the song was racist: so did the college students! If Robert could have taken every listener aside and explained the song to them, we wouldn't have had so many difficulties starting out. Talking his way out of trouble was something Robert was very good at, something he had a lifetime of practice at.

Night by night, gig by gig, we were winning crowds over. On the final night of our residency, I was standing outside on the street in front of the Marquee. In the lull between soundcheck and doors opening, I went out to have a smoke. Behind banks of dark grey clouds the sun was setting, and a gentle London drizzle softened the streetlights and the neon signs in the windows offering 'Escort services'. By the door of the club, there was a poster inside a glass case that listed all the gigs that were coming up. Our gig that evening was the only one with a 'sold out' sticker plastered across the band's name. Big John, the club's bouncer, had just placed a white board on the ground outside the club. In large black letters the sign read, 'HOUSE FULL'.

I stared at the sign in amazement. In a few weeks we went from being unknowns playing to half-empty rooms to this – whatever this was. We'd done it. We were becoming known in London. My reverie was interrupted by a couple of people walking up to the door of the club.

'House full for The Cure? Really?' they snorted incredulously.

'Yes indeed, gents,' Big John nodded as he turned them away. 'Sold out.'

They moved on down the street as perplexed by this turn of events as I was. I went back into the club smiling from ear to ear. I looked forward to sharing the story with Robert after the gig, when the gear was put away and the club had cleared out. I could imagine Robert having a laugh as we polished off the room-temperature beer and cold curry in the dressing room before we went out to conquer the rest of England, Europe and the world. It was the kind of story he liked. People were always underestimating us, Robert especially, and we thrived on it. *Yes, indeed*, I could imagine him saying, a mischievous smile lurking behind his beer glass, *sold out by some poofy blokes from bloody Crawley* . . .

# 9

# THREE IMAGINARY BOYS

The winter of 1979 was the coldest in sixteen years, with harsh blizzards and deep snow. The country slowly crawled out of hibernation in the spring, and by the summer we were generating our own blizzard by playing all over the UK on the *Three Imaginary Boys* tour.

Before that blizzard materialized, however, we played a benefit for our old college/school teacher Dr Antony Weaver. We felt he had been run out of Crawley College unfairly, and because we admired his stance as an anti-establishment figure, we had a gig arranged in the local community centre in Northgate, Crawley.

The building was a drab, utilitarian, pebbledash-finished affair in the heart of a neighbourhood of Crawley with a pub, a school and a church surrounded by row after row of nondescript new houses. It was everything we had planned to escape from condensed into one square mile of suburbia. The community centre was much like a school hall, with a small stage at one end where we set up.

As we had sided with Dr Weaver over the college, the local

skinheads would of course be turning up to see what mayhem they could cause that night. But this was not to be like the night of my eighteenth birthday when they had chased Robert and me over the bridge by Crawley station. No, now we were a couple of years wiser and, having toured England, we had a certain notoriety of our own. We had our followers as well as our brothers' friends – some of whom would certainly be able to stand up to any bothersome National Front skins. Amongst these was Frank Bell, the Cult Hero singer, and Brian 'Headset' Adsett, who would go on to do security for us for a number of years.

After Robert and I had our altercation with a bunch of their followers on my birthday, the Front were never far from our sights in Crawley. Michael even had the misfortune of having to work in the same place as the head of the local chapter for a while. In Crawley you couldn't really escape their pernicious reach, which is why we were totally unsurprised when one of our crew reported their presence at the community centre.

The local paper had turned up to record the bloodbath, and we weren't long into our set when the fighting started. As we played, I watched one of our crew lift up a small, pimply-looking skin by the collar, still kicking and spewing invective – 'I'll fackin' kill yew! Lemme go, you wanker!' – before depositing him firmly outside the community centre with a helpful boot.

The evening served as a symbolic rejection of all the things about Crawley that had sent us on our journey.

The *Three Imaginary Boys* tour really started the ball rolling in the UK. Originally booked to play twenty-six gigs, we ended up playing thirty-two, mostly in clubs and small theatres or a college here and there. We had already played about forty gigs in 1979, including the stint at the Marquee, so people all across the UK were coming back to see us a second time.

Even though we had a proper PA, with Nigel and his assistant Julian and Mac doing some lighting, we still had to pack away all our own gear. It wasn't quite the big time yet but we were getting a good reputation as a live band. We played a lot of gigs in a blur of activity and built up quite a solid following of fans from the ground up. It was a way of doing things in a grass-roots fashion that stood us in good stead for the future.

The tour was originally scheduled to end at the Lyceum Theatre on the Strand in London. I had seen other punk bands like Buzzcocks here, so to me it meant we had arrived. However, the promoter of the concert, not being apprised, apparently, of our burgeoning success, had decided to put us on a bill with The Ruts, who had a hit single with 'Babylon's Burning', to ensure a full house. You couldn't have put together two more diametrically opposed acts.

The Ruts' lead singer, Malcolm Owen, was the antithesis of Robert's approach. He was all skinhead chic and punk swagger on stage, with his Docs and braces. Robert was punk in attitude but his presentation was vastly different, as was noticed that night by journalist Mike Nicholls who dubbed us 'the Pink Floyd of the new wave'. It's true that we had started to pay attention to the way the lights and other elements of the stage might be used to present ourselves, and in Mac we had found a very capable ally.

Gradually, we introduced different colour combinations using blue lights and white strobes as opposed to the red and orange that was typical of rock gigs. We also had smoke and a little dry ice on stage. We were aware that we didn't really move about the stage like some other acts, but The Cure's sound was somewhat introspective, so we presented a spectacle with our light show.

Looking at the bill for the Lyceum gig, I wondered how we would be perceived by The Ruts' hard-core fans. I shouldn't have worried. Like everyone else, Robert charmed the frenzied hordes – much to the chagrin of Malcolm Owen.

In this maelstrom of activity, however, the seeds of discontent were being sown. Touring with Michael was not that easy for Robert. Although they could talk to each other and carry on a conversation, they weren't really friends in the way that Robert and I were. They didn't socialize much when I wasn't around to facilitate matters, which was getting to be both a problem for them and a headache for me.

Robert and I were always able to laugh or get animated or upset at the same things, but Michael was not like that. He always kept his thoughts to himself.

After the tour, we started to plan our next move. Our friend Frankie Bell from Horley had always wanted to make a record. He wasn't a musician as such, but he was part of our crew and had always wanted to be a singer, so we thought we could help by writing him a couple of songs to sing. We also thought that by doing so we might be able to kill two birds with one stone!

Robert and I had hung out with Simon Gallup quite a bit at the pub in Horley and we liked him and got on with him. It seemed natural that we might invite him to play on the record we were thinking of doing with Frankie. It also crossed our minds that if Michael wasn't the bass player in The Cure maybe Simon might become the bassist of choice for us. We asked Simon to come along and play on the Cult Hero single we recorded with Frankie, but in the back of our minds it was a kind of informal audition.

We all had a great time playing together. Besides the drums I even did some drunken back-up vocals. I don't think the light-hearted aspect of the recording was lost on Robert. It was a lot of fun playing with Simon, something that had been missing from our gigs on tour.

We did our first gigs in Europe at the end of July 1979. Having only been out of the UK on a couple of school trips, I had what was termed a visitor's passport: a single-page cardboard document that got me around Western Europe for a year.

Now that I was going to travel further afield, I felt I should upgrade to a full blue passport. Back then the British passport still listed the holder's job on the front page. I filled in the application and put 'musician' under occupation, which felt incredible. I paid the extra fee to have it expedited as we were leaving soon. I got it just a couple of days before we set off for the Netherlands and our first gigs outside of the UK.

We boarded the ferry at Harwich and settled into the trip to the Hook of Holland. From there it was a three-hour drive to the festival in Sterrebos just outside of Groningen.

As the ferry docked at the Dutch port, I stepped off and walked up to the customs control queue.

'Next!' A large, round border guard motioned to me to come forward. 'Passport, please.'

I gave him my new passport and he opened it and took a long, hard look, first at my face then back at the passport. For a moment I panicked slightly, wondering if I'd done something wrong. It was hard to tell from his inscrutable face. Then the reason for his close attention materialized. With an accusing digit he pointed first at the passport details and then at my face.

'Musician? Ha! You have drugs!'

He stabbed his finger at the blue pages harder now.

I'd just turned twenty, and while I'm not sure what my boyish demeanour indicated to him, I'm pretty sure it wasn't that I was an opium eater. Not unreasonably, I muttered a feeble, 'No sir, no drugs.'

Eventually he could see I was no Keith Richards and let me go. He returned the blue passport and sent me off with a desultory wave of his hand, having made a young English musician quake in his boots for a few minutes. Bastard.

I wondered if this was setting the tone for touring outside of England. The thing about The Cure was that although we were very English, we were open to new experiences and trying to live life fully. We wanted to see the world and all it had to offer.

We arrived in a very gloomy Groningen under a lowering sky. The tiny stage was set up in a park on the edge of town. We were due to play late in the afternoon. Being summer there was still some light as we walked on stage. I have to admit that we were apprehensive. Would they like us? Did they know any of our songs?

We needn't have worried – that was the day we discovered that music is a universal language. The Dutch audience took us into their hearts, and even though it was pissing down with rain while we played, we didn't care. In fact, we were so enamoured with the whole affair that when the promoter asked us about playing a second gig later that night we jumped at the chance.

'Just show us the place!'

He took us to what seemed like a secondary school gym about a ten-minute drive from the festival. A couple of hours later, we had performed our second ever European gig, all in the space of a few hours. We felt elated. Then the promoter broke the news to us.

'I don't really have the money to pay for that second show, but if you want to hit Amsterdam on your way home I can get you a hotel for the night so you don't have to rush and get the night boat home.'

A hotel! In Amsterdam! This was an added bonus. Although we had stayed in a few hotels on the UK tour when it was too far to drive home, these hotels weren't in towns quite as glamorous as Amsterdam.

A couple of hours later we were in the heart of the city. With our first European gigs under our belts we were very happy. The promoter pulled the van onto one of the little canal roads that circle the city centre. It was a very charming place and I saw a few names on store fronts I had heard of, like De Beers, the famous diamond dealers. I expected the hotel would be just as grand.

We drove across a small bridge and the promoter pulled the van over to the side of the canal.

'Okay, guys, just go around that corner there and you'll see the hotel. It's all paid for. Just say your name to the, er, owner and have a great sleep.'

He hurriedly started up the van and waved at us as he drove off at an indecent speed for the small canal roads. He was a local, and probably knew his way around like the back of his hand, I mused.

We went around the corner and walked down to the end of the alley to find a rather nondescript building. It didn't look like a hotel. Then I saw the door with the clumsily scrawled 'Hotel' in white dripping house paint. Surely this wasn't the place. We pushed open the door and discovered a winding circular wooden staircase going up for several storeys. As we passed one landing, an elderly man came out of a door.

'You are The Cure, yes?'

We nodded in the affirmative.

'Floor five,' he said, and handed us the key attached to a rather large rubber ball.

We ascended a couple more flights and found the only door on the floor. Opening the door we were assaulted by a strong odour of what can only be described as eau de urinal. We pushed into the room and found several cots with grey scratchy blankets on them and the source of the smell: an open sewer pipe running the entire length of the room. The overall effect was that of a POW camp during the Second World War, which, considering the location, it might well have been at some point in time for all we knew.

We weren't drunk enough yet to tolerate the awful stench so we came up with a very reasonable plan.

'Let's go to a café and get plastered,' I suggested. 'It's the only way we'll be able to sleep here tonight.'

'What a splendid idea, Lol,' Robert agreed.

We proceeded to get properly pissed.

Robert had met Steven Severin, the bassist for Siouxsie and the Banshees, at a gig in London, and they hit it off straight away. That started what I view as a sort of diversion therapy for Robert for a few years.

It was always hard for Robert to reconcile the overt commercialism of the music business with the artistic side. On one hand, he instinctively knew that The Cure were worth something and had definite value. He was very protective and wouldn't let anyone take advantage of us. On the other hand, he did not really want to do things just for their commercial value. That was not his driving force. He was (and still is) an artist who wants to experience life and live with an intensity that he finds fulfilling. Money and fame were not the point. Every so often he would relieve the pressure that was building up from the record company and commercial success in general by changing course dramatically. To my mind that's the genius of Robert Smith: to live a life on his own terms while making a living out of it too.

He always said when we were younger that he didn't want to have a job where he would have to get up every morning and go to work. He wanted to be more self-determined than that. It was not that he didn't want to work; he just didn't see the purpose of working at something he didn't particularly like for someone else's ends. He's still like that, but he's also somebody who has always worked very hard at what he believes in.

Although we had come on the end of the punk revolution and people really wanted to label The Cure 'post-punk', it never felt like that to us. Certainly, we had grown up just a few miles from the heart of the storm, so we absorbed the influences gradually, and not quite at the frantic change of pace that was going on in the capital. This suited us fine, and it was true to our overall temperament. When Robert found something that worked he would stick with it. He was always a most methodical person. This worked well for us overall. Although it took some time to get the band going, it had lasting value because Robert had thought it through, slowly and deliberately.

The *Join Hands* tour with Siouxsie and the Banshees was quite a change for us as a band, and it was probably the beginning of the end for Michael in The Cure. The Banshees had somewhat different views and quite a different set of values from ours, which gave us something to gauge our own path by.

Robert and I both liked the Banshees' music, and Siouxsie had an undeniable charisma. I always got on well with her and Severin. I admired Siouxsie because she had to deal with a lot of misogynist bullshit. She wouldn't put up with disrespect from anyone, and I've seen her deck a couple of particularly annoying characters on more than one occasion. Rightly so.

However, it's wrong to characterize her as an aggressive, hardcore punk. Siouxsie has a very caring, gentle side that doesn't come across right away. For instance, she was always very supportive of girls we would meet on the road who were trying to forge their own way in the world artistically or otherwise. In that way I believe she was the first true punk feminist.

After a couple of warm-up dates in Bournemouth and Aylesbury, we went over to Belfast. The gig in Aylesbury had been quite chaotic, as a bunch of skinheads turned up to try and cause trouble. It's a strange fact that almost all of the violence at UK gigs back then was in the cities surrounding London. Places just like Crawley.

As we rolled into Belfast off the ferry, it was obvious that we had entered a war zone. Soldiers and policemen roamed the streets that were broken up by seriously bombed-out buildings. As we rounded the corner into the main city centre, Parry pulled over and pointed to a policeman standing by a sentry box.

'Lol, go ask that copper the way to the Europa Hotel.'

'No problem,' I said, unbuckling the seatbelt and walking briskly over to the policeman.

What I had not seen was that inside the sentry box was a fully outfitted British soldier with rifle in hand. As I rushed up to the policeman the soldier not unreasonably thought this guy in all black might be some kind of threat. He wheeled around, pointing his weapon squarely at my midriff.

'Excuse me, officer,' I stammered. 'Could you please direct us to the Europa Hotel?'

Hearing my south London accent, I think they realized I wasn't coming to attack the sentry post and relaxed a little.

'Go about a mile down that way,' he pointed, 'and you'll see the Europa. It's the building opposite the bombed-out pub.'

The Europa Hotel had the reputation as the 'most bombed hotel in Europe' having been targeted no fewer than twenty-eight times during the Troubles. I had also heard that bombs were hurled over the security fence with such frequency that the Europa had no rooms on the first four floors. Indeed, when we arrived at the security gate at the front of the hotel, there didn't seem to be anything on the bottom floors that I could make out except the bar. I suppose the thinking was that if you're drunk you're less likely to mind a little bomb now and then.

The gig itself was going to be a little problematic, as the road crew had fallen asleep in Liverpool, and so we didn't have any gear. It was then that we met one of the true heroes of the punk movement: Terri Hooley, who had started up Good Vibrations from his record shop and turned it into the hippest label in Belfast. Good Vibrations was responsible for The Undertones' 'Teenage Kicks' amongst many others.

Terri was a friend of Parry's, so he got one of his other bands, The Outcasts, to lend us their instruments for the gig. The gig went well, even though we had to go on after the Banshees, because there was such a delay starting. Thankfully, some of the audience stayed to watch us. Later, at the bar of the Europa, I sat with Terri and tried to drink enough Guinness so that I wouldn't care about the possibility of being blown up. He calmed my worries.

'If you haven't done anything to anybody you'll be fine, Lol. They'll leave you alone.'

This seemed pretty reasonable to me and we continued chatting, or rather I did, because at some point I realized that although it looked like Terri was squinting at me with one eye open, his head was resting on the back of his comfortable seat and he was in fact fast asleep! Later I found out he had lost an eye as a child, and it was the glass replacement that convinced me he was still awake.

At least he didn't take it out and pop it in my beer, which I hear he liked to do sometimes. Terri Hooley, a lovely man and a true punk original.

We travelled to Aberdeen the next day, where we were in for another radical change. I should have realized it was going to be an unusual couple of days, as we pulled into the hotel to find the place swarming with policemen and still more soldiers. What the hell had happened?

It seemed that Margaret Thatcher, the then prime minister, was staying at our hotel. Hence the large security presence. Unfortunately, that meant we couldn't check into our room right away. It was starting to feel like a police state.

We were directed to a spot at the back of the car park by a small hedge. I hadn't been able to relieve myself since we'd got off the ferry from Belfast. As it was now early evening, I got out to pee next to the hedge under cover of darkness. As I luxuriated in the feeling of release, I noticed several small red dots surrounding me. Nonplussed, I looked up to the roof of the hotel where the lights seemed to be coming from. Then I spied them. Three or four police marksmen with their infrared sights trained on me!

It seemed my penis had gotten me into trouble yet again. I waved at them in a vague hope that they might see that what I was doing didn't pose a threat to the prime minister's security. It worked, as the red lights went off and nobody came to cart me off to jail.

Later that night, after we'd settled into the hotel, we discovered that politicians were much worse behaved than any rock band. Several drunken members of parliament were whisked out of the bar by various members of their staff very much the worse for wear. I made a mental note not to vote for any of that lot in the next election!

The next day there seemed to be a strange undercurrent when we arrived at the Capitol Theatre for the soundcheck. Where were Kenny Morris and John McKay, the Banshees' drummer and guitarist, respectively? They didn't seem to be in the building, as Siouxsie and Severin did the soundcheck on their own.

It turned out that they had all been at a record shop signing earlier that day and had an argument with the owner about giving away free copies of the *Join Hands* album. Kenny and John stormed out of the signing and got on the next train back to London, leaving the tour in jeopardy.

We went on at our allotted time and played our set. Afterwards Dave Woods, the Banshees' manager, came up to us.

'Do you think you guys could go back out and play some more songs? I don't think the Banshees are going to be able to play tonight!'

Robert said that we would, and after Siouxsie and Severin went out and told the audience the bad news we went back on and played some rough versions of songs we were writing, most of which didn't have lyrics yet. Then Siouxsie and Severin joined us on stage for an improvised version of their song 'The Lord's Prayer'. It was a very chaotic evening.

Later that night, we all hung out drinking, and Robert nobly said he would play guitar if they needed, and I offered my services too. We all wanted the tour to continue. However, for the moment, it was going precisely nowhere.

We went home and into the studio to record 'Jumping Someone Else's Train', which would be our final recording with Michael. We also slotted in a headlining gig at a new pop festival in front of 10,000 very enthusiastic Dutch fans. We were making our own inroads into Europe.

While we were recording, Siouxsie and Severin turned up to the studio to ask Robert if he would help them out by playing guitar for the final tour dates. They had a new drummer in Budgie from The Slits, so now they were ready to continue.

Continuing that tour was difficult for Michael and me, especially for Michael. I was naturally more easy-going with the Banshees than Michael, who could come across as stand-offish. Although I suspect that had more to do with his deteriorating relationship with Robert.

I also took a more pragmatic approach to what was going on. Although I thought it must be tiring and mentally exhausting for Robert to have to play our gig then turn around and play the Banshees' set, I always felt in my heart of hearts that Robert's real loyalty lay with what we were doing with The Cure. Even after the tour, when he got more involved with the Banshees, I never felt that he would end up in that camp for ever and ever. He needed somewhere to put the stress he felt as leader of The Cure, and playing other people's songs relieved him of that pressure.

The one thing that we did learn from the Banshees was to be far more assertive in doing business in the new world in which we found ourselves. Siouxsie and Severin had to struggle in the early days of punk to get the Banshees taken seriously, but they quickly learnt to assert their opinions, inject their art into the equation, and it had worked. It took us a while to learn to be that insistent about our wants and needs. We were, after all, nice polite middle-class boys who had never been exposed to the cut and thrust of the nasty old music business.

Although the Banshees may have made all kinds of plans to keep Robert in the band, that wasn't ever going to happen. I knew Robert too well. He needed to have his own thing, and the Banshees were never going to be that. He needed to be the captain of his own ship, not just a trusted lieutenant.

We were at the Smiths' house back in Crawley when Robert presented a cassette for us to hear.

'These are some ideas I have for the next album,' he said as he inserted the tape in the player.

He asked me if I remembered that fucking awful night in

Newcastle and I nodded my head. Robert had been in a fight with three businessmen inside our hotel lift on the *Join Hands* tour, while Michael and I were fast asleep. He was badly beaten but used the energy and pain from that night to write his feelings into songs for the next album.

'I got a lot of ideas that night and I've been working on them.'

With that he pressed play on the machine. As I listened, I was amazed by the minimal beauty of the songs. Some had lyrics, but not all of them. They were sparse sketches that he had done mostly using his guitar and the electric organ in our practice room. He utilized the rudimentary drum machine on the organ for rhythms and recorded it all on a small tape recorder. It was a departure brought on by our exposure to the bleeding edge of new music, like Wire and the Banshees. However, I felt that more than the Banshees, the real influence was Wire. Their subtly shifting minimal punk soundscapes were far more in line with what we were thinking and doing than the more bombastic drama of the Banshees. Lyrically, we were like neither of them, to my mind, but musically I see the connection with Wire.

As much as I liked the new songs, Michael was fairly non-committal.

Inside this preview of what would become *Seventeen Seconds*, I heard a glacial sonic landscape that mirrored my own lonely feeling at the time. I don't think Michael related to it on that level, so perhaps to him it felt like a step in the wrong direction. I felt he wanted to do something more melodic and intricate than the song fragments Robert played for us suggested. I, on the other hand, connected immediately, even though they were just skeletal ideas, the bones of the songs to come.

Underneath all of that, the real problem for us was that we were English boys from suburbia. Somewhere out there on the road things had changed for us, but we didn't really have the emotional tools to deal with each other's feelings in a constructive manner. Instead of talking about the different ways we felt about the songs, we kept the conversation polite and stuck to discussing their mechanics. We chose a very English way of dealing with our emotions: by not dealing with them at all. We figured if we ignored our problems, they would go away. This mindset was the biggest barrier to the continuity of The Cure as years went by. It destroyed far more than it created.

Before long the gulf between Robert and Michael had widened. If we had all been less emotionally stunted, perhaps we might have worked out our differences. Maybe it's just a product of youth, and experience is the only way to get to that point.

In any case it fell to me to tell Michael about the rift that had opened up, and the fact that Robert felt like it wasn't going to work out anymore. To his great credit, Michael has never held any kind of grudge about this with me. I think he realized this was inevitable, although it couldn't have been easy. I know it wasn't easy for me.

I also think that in a way it was a kind of relief as the pressure had built up so much in the preceding months that it was impossible to go on without some kind of change. This was the first time that I saw Robert's stubborn side. I don't think he planned Michael's removal. I never believed he was as Machiavellian as that, but he definitely had an idea of the direction in which he wanted to take the band, and he was determined to stick to his plan until someone proved him wrong.

He did call Michael after I had made the first inroad and said that if Michael wanted he could keep The Cure name and we would start a new band. It didn't turn out that way, obviously.

Robert and I went around to Simon's house and asked Simon if he wanted to join the band. Of course he did. We knew that he would fit in well with us both musically as well as socially.

We thought we should change things a little. We were aware that Parry had this image of us as a three-piece power pop trio and we definitely wanted to disabuse him, or anybody else, of that viewpoint. From the very early days, Robert always defied expectations. Not in a bloody-minded way, but to keep himself vibrant and connected to what he was doing. He's never been one to sit and rest on his laurels. That would be anathema to him.

Robert and I discussed what we could do to make things different. Listening to the *Seventeen Seconds* demos Robert had it seemed like a good idea to introduce some other instruments to the songs, as they were almost begging to be coloured in a little. One of Simon's friends was Matthieu 'Matty' Hartley, who played keyboards. I had seen Matty around town with various different coloured hairstyles, and both Robert and I thought he could add something to the songs. We wanted Simon to feel at ease within The Cure and figured if his friend came along that it would make him more comfortable in the band. There was bound to be a little fallout from Simon's old band for leaving to play with us, and we thought if he had his mate with him he would probably weather the flak a little better. The music scene was changing, moving forward from straight-ahead punk thrash and into new territories. We felt we were at the forefront of whatever was coming next.

*

So we had a new band and some new songs. It seemed like a good idea to put the two together and go play some live gigs for people to get a feel for what we could do. We went on the road with our labelmates The Passions and The Associates on the 'Future Pastimes' tour. I think that's the reason *Seventeen Seconds* is such a fully realized album. We had fresh new musical minds working on the songs, as well as time to figure out what worked and what didn't in a live setting. We began with some shows in the UK. It was the first time we had played songs that were not fully formed for quite a while. We'd been playing the same set during the *Three Imaginary Boys* and *Join Hands*, tours so it was refreshing to have new songs to play and experiment with.

Shortly after the UK leg of the tour, we were on a ferry, going off to conquer Europe proper. The wave had crested for punk and we were going to be the new sound. We could feel it. The tour was hard but great; I felt people got what we were doing. However, as I would soon find out, it wasn't to be all joyous good times.

We played in Eindhoven in Holland for the first time as a four-piece. Afterwards, it seemed appropriate to celebrate, which we did. I drank so much red wine I felt like I wanted to die. Somehow I ended up lying in my shower with the water running over my face, trying to make sense of what had happened to me. I felt so bad from drinking. It didn't seem like fun anymore, but I also didn't seem to be able to stop. It was very scary, but I didn't see the connection between my alcohol intake and that dark depressed feeling I carried around with me afterwards, which made me want to drink even more. The chaos and pain kept building and building until it exploded. Once again, Robert came to my rescue.

*

I think it's called a 'glassing'. That's the common term for what happened to me. I was not overly concerned with the definition, rather I was acutely aware of a sharp pain on the left side of my face just below my eye. I instinctively put my hand up to the place where the pain emanated from, finding a warm, sticky ooze on my fingers combined with broken bits of something crystal. It took a few seconds for the realization to dawn that my attacker had smashed a Pilsner glass into the side of my face, which then peeled open like an onion under a paring knife. I glanced downward to see my once pure-white shirt wet with brilliant red blood. In shock and anger, I sobered almost instantly to the realization of what had just been done to me. I grabbed my assailant by the shoulders and flung him backwards, furiously jettisoning him away from me and back into the dark orbit of the club.

Propelled by hands I couldn't see, I staggered towards the small bathroom where, as I looked upwards into the hazy, mottled bathroom mirror, an awful picture awaited. My facial features were contorted and swirled in red like a Francis Bacon portrait. They were almost howling at me from my murky reflection. I dabbed a proffered towel on my stinging face to staunch the blood flow, but soon a bloom of red poked through this too.

'Shit!' was all I could manage.

This required a bit more attention than I could give it. Suddenly Geil, the local record company guy, spun into the bathroom with me.

'Come, Lol. I'll take you to A & E. You need to get that fixed up.' I glanced up from where I was watching drops of red fall into the white porcelain sink.

'Yeah, you're probably right,' I managed to croak under my

breath. I was in shock and shutting down a little. Geil anticipated my next question.

'Robert knocked that asshole clean out! Security have him now and he's going straight to jail, I promise you.'

Robert, my boyhood friend, teenage companion, and now adult defender, had meted out punk justice and protected me. Once again.

We raced through the damp, dark streets of Ghent, Belgium, in Geil's car to A & E. Once inside the brightly lit hospital, it became evident just how much blood had spilled from my slashed face. One of the crew had rustled up a T-shirt from merchandising for me, so I removed my blood-soaked shirt and deposited it in the nearest bin.

It had started out as a celebration of the end of the tour. The Cure, together with our road crew, were invited to Ghent's only alternative nightclub to drink and dance the night away. It was a great chance to wind down after a long, arduous year of touring. We played an exhausting 125 gigs that year. It was the night before Christmas Eve and we were to go home at last the following day. I had been talking to a couple of Belgian girls who had been at the gig, and was getting pleasantly drunk when a swaying individual to my side grabbed hold of my drink and took a hearty slurp from it. Although I was somewhat irritated by his oafish behaviour I chose to ignore it. The record company was paying for the drinks, so what did I care? I just ordered another one. However, the oaf had other thoughts and was now turning his drunken attention to my companions. He roughly pulled one of them towards him, at which point I intervened and pushed him away. He fell awkwardly and drunkenly backwards over an empty table, glasses flying everywhere.

Then it happened. He sprang madly to his feet, grabbed hold of a glass and I felt a quick, sharp punch as the glass exploded into my face. It took a second or two to register just what had occurred. It was like a car accident in that way, and then reality returned and slapped me very hard indeed.

The sight of the doctor brought me back from my waiting-room reverie.

'Okay,' he said in perfectly balanced English. 'Looks like you've been in a war! Let me take a look, please.'

He peered at my mangled face and brushed away the hair that had matted into the blood.

'Is it bad?' I asked.

'I think we can fix you. It will look like you've been in an old-fashioned fencing duel, but that's okay for a man's face, gives him some character, no?' He laughed a little nervously.

I didn't think it was very funny.

'You're very lucky. It missed your eye by about a centimetre.'

I pondered what I'd just heard. I was worried and suddenly very cold. I shivered uncontrollably as I followed Geil and the doctor into a sort of surgical room.

'Lie on the table on your back, please.'

I complied and a sheet was placed over my face like I had just died. I noticed a small hole in the cover through which I could just make out the doctor's hand with a pair of forceps. He pulled broken bits of the beer glass from my cheek.

'I'm going to give you a shot for the pain, but you're probably fairly numb anyway.'

I couldn't help but notice the strong smell of alcohol in the air. I figured it was probably me rather than the doctor, or maybe the solution that he used to irrigate my shredded face. The first of fifteen stitches pierced my torn flesh. Mercifully, the shot he'd administered worked and the pain was dulled. It felt like someone was pushing fishing line through my cheek. Which was, I suppose, fairly close to the truth. I relaxed and let the medic do his work. At least I was alive, right?

'Bloody hell! Is he dead?'

I came out of my narcotic fugue to hear the voice of Elvis asking the doctor about my apparent demise. Not 'The King', I hasten to add, but our roadie of the same name. That would have been way too much Demerol even for me.

'No, Elvis, I'm not bloody dead,' I rasped from beneath the covering sheet. I didn't blame him for thinking I'd died. It probably looked like the doctor was working on a corpse. I felt cold, bruised and much, much more sober.

'I'm so glad you're alive, Lol!' Elvis exclaimed in his broad Yorkshire accent. Our crew was like an extension of the band. We had spent so much time with them over the last few months, crammed together in hotels and smaller backstage areas where the gig was the only thing we were all focused on. Brothers of a sort.

Eventually the doctor finished his expert needlework and I was encouraged to sit up. I felt a little woozy at first. He handed me a small mirror in which to inspect his handiwork. This struck me as perhaps a little cruel, but I was still in enough shock to take the mirror and look. Like cuts from a fencing foil, a couple of straight slashes to my left cheek were now held together with black threads barely visible through translucent tape. The doctor's handiwork was obscured by redness and swelling. At this point

I sensed the slightly nagging, irascible voice rising up inside me: I needed a drink.

I bade farewell to the good doctor and thanked him for his work. Geil, Elvis and I walked out the doors of the A & E.

'Where to, Lol? The hotel?'

My voice was a little hesitant at first but found its confidence. 'Umm, no, I think I'll join everybody back at the club.'

My companions looked a little dumbfounded, but Geil quietly started his car and we pulled out of the car park past the big red neon sign that read 'Hospitaal' in that double-vowelled Flemish way and back onto the two-lane motorway towards the centre of Ghent and the club.

As I walked in I heard gasps from various people. I ordered a drink and soon everything was like before. Sort of. Looking across the bar, I caught sight of my rather macabre features in the mirror at the back of the bar. The bruises were starting to show. Tomorrow I was bound to look much worse. I decided to drink until I no longer cared how I looked or felt. And so I did. It was three in the morning on 24 December 1979.

Merry bloody Christmas, everybody!

## 10

# SEVENTEEN SECONDS IN THE USA

With *Seventeen Seconds* we combined elements of music we really admired and gave it our own twist. Both Robert and I really loved David Bowie's *Low* album, and Robert was also a fan of Nick Drake's music. Listening to it years later I can hear those influences in *Seventeen Seconds*, but more than that, I hear Robert's musical genius coming through for the first time.

Once we had all the elements in place, we went into the studio. We worked again with Mike Hedges, who by now understood our methods and drives and complemented them perfectly. Hedges was open to new ways of recording and constructing music. He would help us in myriad ways, and I know that we all found him very encouraging and creative.

We still didn't have much money, so recording time was at a premium. We experimented, and at one point we even tried swapping our instruments with each other to see what would happen. Those tracks weren't used, which I think tells you what it sounded like. We slept in the old Morgan Studio 1 for some sessions, which was kind of creepy, as it used to be a church.

Above the new ceiling was an old, stained-glass roof. When the studio was dark it was visible in a ghostly kind of glow. At 4 a.m. it looked almost otherworldly.

It was a very happy time for myself and Robert, as we had a new band with Simon and Matty, and Parry had given us the freedom to record what we wanted. We all helped in the production. When Robert was singing, we were all in the control room giving our input. It felt very cohesive for a while. We were really alive with the music, and I know that Robert felt especially good about being able to produce the album ourselves.

Matty was a competent player but he generally wanted to add more colours to the palette than Robert wanted to use. If *Seventeen Seconds* was going to have a shade, it was going to be very muted, almost monochromatic. At the beginning, it wasn't such a problem as we managed to get what we needed for the songs to work their hypnotic magic. Matty went along with it. Eventually, however, he would feel constrained by this minimalist approach.

It is obvious to me now that one of the main things I got out of being in The Cure was that emotional release and understanding of where I was spiritually at any particular time. The lyrics have always spoken to me in a very helpful and healing way. To me it was our diary. The things we wrote about were personal yet applicable to all, which makes them almost sacred when I reflect on them. Personally sacred, if you like.

In the early days, when Robert had difficulty finishing the lyrics to a song, I would always help out with a sheet here and there of my own words. Even though I was as emotionally damaged as anyone else coming from our time could be, the lyrics had an effect on me too, despite seeing them come together bit by bit. To me that was the real magic. That was the real purpose, if there ever was one, of The Cure: to serve as the template for a kind of emotional therapy we created with our sounds and fury.

Years later, when people would try to hold us responsible for someone's depression or even suicide, it seemed to me that they were missing the point. We created these songs to help alleviate those same feelings in ourselves, a horror of the world that we could cope with only by singing and playing our particular music. That in a nutshell is where our English self-loathing and emotional repression really helped create the path forward. I think we were pioneers in that, especially in helping other repressed young men. I have always been both humbled and amazed by the number of people who have expressed that very thought to me over the years. It was certainly one reason I kept in the back of my mind for keeping on when things were grim.

It's weird to me that all of the various members of The Cure over the years, almost without exception, fell into a category of people halfway between introvert and extrovert. Ambivert is the term. I suppose it describes nearly every one of us at one time or another, but in The Cure I really feel that we were the extreme version of that. Especially Robert. He was either very social and extroverted or entirely the opposite. I believe to a certain extent to perform in front of people you have to have elements of both, otherwise you simply can't do it.

I've never felt stage fright before going on stage, just an excitement to get out there. I believe it helps to reflect and be introspective at times, but sometimes spontaneity is the better path.

*Seventeen Seconds* is the first album by The Cure where we were able to start communicating our feelings. Even the cover art, which Robert demanded to have input on, reflects this. The photos of the band were all blurred, which we felt correctly mirrored what we felt our fans should take from the album. We wanted people to focus on the music, the actual songs, not our appearance. For the first time in our career we had been correctly represented both in the album art work and the sonic territory of the music. It felt good, and I think if that had been the last the world had seen or heard of The Cure, then we would have made our mark. It meant that much to us.

If there was ever a spark of genius in Parry's management of The Cure, it was that day in early 1980 when he listened to Robert telling him he didn't need to come to the studio for the recording, that we could do it ourselves. He realized that by taking his own ego out of the equation and letting us just get on with it, he would start us on our way to a place we might never have reached otherwise. I truly believe that. Like a plant that you fuss over too much and kill with overcare, Parry realized (or at least hoped) that we just might flourish on our own. Although he would still drop by the studio to hear what we were up to, he rightly surmised that too much attention might kill off the beautiful flowers about to burst forth.

Our first ever tour of the United States was nearly our last.

First of all, we had trouble getting in. After landing at JFK in New York we were all waiting to go through the usual immigration process. Although things had obviously improved since Ellis Island, I think our appearance and general demeanour was probably disturbing to the 'regular Joes' manning the border posts.

'So what are youse guys doin' in Noo Yawk?' The large man in uniform holding all our passports in his hands motioned to the four of us.

'We're a band. We're playing at Hurrah's,' said Robert.

'A band, really? So what are youse called?' he eyed us suspiciously.

'The Cure,' Robert said.

'Liqueur? Hmmm . . .' he rolled the word around in his mouth like a bad taste. Then the *coup de grâce*.

'So are youse a faggot band, then?'

Of course we had not the slightest idea what he meant. Popular in wartime rationing, a faggot was a meat dish in England. Is that what he meant? He saw our puzzled faces and offered, 'Well, seeing as youse all have earrings in your ears!'

He elbowed his compatriot in the ribs who chuckled at these effeminate-looking English guys.

After a minute of inspection, he handed everyone their passports – except mine, which he placed in a large red folder.

'Mr Tollhouse, come with me.'

I assumed he meant me and duly followed. Looking behind me I could see the concerned look on Robert's face. I was led into a small room with a glass partition through which I could see the baggage hall. The large man opened an even larger book on a table in front of him and scanning the pages he found the relevant section. It seemed one of my youthful indiscretions outside the Maid of Sussex pub while I was still a minor had registered on the US government's radar. Looking up, he pronounced his sentence.

'Well, we let those other limeys in, The Beatles, so I guess we can let you in, too!'

He closed the book firmly and handed me back my passport. A little bemused by this sequence of events but grateful nonetheless, I left to join everyone collecting their suitcases on the other side. Robert had a grin on his face while Parry's wore a look of relief.

Several days later, someone explained the faggot reference. Aha! As Oscar Wilde would have it, 'Two nations divided by a common language.'

We drove into NYC in our rented car and the grandeur of the concrete avenues and buildings overwhelmed us all.

'It looks just like the movies,' I said as Robert slid further into his seat, sunglasses firmly pushed over his eyes as he looked out of the window and took it all in. We arrived at our destination: a small hotel on the edge of Central Park with a coffee shop on the ground floor. We had made it to America.

Having dropped our bags off at the hotel, we walked outside to explore this brave new world.

Growing up in England, most of our knowledge of the United States came from American television shows that made it to the UK, most notably *Dallas* and *The Rockford Files* with James Garner. We marvelled at the fact that Jim Rockford was able to live in a caravan on the beach by himself and had an answering machine. Very cool, but totally outside of our experience in cold old England. *Dallas* was even more alien to us. Strangely enough, we met Larry Hagman, the actor who played the character J.R. many years later, on the French TV show *Champs-Élysées*. He probably viewed us as aliens, in our colourful man dresses!

The other touchstone was Marvel comics. They were readily

available in England in the 1970s. The stories were the usual good vs. evil stuff and often set in the very city we were in, but what intrigued me and Robert as teens were the adverts in the back for items unavailable or unknown to us then in the UK. Twinkies, for one. So as our first foray into America we set out on a mission to find and consume a Twinkie. It didn't take long to locate one or figure out why the 'Twinkie defense' was used as a mitigating factor in the Harvey Milk murder case. Many years later Robert told me he still has one from our first trip in his kitchen drawer. Perfectly preserved!

New York in the early 1980s, the New York of Mayor Ed Koch, was not beautiful. Run-down, covered in graffiti, and plagued by violence and crime, it was a gritty place, to say the least. We had arrived a few months before John Lennon was gunned down outside the Dakota by Mark Chapman. The era of Peace and Love was definitely over and, as in the UK, the punk scene had emerged from the maelstrom. You can see the tension in Allan Tannenbaum's beautiful photo of The Cure standing on Columbus Avenue, being eyed uncomprehendingly by some of New York's finest out on their beat.

The first gig we ever played in the US was not in Manhattan but at Emerald City in Cherry Hill, New Jersey, on the edge of Philadelphia on 10 April 1980. To us it could have been Mars. It was that different from our own experience. A former disco club, its patrons spent most of the gig with their plaid-shirted backs to us while nursing their drinks. Robert bravely tried to rally the troops.

'We're The Cure and this is our first time playing in America!'

Although it could have been a disaster, we won them over

eventually. Polite applause turned into whoops and hollers by the end of the set. It was a very small, almost miniscule beginning to what was to become The Cure's huge success in America.

In Washington, DC we experienced the sharper side of American life. We were shocked when we pulled into town and realized it was divided into the haves and have-nots, ghettoized in a way we had not experienced before. It was an eye-opening experience. In London it appeared to us that all the races mixed together, but here it felt distinctly different to us in a way that was immediately apparent.

We stopped at a fast-food restaurant to get lunch. Since arriving in the US we'd been overwhelmed by the sheer number of options for everything so naturally we wanted to try as much as possible. Our bus pulled up and we went inside to eat. Afterwards, Simon and I were standing outside the place for a minute or two chatting and smoking. A man walked up to us, pointed at Simon, and hissed, 'You're on my death list, man!'

Simon turned to me as he hadn't quite heard what was said.

'Lol, what did he want?'

'I don't know, Si. Directions?' I said, diplomatically.

I didn't want a street fight to erupt right here in unknown territory. We got back on the bus. I felt a chill. It seemed here in the US things were pretty polarized. You were either with us on the bus or off the bus.

Back in New York City we played our first gig to the New York cognoscenti. There was a difference in how the UK and US punk scenes evolved and this was evident at that first Hurrah gig. In the UK punk was more of a cultural/political movement – it had to be, given the circumstances – whereas in the US it felt more like a social/fashion happening. It was confusing initially for both sides. There was a heckler who shouted something strange about 'pissing on Portobello', and Robert answered him in a perfectly reasonable way.

'We don't understand. We're from England,' or words to that effect. We played some songs from the first album and *Seventeen Seconds*. By the third gig I felt like we had weeded out the people who came and didn't understand or like us, and I remember the last gig being pretty good, like there could be something here for us. After the gig I sat in the bar and then got up and danced to 'Ready, Steady, Go' by Billy Idol, a new transplant to NYC apparently. Looking in the mirrors around the club dance floor, I felt a certain synchronicity.

Of course, this being New York, we had our first brush with the celebrity circuit. Debbie Harry and Chris Stein of Blondie, along with David Johansen of The New York Dolls, turned up to our first-night gig at Hurrah's. I had a badge for *Seventeen Seconds* on my lapel that had been abbreviated to '17 Secs' to make it fit.

'17 Secs?' David Johansen said as he peered at the badge. 'They call me sex seventeen!' he grinned at me, and I laughed. It broke the ice somewhat. Gradually, it seemed we were getting to know the US on equal terms. The relationship was to be further cemented in Boston. We played the Underground, a club that was in the basement of a building owned by Boston University. It was a strange venue because it was an L-shaped corridor with the stage area at one end of the L-shape, which meant half the audience could hear us but weren't able to see us play.

Here we had our introduction to some new American music in the shape of Mission of Burma, who we immediately liked and felt a kinship with. This meant more to us than meeting Debbie Harry and Blondie, or even The New York Dolls. To my mind they were the precursors of bands like Sonic Youth. They were pioneers.

The gig was filmed by a guy from MIT. He had a rather unique set-up, with three cameras filming in separate primary colours and one in black and white. Viewing the footage many years later, I am utterly amazed at how young we are. After the Boston gig, we went back to the film guy's rooms in MIT and viewed the stuff he had shot that evening. It had a very surreal quality with the four cameras being mixed together. We watched it for a very long time and drank the rest of the night away, toasting our first US tour.

Sometime later I looked out of the window of the room and noticed that the sun was coming up. We decided we should get back to our hotel, as in a few hours we had to drive down to New York to catch the plane home. Miraculously, 'A Forest', the first single from *Seventeen Seconds* was on its way to becoming a minor hit, and we were required back in the UK to play on *Top of the Pops*.

As we careened unsteadily along the road in our rented car, we realized we had a flat tyre. We pulled over and decided that we had better change it, as we still had to drive the 200-odd miles to New York later that day. We all piled out of the vehicle and proceeded to take the tyre off. Somewhere we found the jack and took the nuts off the wheel. Manhandling the spare over to fit on the wheel took quite a bit of dexterity considering how wasted and tired we were.

'I'll put it on, don't worry,' I heard Robert say, a little slurred.

Then I looked over and noticed he was putting the hubcap back on by kicking the edge with his boot. Unfortunately, his thumb was still under the hubcap, but for some reason he didn't notice.

'Shit,' he shrieked. 'That hurts!' and he proudly displayed his bloodied left thumb.

We all piled back into the car and drove to the hotel for a few hours of uneasy slumber. The alarm rang in my room and I summoned all the energy I had left and stumbled into the shower to try and wake up for the drive to NYC and then home. Miraculously, the tyre on the rental car was still inflated so Parry slipped behind the wheel and we started the four-hour or so drive to the airport. Pushed together in the back seat we all slumbered on and off for the next hour and sixty miles or so.

'I'm going to stop for petrol, boys.' Parry's New Zealand-accented voice brought us back to the present day.

We pulled over at the next gas station.

'Excuse me, chief.' For some reason, Parry always called people he didn't know 'chief'. Perhaps it was a Kiwi thing.

'How far to the airport?'

'Which airport would that be, sir?'

'JFK, of course,' Parry replied, slightly irritated by the question.

'Well, I'd say you're a little off course, sir. This is Cape Cod.'

In our somnambulant state, we had taken a wrong turn on the highway and ended up on the little peninsula that is Cape Cod. Now we would have to race down to New York to catch our plane back to the UK in time to play on *TOTP*. It wasn't the last time we would take a wrong turn in the life of The Cure. It was 21 April 1980, and Robert's twenty-first birthday.

*

We arrived at the BBC Television Centre jet-lagged and hung-over. We had travelled back on the plane with our old festival buddies The Specials, who had just been in New York themselves, which of course meant a few drinks here and there.

Any band that has ever played *TOTP* will tell you how mind-numbingly boring the day of the actual show is. Endless rehearsals for lights and cameras start at a very ungodly hour, and you spend most of your day confined to a small, bare, utilitarian dressing room somewhere in the bowels of the Television Centre. It's no wonder that at 5 p.m. when the bar opens upstairs, everybody makes a beeline for it.

I think *TOTP* was one of those venerable old institutions by this point. Like the Queen, largely irrelevant to the average citizen but still acknowledged for old times' sake and a certain 'Britishness'. You simply had to do it despite the fact it was so old-fashioned and not part of what you really wanted to express with your music. As Robert pointed out to me, 'If we don't do it some other rubbish band will, so I suppose we should.'

Quite right.

I think for our first performance we come off quite well. It was always mimed. I think only The Who and The Clash managed to persuade the BBC to let them play live. I have the stone-faced look of indifference I was using at the time behind the kit, and Simon looks suitably hunky and young. There was a large bandage on Robert's left thumb from the accident with the car hubcap in Boston. If you look closely you can see it in the footage, incongruously sliding up and down the fretboard. After he had been to the doctor to get it seen to, Robert told me the doctor had had to drill a hole through the nail to let the pressure out. It looked painful, so it was a good thing that we didn't actually have to play.

This was our first time at *TOTP*. We would be back for quite a few more performances. One particular encounter there sends shivers down my spine even now. We were there to perform 'The Walk', and Porl, Andy Anderson and myself were standing around the edges of the studio when somebody crept up behind us.

'Oh, sons of Dracula! You are looking ten thousand per cent!' Eyeing us up and down it was none other than the old sex offender himself, Jimmy Savile.

# 11

# SOS

1980 and 1981 were the years The Cure became an international band. Of the 250-plus gigs we played during that period, the vast majority of them were outside the United Kingdom.

The Cure appealed to so many different types of people around the world because we were never tied to a particular fashion. There have been attempts to pigeonhole us and make us into a kind of brand, but these attempts have failed miserably. I don't think you can say that we represent one idea at all.

The beginning of the *Seventeen Seconds* tour in the UK took us to one of the coldest spots in the country: Cromer, West Runton Pavilion. Even the name conjures up old shipping forecasts and freezing seas. I vividly recall sitting in the ancient seaside hotel after our gig, seriously thinking about chopping up the furniture to make a fire. It was that cold. The kind of deep wet English chill that makes your bones creak.

When we got up to Newcastle, something seemed to be stirring in the ether, an undercurrent of violence that we just couldn't quite shake. Halfway through our set it was obvious we would have to do something about the annoying guy in the audience who kept throwing things and upsetting everyone else.

I heard a clang as something hard hit Robert's guitar neck and he spun round and gave me an exasperated look as he firmly put the guitar down. I knew that look from our early days. It meant we were going to have to engage again with some idiot. I really wanted to believe that all of that stuff was behind us now. Whenever trouble popped up, it just made us more determined to be heard. I got off the drum seat and together with Robert and Simon and one or two of the crew, we chased the interloper out of the university hall.

With the English leg over, we were off to Europe again to consolidate our success there. We went to Rotterdam and had a fine old time in the appropriately named Heavy Club. The thing about touring is that most of the time is spent either travelling or hanging about waiting to travel. As a young band, we spent a great deal of time looking for diversions. Nowadays, I'm quite content to read a good book or some such, but back then the only reasonable (or maybe unreasonable) diversion was to drink in our hotel or go out to drink, which was why we found ourselves at this nightclub. It was getting very heavy in there. The drinks were flowing even though it was very early in the morning. I think Horace Panter and a few other members of The Specials were there as well. We had become friendly with the band, having played a few festivals on the same bill. As we were veterans of the same wars, so to speak, we had a bond of sorts.

Once again, I was searching for a place to pee in the crowded club and I was having trouble making out where the lavatories were located. I stumbled into a small room that looked like it might be the toilet. I looked for a light switch, but no luck. In the darkness I decided it felt right to pee even though I couldn't see the urinal. It certainly smelled like one, so I decided to relieve myself.

At that precise point a warm glow infused the room from a small electric light above me and a woman's voice said, 'Hey, not here! This is not the toilets. You must leave now!'

All at once I realized my mistake. I couldn't find the light switch, mainly because it was on the outside of the phone booth. My penis, or more precisely my bladder, had got me into trouble yet again.

My propensity for bladder trouble came to a head later on in the tour. Mac had arranged some screens at the back of the stage against which he would throw vast washes of lights. By this time we were playing longer sets and consuming more beer before and even during the gigs, which necessitated a short break so that I would be able to relieve myself.

One of our songs, 'Grinding Halt', had a long intro. If I gave Robert a signal he would spin it out even longer, thus enabling me to get off the drum riser to nip behind the screen, where the crew had thoughtfully stashed a large bucket to enable me to pee without leaving the stage.

The rest of the stage area was designed to be private and closed off, so it was in fact very discreet. Nobody was able to see me until I reappeared looking much relieved. This arrangement had worked very well throughout the tour and nobody but the band and our crew had any idea that halfway through the gig I was in fact pissing while on stage.

That all changed in a very big way, and I say big because it was massive.

Lights were positioned to project coloured washes of light up on the screens. My bucket was strategically placed between the screens. As I accessed the onstage 'facilities' Mac would extinguish the wash lights from the lighting desk out front, plunging the backstage area into darkness, with the exception of a single torch held by one of our crew that was guiding me to the correct spot and then back to the drums. Perfect.

One night Mac absentmindedly (at least I hope that was the case) pushed the faders up on the lighting channel directly by my bucket. The effect was immediate and dramatic. The audience waiting for the extra-long intro to 'Grinding Halt' to finish were treated to a spectacularly outsized shadow of yours truly peeing into a bucket.

I suppose there are times when it's hard to believe your eyes and equally hard to comprehend what has just occurred. Both arrived at the same time that night. I heard a gentle titter, then a full-throated guffaw from someone in the audience. It was joined by a few more and then even more. As anyone who has ever worked onstage for his or her livelihood will tell you, there is one incontrovertible truth: the show must go on. No matter what illness, injury or tragedy may befall you, you have to get out there and get on with it. People have paid money and your reputation depends on it. Secondly, if something bad or strange happens on stage, incorporate it into your performance and the audience will be none the wiser.

So in the tradition of music hall comedians around the globe, I zipped up my trousers and strode back to the drum riser, my face a mask of inscrutability as I sat on the throne as if nothing had happened. Like that old movie *Gaslight*, where the husband tries to drive his wife mad by suggesting the things she sees and hears are all figments of her imagination for his own nefarious ends, I dared the audience to think that they had only imagined what they had just seen by keeping a completely straight poker face.

You know what? It worked. Because after the gig nobody mentioned it. Had I fooled the audience or were they just too polite? Maybe they thought it was part of the act . . .

Anyway, as a result of my unruly bladder, we were shown the door at Club Heavy and we decided to go down to the sea as the morning light was just coming up.

We jumped in the van and drove ourselves down to Rotterdam's seafront at the village of Monster by the Hook of Holland, and thence down to the beach. The van was full with the band, Mac, and a few extra people we had met at the club. The dawn light was coming up as we parked and tumbled out onto the grassy edge of the sandy beach. A strong wind blew across the sand, reminding us we were not on the Mediterranean but on the edge of the North Sea. It was a fairly nice-looking place but was directly across from a huge international port for container ships that was full of large grey vessels and massive cranes they used to load the goods onto those ships.

'Bit parky,' I said to nobody in particular, and started to wander off towards the sea. I noticed a small path veering off to the left and decided to go down it. It was the opposite direction from the beach where most of our crew was headed, but a young lady from the club followed and eventually caught up to me. We chatted as we strolled along the early morning coast.

A good twenty minutes or so had passed, and as we were getting nearer the containers and colossal ships, I suggested we turn around and go back towards the van. I hadn't really noticed how far we had walked. We were completely out of sight of the others and I couldn't see or hear any sign of them at all. It took several minutes of fast walking before I could see the van again.

As we drew closer, I noticed there was another van parked in close proximity to ours. In fact, it seemed to be blocking our van. It was unfamiliar to me but the letters on the side had a familiar ring: 'Politie' looked a lot like 'Police', and my walking companion confirmed it.

'Shit! What's happened?'

I could hear the raised voices of people remonstrating with the police. That didn't sound good. As I got closer, I could see that everybody was inside the police van with bars on the windows, and a policeman was about to get in the van and drive them off to the station and put them in jail!

It seems that when we arrived at the beach we had failed to notice a small sign that said 'No Swimming'. It's no surprise that we missed it, because the sign was in Dutch. Nevertheless things would have been fine if it hadn't been for the little old lady who looked out the window of her beachside cottage at the normally deserted beach and spied several drunken Englishmen running full tilt along the beach, whirling the 'No Swimming' sign above their heads before depositing it in the ocean. Then some of them decided to strip off and go for an early morning skinny-dip. This apparently was too much even for the normally phlegmatic Dutch disposition to tolerate, and the old lady called the coppers on my friends. Hence their current residence in the back of the Rotterdam Police paddy wagon.

I approached the policeman as deferentially as I could muster, being two sheets to the wind myself, and asked what crime my compatriots had committed to land in such hot water?

'Ah well,' he said, tilting his hat back on his head in the manner of exasperated constables everywhere.

'You see that house up there on the top of the sand dune?' he asked.

I nodded that I did.

'Well a very important old lady lives there and she called us to report that drunks were running up and down the beach, smashing things, and one of them was naked.'

A cursory look into the van and I ascertained that this was the man from the Isle of Iona, none other than Mac, our lighting designer, shirtless still. At this point the occupants of the van were getting agitated and starting to shout things like, 'Call the British embassy!' and 'Fascists!'

'Will they be charged, then, officer?' I asked in my best un-drunk voice, which wasn't that convincing, I have to say.

'Well they might have to wait a day in jail before they see the judge.'

He looked around in both directions to see if anyone else was in earshot before taking out his notebook. I stole a look at everyone and, with a finger pressed to my lips, motioned to them to quiet down.

'But maybe we can forget the whole thing,' he said, hesitating slightly, 'if you pay the fine right now in cash. I'll be sure to tell the old lady you're very sorry and that I gave you a stern warning.'

Even in my intoxicated state, I realized that I was being offered a chance to keep my criminal companions out of jail.

'How much is the fine, sir?'

The policeman flipped open his notebook again and wrote a figure on it and showed it to me surreptitiously. It said 450 guilders – about £350. I opened my wallet. I had about 250 guilders. I gave it to him.

'That's all I have, sir.'

He looked at me then motioned to the van. I walked over and explained the situation. Robert, being totally pragmatic about the situation, gave me another couple of hundred and we paid the fine. The policeman quickly put it in his back pocket.

'Your friends are now free to go. Be good boys, now.'

He opened the back door of the van and they tumbled out, cursing slightly under their breath, but now the fight had gone out of them. We all got into our van and Matty said he would drive. The driver of the police van left first and drove out down the beach road into town.

Matty drunkenly steered the van into town. That's when the absurdity of the situation really struck home. They let us off with a bribe to drive the van home drunk.

A few days later, we played our first gig in Berlin. Keep in mind that in the early 1980s Berlin was a city divided, as the Berlin Wall was still in existence, and it was a little difficult to enter the small enclave that was West Berlin, even for Western Europeans.

Back then, there were two main ways to enter the city: by car, or by train. If you came in by car, it was along the heavily policed Berlin corridor to make sure you didn't pick up people from the eastern part of Germany. If you made a wrong turn and drove off a motorway ramp, within a few hundred feet you would be greeted by a gated guard post with heavily armed police inside who would quickly turn you around.

The border between West and East Germany was marked by two border posts with a no man's land in between that was full of barbed wire and looked heavily mined. Your passport was stamped with a time to ensure that you kept to the speed limit, as it would be matched with the time at the other end of the corridor. If you went too fast you would get a speeding ticket; too slow and the car would be dismantled as they searched for stowaways or contraband.

The bus stopped at the border post and a heavily armed and greatcoated East German border guard got on the bus and asked for our passports. As soon as he realized we were a band, the following conversation ensued.

'You are a musical group, yes?'

After we answered in the affirmative (and why wouldn't we, as any other explanation would seem very suspicious?), the conversation continued:

'You have T-shirts, yes?'

This question was usually asked after the guard had everybody's passports in hand. Road-tested tour managers usually kept a small box full of such goodies close by at border stops to facilitate the next exchange.

We produced two or three T-shirts and gave them to the guard, who furtively stashed them under his greatcoat with a nervous look. Then he handed back our passports with a flourish and waved us through the border post.

In the space of a couple of days we had paid two bribes to officials. Whatever it takes. The show must go on.

Berlin in the early 1980s was a very different place than it is today, with the constant anxiety of living in a totally walled-in city (albeit one of two million people) combined with the presence of the Red Army on one side and the Second World War Allies on the other, creating an air of constant paranoia. It was a place that was on edge all the time.

Our first gig was at SO36, a club in the heart of Kreuzberg, which was the alternative subculture district, because it was in the poorest area of the city and home to the largest Turkish population outside of Turkey. Truly a place where east meets west, which made it very exotic to us.

We had been playing in front of people for a while now, and usually the reactions were positive. If on rare occasions the results were not quite as good, we at least understood why we were being ignored or even misunderstood. The reception we got at SO36 was very odd: I felt like we were being studied under a microscope. The club was long and narrow, with the stage at one end. The place was absolutely packed with people, but no one talked. The silence in the room was complete. All 600 or so people just stared straight at the stage with tremendous intensity.

We started with 'Seventeen Seconds' – not the liveliest opening song, but it suited this very intellectual and introspective audience. From there we went straight into 'Play for Today', and I couldn't detect so much as a tapping foot among the stone-faced crowd.

I shouldn't have worried, because by the time we got to the end of the set, with 'A Forest' the joint was, as they say, jumping. I think Robert won them over by changing the lyrics to 'Killing an Arab' to 'Killing Kevin Keegan', an English footballer of some repute.

*

The last gig of the year was in London, and in a way it was a swansong for our innocent youth. Those years were now over and we were a serious rock band – whatever that meant – completely professional and road-tested in every way. We had played over 250 gigs in two years and the strain was beginning to show, so we decided to have a Christmas party!

The occasion illustrates the two sides of Robert: on one side he is a creative artist with a very sincere and singular message to give the world, but on the other side he absolutely loves Christmas.

We looked around for a suitable place for a combined gig and party on the last Thursday before Christmas. We found it in the Notre Dame Hall in Leicester Square, which coincidentally was connected with our old schoolmaster Dr Antony Weaver. He was running a cultural exchange centre there for French students. We decided to invite our friends to play with us: The Associates, The Scars and various members of the Banshees. The evening was a huge success, as the audience was made up of our friends and colleagues. It couldn't be a party any other way.

It was really loud, and it seemed as if somebody was screaming all the time, which was a little disconcerting, but I took it as a sign that everyone was having a good time. There was much drinking from 7 p.m. until 1 a.m., and the year ended on a high. We had weathered the storms of the road and emerged reasonably unscathed. We were twenty-one years old and we were now adults. The playfulness and lightness of our youth was being washed away bit by bit by the harsh realities of the artistic life we had chosen.

# 12

# FAITH

Although we had managed to wrest control of the recording process from Parry on *Seventeen Seconds*, and made the record we wanted to make, we were in a time of turmoil as a band. This wasn't due to a particular situation within the band but more to do with outside issues and family matters; Robert's grandmother suddenly passed away and my mother was terminally ill with cancer.

Robert and I had both been brought up Catholic, and while we had moved on from the beliefs of our early years, we were actively looking for something new, something different to replace what we had been taught as children. It started with the single, the first thing we recorded for the new album: 'Primary'.

We wrote a lot of *Faith* in the studio. We had been on the road constantly, switching between recording an album and touring. It needed to end, but we didn't know how to get off the rounda-bout. Our friend Billy Mackenzie came to see us while we were recording. I miss Billy. He was one of the most charismatic people I have ever met, a truly creative soul – unique and wonderfully familiar at the same time. Michael had joined Billy's band, The Associates, after he left The Cure, and had a very interesting time playing bass for Billy.

Unfortunately, although Billy had many great qualities, he was also just a little too eccentric to last long in the crazy world of rock and roll. This may sound strange from the outside, but rock and roll, like most art forms of the last century, is now controlled by corporations and outside influences which have very little to do with artistic processes. The trick is to be able to surf along the wave of commercial success without destroying that which gave birth to your art.

That's something Robert has always managed to do well. He's most definitely an artist, but he is also a pragmatic person when it comes to the business of music and, believe me, it's a business. A right old business.

As we went along in our contract with Fiction Records we would have yearly options, which meant once a year Fiction would pick up the option to our contract and agree to make and market another record. It was an unfair arrangement in some ways, as it kept us on a very short leash with only the next record as a certainty. They dangled the carrot of an advance for each option to help sweeten the deal. Many bands in this situation splurged on items they perceived would make them look like rock stars, i.e. flashy cars, expensive clothes, etc.

But not The Cure. Under Robert's leadership, we took that advance, put it in the bank, and paid ourselves a wage each month that helped us all have some kind of financial security.

Not so for Billy Mackenzie, who spent his money on a posh flat and a vintage Mercedes despite the fact that he didn't have a licence to drive a car! Michael drove it for him and one night they crashed, so that was the end of that trapping of excess. Billy also liked to hire famous orchestras for recording sessions, so his recording budget was spent pretty quickly.

I always remind young musicians that record labels are like banks. They give you a loan to make your music, then tell you how to use the money, and at the end of the day they want it all back and then some! But Robert, despite his otherworldly side, was always smart enough to not go down that particular road, and for that I'm eternally grateful, as The Cure has provided for me for most of my adult life.

As I've said, a lot of *Faith* was written in the studio, and we were now a three-piece again consisting of myself, Robert and Simon. Matty left at the end of the tour in Australia. The tour had been pretty damn great, really. We sold out the gigs everywhere we went, as Parry had a lot of connections in that part of the world, having grown up in New Zealand. Unfortunately, Matty was one of those people who was not really designed to be in a band that's on the road for any length of time. Being in a touring band is rather like being married to the people you work with. You live with each other 24/7 for months on end, and the smallest irritant can become a very large dispute if you're not careful.

On our trip Down Under, Robert, Simon and I spent a lot of time together, but Matty went off on his own, both before the gigs and after. We didn't see much of him and that destroyed the camaraderie of the band. For instance, we spent about a month on Bondi Beach. We stayed at one hotel and went out to play gigs nearly every night all over Sydney and environs. It was a glorious time, really. We would play the gig to hordes of people, go out to the clubs of Kings Cross until 4 a.m., then sleep a few hours before getting up to jog (yes, jog) along Bondi Beach and go for a swim. That's how we got ready for the next night's gig. Everyone, that is, except Matty.

Matty also had a different view of music. He wanted, like Porl before him, to play much more complicated versions of the songs than we felt was necessary. The beauty of The Cure has always been 'less is more'. That is especially true with the songs from *Seventeen Seconds*. They rely on simplicity. Their ultimate strength is their minimalism. Some of that minimalism came from a conscious wish, and in my case from a limited ability. That wasn't exciting enough for Matty. Occasionally he would sneak in a little frilly embellishment to his part on a song and I would see Robert grimace. While it's true that we were pretty democratic in the way the band was run (we each received an equal share of the tour income and a portion of the music royalties) and everyone had a say, if the majority of the band wanted something done a particular way, then that's the way it was done. Either Matty never reconciled that part or The Cure weren't meant to be his band.

At the end of the tour in Perth, we had about a week to wait before we got on a plane home to the UK. It was pretty obvious to all that after the tour Matty wouldn't be in the band anymore. To his credit, when we got home he called up Robert and said he didn't think it was going to work anymore. So it was an amicable ending between Matty and Robert and a relief for the rest of us.

Robert and I had spent a lot of time talking about death on that tour – not as a morbid preoccupation, but how it is something totally abstract until someone you love or know dies. As I've said, my mother was very ill and his grandmother had passed away, so it was on our minds a lot. There was a period during the recording of *Faith* where we were swapping studios and it was just going on and on. We were redoing everything, nothing was getting finished, and we were all rather exasperated about it.

Our frustration reached its zenith when we recorded in Abbey Road's new room – the Penthouse, I think it was called. They had some new equipment in there and we were getting used to it when Billy Mackenzie came to visit. Just his presence had an uplifting effect on us, and the next few days we got quite a lot more done than we had previously. I recorded the fast tom fills on 'Doubt' in that room at the top of Abbey Road, and then Robert came in and really nailed the vocals. Things were finally coming together, but I was about to learn the truth of the phrase 'Art imitates life.'

'I am not afraid to die,' my mother said in an airless whisper. She was certainly dying. She had a large black mass in her chest that had been diagnosed as terminal cancer. It had grown, undetected, for some years now. It was too big to operate on, so they tried chemotherapy and radiation treatments. It was a hard thought for me to process when she informed me she had been told by her doctors that she had just three months to live. She didn't want to lose her dignity and become a drooling, incontinent mess at the end, so she told me she would go as soon as she'd said goodbye to everyone she wanted to say goodbye to.

'I know where I'm going after this world and I'm just going to say goodbye to everyone and go.'

With slow, painful movements, she showed me the newly pricked blue-black target tattoo on her skin where the technician would aim the deadly beam in the hopes of destroying the tumour, while leaving the healthy cells untouched. Her hair was falling out in clumps because of the treatment, leaving a grey wisp across her once full head of hair.

I was twenty-two years old. Everything told me this was the end for her, but I didn't want her to die. Not now, with all the good things that were just starting to happen for me.

The Cure were about to go on a month-long tour of Europe that would end in Holland with our unique circus tent show. We had finished the *Faith* album sessions, and before the tour started I went to visit my mother in my sister's house on the south coast of England in the very English town of Poole. My father was a full-blown alcoholic by this time and had elected to stay home and ignore the terrible future by clinging to his oblivion, unaware of anything but his own wants and needs, selfish bastard that he was.

My sisters despised him for this, especially the youngest, but I had no feelings one way or the other. It was just what he always did. I knew no different. I didn't expect him to change his behaviour. My father, a Second World War veteran, had never really figured in my life, mostly by his own volition. He returned to England in 1945 after fifteen years' service in Her Majesty's Royal Navy to find a country locked in post-war austerity, and the thrill of world travel and battle became a diluted and fading memory.

He came home to a young wife he didn't really know with a four-year-old son to take care of, a four-year-old that he doubted was his in the first place. There have always been dark mumblings in my family about Canadian soldiers stationed near our wartime home and my Canadian 'uncle's' valiant efforts one dark blackout night to save my twenty-one-year-old mother's virtue from marauding drunken squaddies. And darker still, the hint of a thankful reward from mother that may have been the reason for my father's frown and my elder brother's certainty that 'Dad never loved me.' Either way, my father retreated into introspection and drink upon his return and this never changed. People are still amazed when I tell them that I cannot recall a single pleasant talk, hug, or kiss from my father the whole time I grew up with him. Nowadays we might subscribe to the theory he had PTSD as, truth be told, he had seen and experienced some horrific events in the China Seas, but back then all he was to me was a grumpy recluse that I tried my best to avoid.

I suppose this explains why, at the end of his life, I cut him a little more slack, but my sisters never forgave him. One of my last memories of my dad was a cold, wet winter afternoon at his home when he played another ramshackle sea shanty on the piano to drunkenly accompany his rasping vocals. I don't think he ever knew what I did, or what any of his children did in the world, really. He was on his own course into the setting sun, and damn and blast anyone else. He was the epitome of slow, simmering resentment. I had long ago decided that I would become the polar opposite of my father, whatever it took.

We sat silently for a few moments in my mother's stuffy, over-heated room. I couldn't catch my breath. The clock on the wall ticked the only sound in the room besides my mother's laboured breathing. 'I guess you're off to see that girl now,' she said, except she used a more canine term, which shocked me a little. I suppose she realized she'd reached the end, and such desperation, although unseemly, was only to be expected. I was, after all, her youngest son, and she was right: I was going to leave and meet my girlfriend Vivienne before I left for foreign shores. I kissed her goodbye, and I would never see my mother alive again.

I started our Dutch tour with the knowledge that I would be one parent less when I returned.

It was a strange convoy for a rock band; the artics with lights and equipment, the band and crew buses, and then the trucks and caravans from the circus. Rock and roll gypsies indeed. The Cure circus tour of the Netherlands.

Sometimes we set up in a park, sometimes in a car park, playing each night to a couple of thousand ardent Dutch fans. This was the first place outside of the UK where we'd started to get a proper following. Normally it would be a very joyous occasion, but my mother's impending end weighed heavily on me and tainted the tour with a sullen, insistent throb, like a bad toothache that robs you of calmness and equanimity and permeates every facet of your existence.

I told the tour manager that if he heard from my brother about my mother's condition, not to tell me until the gig was over. I felt I owed that much to the fans who had saved up their hard-earned money to see us. My problems were not their concern, and besides, I felt my mother would approve of that. She was always a champion of our endeavours as a band.

The circus tent was arranged by our Dutch promoter, Fred Zylstra, a slightly older counterculture type, as were many promoters of The Cure in the early days. I think he loved our youthful spirit and was determined to help us realize some of our more outlandish ambitions. By this time we had played in many of the clubs of Holland and we were looking for a different venue, one that wasn't so rock and roll, to perform in. We felt it would differentiate us from the rest of our peers to do something like this, and we were right. I can't recall if it was us or Fred that thought of the circus tent idea but it was a great one. Every day, around 30–40 circus people hoisted this huge blue and white striped canvas tent up into the air and prepared it for a most unlikely stage show: The Cure Circus! There were no other performers besides us, and at first I was concerned it might be too ambitious, but we sold out each gig, and every night the tent fabric was sodden with sweat from the new religion we were bringing.

There were lighter moments amidst the dark, impending doom. Fred would reply to every request we made with a curt, 'Is possible.'

For example, 'Can we get some beer, Fred?' would be met with, 'Is possible.'

'How about more ice, Fred?'

'Is possible.'

We expected and received this reply no matter what we asked for. Fred's stoic demeanour, probably born of many, many tours with drunken English hooligans masquerading as musical artists, never changed. This both intrigued us and piqued our imagination. Perhaps Fred was not as docile and calm as he seemed; maybe under that relaxed, cool facade lurked a darker heart . . . We needed to know.

One day Simon asked, 'So, Fred, are you a murderer?'

Fred looked him straight in the eye and deadpanned, 'Is possible!'

We all liked Fred. He was our champion for Holland.

Then the dreaded call came. My brother informed me that my

mother had taken a turn for the worse and I should come home at once. I talked with Robert and Simon and we agreed that I should leave immediately. They graciously offered to cut the tour short, but I insisted I would be back as soon as possible to play the few remaining gigs. It's what mother would have wanted, and I felt I needed to have some normality in my life at that time. And normal was playing in a circus tent.

Our roadie Gary Biddles and I were chauffeured in a car to Amsterdam to wait for a plane to Gatwick. We checked into a hotel, but sleep didn't come very easily. Eventually, I drifted off in the wee hours. The alarm came too soon, and after a brief shower we got on the plane home from Schiphol. In a strange twist of fate, Gary had to appear in court in the UK on the very day I had to run home, so he was at least able to be company for my horribly screaming head.

*Dead. She's dead. I know*, it said.

I'm not sure if this is the point where I pushed off into unknown territories with no lifeline, or if it was simply the very small start of my real adult life. Up until this point Robert, Simon and myself had existed in a kind of bubble of pre-adult life. We were granted the freedoms of maturity but with few of the real responsibilities. Rock and roll is like that: it makes children of you all if you're not careful.

We actively fought against being babied too much, mainly because we at least realized that we were ripe for being taken advantage of. We considered ourselves reasonably intelligent, but a sixth sense warned us that we might be fair game for the sharks of the music machine. So we cloaked our uncertainty in an adolescent bravado bolstered by the punk manifesto we subscribed to – along with a fair amount of Tennent's Lager (the one with the pictures of lovely Scottish ladies on the cans).

I was met at the airport by my brother Roger in his VW Beetle. He hugged me as I came through the gate.

'Lol, you're too late, I'm afraid. She died last night.'

The words stabbed like knives into my heart. Of course I expected this, but you're never really ready when the moment comes. I've since had other dealings with death, and each time it's as if the world is simultaneously both too fast and too slow. You want time to pass quickly so the pain will subside like a badly stubbed toe or a bit tongue, but you also wish the moment to be frozen by some magic so that its horrible power will be diminished or destroyed. Impossible, really.

Gary and I said goodbye and he departed to the courthouse.

'See you tonight to fly back?' he asked.

I nodded in the affirmative. I recalled the first time my mother met Gary he was face down, spreadeagled on our front lawn, hopelessly drunk on Christmas Eve. Classic. No more of that, I supposed.

We got in my brother's car, my eyes moist with tears, and drove to the funeral home to 'see' mother one last time. Along the way he filled me in on the grisly details and at some point I noticed we weren't driving on the motorway anymore but had pulled into a lay-by.

'Where do you think Mum is now, Lol?'

'I'm not even thinking about that yet, Rog,' I said, somewhat surprised. 'My head can't even get around the dead part yet even though I knew it was coming'

'Well, Lol. I think . . .' and then I realized he was giving me the pitch. My brother Roger was a recent convert of the Jehovah's Witnesses. God bless him. I was not in the mood right then for his latest religious theory and I told him so.

'You need to stop with the sales stuff here, Rog.'

Because he was my brother and loved me, he did, for the moment.

We pulled up in front of the mortuary in Crawley. I hadn't been to Crawley for a while, but it still had that dark drizzle of despair soaking everything and holding everyone down. As we were parking I idly wondered how mother's soul would manage to escape this sodden earthly prison.

Inside the fake oak doors of the funeral home my sisters appeared. We were going to see our freshly embalmed mother together as a family. I thought it was funny how it took death, to get the Tolhursts together. We awkwardly shuffled into the room where nobody ever really wanted to be. The room of death where we must all end up. Shit, I hated being there.

There was a curtain of red velvet that the funeral director beckoned us over to, and then pushed aside so we could go in and see mother lying in her coffin. The smell of formaldehyde and dead flowers that is familiar to anyone who has ever entered one of these places lingered in the air.

Then I saw her: my mother, Daphne. I had often thought I would want to place a last kiss upon my mother's face to bid her farewell, but when this moment came the grotesquely twisted mask her face now resembled was nothing like the mother I had known and loved. I gasped a little. The lipstick was just a little too bright and too red, and her face was set at a strange and unnatural angle. I also felt very strongly that my mother's spirit was no longer present. This resembled nothing more than an empty glove without a hand in it. Wherever she was, she wasn't there. Whatever remained in this wooden box was not the mother I had known for twenty-two years, but just an empty shell. So I did not, could not, touch her. My lips did not kiss hers one last time.

I stood to the side, holding my oldest sister Vicki's hand, and then it started, the comments, a whisper from one of my sisters about the hideously presented mannequin, then gradually we started to laugh, and eventually doubled up in screaming guffaws at what we saw before us. It was a terribly human reaction to a horrible surprise. We were in a state of shock, I later surmised.

Slowly I released my grip on Vicki's hand as we realized that this was how it was going to be now – the parent we loved was gone, and the one we didn't love would need to be looked after. That little realization came fast in the cold, sterile little red-curtained room, and as we walked out together we knew our family would never be the same again.

Outside I discussed the grim but necessary details with my brother. Father was too drunk to comprehend much, so we had to organize what was needed. The funeral was arranged for the day after the last tour date in seven days. We adjourned for a very sombre lunch.

I met Gary at Gatwick at 5 p.m. and we boarded the plane back to Holland just as the dying sun was disappearing into the black night. I looked out of the small window of the plane and saw at the side of the runway the silver birch trees so familiar to anyone who ever lived in southern England. They looked like silver arms thrust up into the sky, pleading for something from the angry gods, and I knew everything had changed.

We landed in Schiphol, walked through the airport entrance, and saw a man with a crudely handwritten sign saying 'Tokhuurst.' I took that as a Dutch version of my last name and approached the driver. 'Yes, that's me,' I said, and we walked to the car just a few yards away from Schiphol's main exit. I climbed in and Gary plonked down in the other seat and the driver said, 'I'll take you to the show, okay?' I said yes, and off we went to the circus tent. Within an hour we had arrived, and I was ushered into the little blue and white caravan we were using as a dressing room. I could hear the noise of the soundcheck. Gary went off to investigate. A few minutes later, Robert and Simon came into the caravan. They both came over and hugged me. We didn't say anything, just sat there in the gloom for a couple of minutes.

'I want to play tonight,' I finally said. 'Daphne would've liked that.'

'You know if you don't feel like doing the rest of the tour we can go home,' Robert offered.

'No, I think this is the only thing that's going to keep me sane. I'd rather we did the gigs.'

Both Robert and Simon nodded in agreement, and so we did the remaining circus tour. That first night back is burned into my mind for ever. I was playing the songs with a ferocious intensity, madly slashing and berating the God that would let this happen to me when I was so young. I felt cast out of heaven and thrown down to earth like a damaged archangel.

After the gig we all sat in our trailer with nobody else, just us, The Cure. We meditated on the finality of death, which, strangely enough, helped lift my spirits to a place where I could carry on.

'My first drum.'

Going to the fair

I see a caravan going
to the fair,
Come along, come
along llet)s go there

'Already dreaming about making my escape.'

'Me at eight with my sister.'

'Dad in Syria in 1944.'

'My parents at the beach with my cousin.'

'First ever Cure gig poster, except we were called Malice back then'.

'After the Malice gig we had to change our name!'

'1978 flyer – we handed these out personally at the door of the Marquee. Punk self sufficiency!'

'1981 at Hammersmith Odeon
(notice the convenient screens!)'

'Printemps de Bourges Festival,
France, 1982.'

'Robert and me outside the Hammersmith Odeon, London, 1985.'

ABOVE: 'In the pub opposite Fiction's office, London, 1985.'

LEFT: 'Printemps de Bourges Festival, France, 1982.'

ABOVE: 'Athens, 1985.'

LEFT: 'On drums, France, 1982.'

BELOW: 'On keyboards, Switzerland, 1985.'

BELOW: 'Canterbury Odeon, England, 1981.'

'Me and John Hurt, London, 1987 –
"I look like a man whose soul has
been zapped."'

'Me and my soulmate Cindy.'

'Robert and Mary's wedding, 1988: a wonderfully happy day.'

ABOVE: '"Reflections" at The Royal Albert Hall, London, 2011. Standing on the stage, staring at Simon's arse!'

ABOVE: 'Open Air Theater, June 1st 2000. Robert and me reconciling.'

LEFT: '"Reflections" at The Pantages Theater, Los Angeles, 2011. Gray, me and Robert on Gray's twentieth Birthday.'

Sometime later in the hotel bar Ted Page, our sound guy, proffered a cassette tape to me.

'Tonight's show, Lol. Thought you might like it.'

I took it from Ted, thanked him, and slumped back into my seat in the dark and smoky bar. It had been the longest day of my short life, but I knew I wouldn't sleep without copious amounts of alcohol and drugs, so I started with a large glug from my bottle. Sometime later, I imagine, I passed out.

Coming to in my cold hotel room, I prepared for the day, and suddenly it hit me again. Brown bread, dead. Mother's dead. Time passed in a stupor of sadness. Several days later we went up to Groningen in the north. I looked at the map on the bus and saw something strange. We had to pass over a long causeway on the A7 motorway – the Afsluitdijk dam – on the way to Friesland and Groningen. The sea was on one side and a huge lake of fresh water on the other made by damming up the Zuiderzee. In the process, the truncated Zuiderzee miraculously turned from salt water to fresh and became the IJsselmeer, the largest man-made freshwater lake in Western Europe. It served as a symbol to me of the metamorphosis I must now undergo, even though in my grief I was unaware of what those changes might be.

As we were driving and approached the dam, I realized that the causeway was just the width of the road. I could see water on both sides at many points. It was remarkably beautiful, both inspiring and calming in its grey-blue bleakness. I was staring at nothing in particular out of the window when it occurred to me that there were mute swans swimming on both sides of the causeway in both the lake and sea. Very curious. I had never seen that before. But these were strange days, and soon they would become much, much stranger.

A week after mother's death, the Dutch tour came to a close. These were sad, bleak days. In the cold, damp afternoons I wandered around the town square, or wherever we were that night while the tent was being put up, and watched the Dutch people go about their business. They were stolid northern Europeans used to travellers and such, and paid me little heed in my grief, and really, why should they? They had their own lives. It was not until I entered my own small world of the travelling circus tour that people acknowledged my loss. Or as was normal with the English, they politely avoided much talk of it and instead were solicitously overkind to me, going out of their way to be helpful. I understood, but when I turned my head I caught the looks of pity and confusion on the faces of the tour personnel. Surely a rock tour was not meant to be this way? Truth be told, it wasn't usually like this, but this was The Cure and nothing was the same as before.

On the day of my mother's funeral, both Robert and Simon were there to help me say goodbye. Michael, too, had come to say farewell, having already got on a plane to see me in Holland when he heard of her passing. He thought I might be in need of his company and he was right. It is one of the kindest things anyone has ever done for me.

The funeral finished and we all went to the graveside. There, on a chilly wet afternoon, The Cure played our melancholy songs for my mother as she was lowered into the earth, Robert and Simon with a couple of acoustic guitars and me with bongos. I threw the cassette tape Ted gave me of the show into the dark black hole where her remains at last rested. I pulled my leather jacket tighter around me and again cursed the God that would do this to me.

After the funeral we adjourned to my parents' house for a small and joyless wake. The house when my mother was alive had never been a place of much hospitality. Now it was overflowing with people, teacups in hand, or something stronger in my case. You should realize that it was not my mother that shunned company but my sullen father, sitting glowering at the priest, or 'sky pilot' as he would call him, slumped in my mother's now empty chair at the table in the sitting room. People offered their condolences to my father and he grunted something back at them. I suppose they took this as him being overcome by pain and sadness, but my sisters and I knew it was really the only way he communicated with the world. It was the most he ever said to us unless he was in his cups, and then it would be totally the opposite, a torrent of expletive-laced invective. We had learnt to avoid him at such moments.

I wandered out into the garden of my childhood. The hedges, bushes and shrubs were so much smaller than I recalled from my boy's perspective. They now looked as tiny and shrivelled as my father did.

I climbed up high into the sycamore tree at the end of the garden just as I had done as a small child. The boyish sense of excitement may have faded just a little, but I still got that frisson of fear and joy clambering about the shiny black and green limbs. All at once, I slipped drunkenly on a branch and tumbled down about ten feet. I grabbed at the air wildly and my fall stopped abruptly, knocking the wind out of me.

It occurred to me in that breathless minute. *This is it, Lol, your youth is over. A new life calls.*

Damn.

All hindsight is 20/20, but after the exhausting year that had been *Faith*, we had been around the world for the first time and, as Robert had noted, it seemed 'a lot smaller than I thought it was going to be.'

We now knew the bad and the good of the music world and we had seen many places. In a way it was heartening, because we found people just like us wherever we went. In other ways it was soul-destroying, as we found there were also the kind of people we had tried to leave behind. This last observation came to a head during the one and only time we played in the Grand Duchy of Luxembourg.

Growing up in suburban England in the 1970s meant that there was a complete absence of any decent music on the radio. There was only one station that played pop music, for want of a better phrase, that being Radio 1. The one exception was Radio Luxembourg, broadcast from the Grand Duchy of Luxembourg, which I remembered listening under the covers with an earpiece plugged into my little transistor radio. The DJs had exotic names like Emperor Rosko (actually an American relocated to Europe). It was so far removed from my experience as a teen growing up in Britain, with only one state radio station that was very drab and very British. Along with Radio Caroline, which was broadcast from a ship outside British territorial waters, Radio Luxembourg seemed exotic and a little anarchistic, too. They didn't play just Top 40, either.

So when we got the chance to play in Luxembourg I imagined that it would be a radical place, something like Denmark's Freetown Christiania, an autonomous, anarchistic neighbourhood in Copenhagen, something that both Robert and I would enjoy. Luxembourg was nothing of the sort. Surrounded by France, Germany and Belgium, it was conspicuously bland.

We were exhausted from playing so many gigs that year, and a certain aggressive sheen had come into our psyche. This was to set the scene for the making of *Pornography*. Despite it being autumn, an unpleasant, sullen humidity hung over everything. The club was small, dark and damp. An utterly inhospitable dump with scant comforts.

We set up our gear and played our normal set for the 118th time that year, a year that had seen us change from a fairly loose four-piece to a very compact three-piece unit. There wasn't a tour manager for this trip, just us and a bare-bones road crew.

We felt the absurdity of our situation but, as always, Robert was determined to give the best show possible to our smallish audience. That's something that's never changed. Robert doesn't play half-heartedly; when he plays his songs he has to inhabit them for them to work. I remember some tours where he would literally collapse after the gig and lie on the floor for thirty minutes to recover from the effort he put out. It's always been a cathartic experience for him.

In a three-piece, everyone must play to the best of their abilities. There is no room for mistakes. It tends to make you very accurate and tight as musicians, but it also means that each gig has some tense moments as each member has to literally carry the show at certain points in the set, because any bum notes or miscues will be very obvious in the skeletal structure imposed by the three-piece format.

When the gig ended we were physically exhausted and just plain tired of being on the road. We convened in the pitiful dressing room and waited for the local promoter or whoever had organized the concert to come see us and pay the agreed fee. I believe Martin Hopewell was acting as our agent, and as professionals we expected to be treated that way. Apparently that was a bit of an assumption, as the local promoter had little intention of paying us, and Robert wasn't very happy about it. I looked around the room for something to drink, and the next thing I knew Robert and the promoter were locked in a struggle and went tumbling down the stairs next to the dressing room, with Robert shouting to me and Simon to come and help as he rolled out the door of the club.

Simon and I rushed down to assist Robert as he shrugged off the promoter, who now saw that further fighting would be an unwise proposition. An uneasy peace ensued. We asked Robert what had happened, and he told us that we weren't getting paid for the gig. We decided to leave it up to our agent Martin to get some recompense, but this was a stinging slap in the face (literally and figuratively). Infuriated by this turn of events, we shoved off into the night towards the British Isles, where a mere five days later in Newcastle we would have to chase that large oafish man out of the hall who wanted to fight us. It felt like the storm clouds were gathering for a downpour, and out of that tempest would emerge the most intense album of our career.

# 13

# PORN

Things had changed in my head and heart now that my mother was gone. I was adrift. For a few months I didn't do much but drink and feel sorry for myself.

Things had also begun to change in the band somewhat. Parry had not been a great fan of *Faith*, as it hadn't spawned any major hits. 'Primary' was the only single from the album and it only got to 43 in the UK charts. We had spent the previous three years working non-stop. When we weren't on the road, we were recording, and vice versa. One reason *Faith* took a while to make was we didn't have enough time to write on the road and get the material prepared before we went into the studio. We were just go, go, go.

In the course of those three years of working and touring, my alcohol consumption steadily increased. Although I tried many different drugs, I was mostly a drinker. Parry decided that if we were going to fulfil his version of success for his label, he would have to get more deeply involved. He said that for our next record he didn't really need to come to the recording sessions, as we were such a closed-up unit, which was true, but he wanted to make The Cure into a bigger concern.

*Pornography* was a very difficult record to make. I feel that it represents the highlight of our sound as a three-piece. It also represents a creative peak for everyone involved, especially Robert. We operated a pretty closed studio, with only ourselves, our producer Phil Thornalley, and Mike Nicoto, the assistant engineer, in the room, with occasional visits from Gary Biddles. One night Siouxsie was allowed to visit, but most of the time the three of us were wrapped up in the fury of what became *Pornography*. It's a big, monolithic slab of sound. We had hoped to get Conny Plank, Kraftwerk's producer, to help us record it. In fact, Robert and I had a meeting with him at Fiction's offices one afternoon. He was a great, brooding German man all dressed in black leather. He regaled us with stories of his last recording sessions, 'where the sound was like a wild animal'. We were quite impressed with what he said he could bring to our music. Unfortunately, he passed away before it could happen.

We may not have generated as many hits as Parry would have liked, but the gigs were getting bigger and the audiences larger. Although we definitely grew at a slower pace than some of our peers, it was, I think, due in part to Robert's steadfast but stubborn insistence on taking our time to make sure that what we did was the highest possible quality. I think time has proved him right on that score.

In many ways *Pornography* is my favourite Cure album. I love the great big sound of the drums and the huge slabs of music used to make the songs. It's the pinnacle of the three-piece Cure sound, though we incorporated a variety of instruments. On *Pornography* you'll hear a smattering of keyboards, bass pedals and other things (cello, anyone?), but the main triangle of sound is created by the drums/bass/guitar structure, with Robert's immense vocals on top.

It represents one of my proudest accomplishments with the band. The circumstances surrounding its making were certainly intense, but that made it the album it is. It stands the test of time to me because it's not a slave to whatever the current fashions of the day were. It was born out of our own desperation and peculiar madness.

It was an unusual recording process, which at the time seemed perfectly normal. As our sessions progressed we would arrive at RAK Studios in St John's Wood later and later in the day, until finally we settled into a groove of coming in late in the afternoon and emerging the next morning, having seen the dawn rise yet again through the control room windows.

I think that Mickey Most, the studio owner, was as bemused by our schedule as everybody else seemed to be, but having been in the music business for many years and worked with many people, he knew enough to give us our space and not intrude too much. However, some days he'd bring us the occasional gift, like the guitar that Jimmy Page played when he recorded 'Stairway to Heaven', for Robert to use.

The rest of the album continued in similar fashion. We made an arrangement with the owner of the off-licence across the street. Basically we would come in every day and place what we wanted on the counter, and his son would deliver everything in a box that night. We kept a tab going to be paid once a week, and must have doubled his income for those months we were there. We were living in the offices of Fiction at the time, which added another level of claustrophobia to the mix. We were with each other 24/7, which wasn't a good idea, considering the amount of substances that were being consumed every day. I am grateful that Phil and Mike kept a sane and somewhat sober eye over everything, otherwise it might have ended in catastrophe.

The drum sound was obtained by putting the kit in the large recording room and removing all the acoustic shields so there was an immense natural reverb. I had my own sticks made to my own specifications, so they were basically thicker in the middle and thinner at each end, giving them a great 'throw', or power, whichever way I chose to use them. For most of the album, I turned the sticks over and used the thicker end to play the snare, which I had bought from John Bradbury of The Specials. It was a military snare 10 inches deep, as opposed to the usual 4- or 6-inch deep snare drum. The combined effect of all of this was to make a huge crack with every snare beat. No ambiguity or ghost notes, just the metronomic mantra of the drums!

Both Robert and Simon had new Peavey amps that were bigger and more powerful, so the combined effect produced aggression in the songs. Many of the cymbal crashes I overdubbed later in a separate room of the studio that had just been built. It didn't have any acoustic padding or finished walls built in it, and was just a bare concrete box. Phil and Mike set up some microphones, and I put my new Ray Man Chinese cymbal in there to record. That thing was so loud when I played it that I had to turn my head sideways to avoid being deafened. You can imagine the noise it made in a concrete box! I think that was the start of my hearing loss right there.

However, after we recorded *Pornography*, there was a sense of urgency to get the music out and then go on the road to promote it. The thinking was to keep things fresh and vibrant, which usually worked for us, but on reflection I think we should have waited a little bit instead of storming out of the studio and going back on the road so soon. Even a short break of a few months would have helped the band, and might have possibly avoided what was to become the death knell of the old Cure.

If the *Pornography* album sessions were difficult, the *Pornography* tour of 1982 was even more so.

The initial shows of the 'Fourteen Explicit Moments' tour for *Pornography* in the UK were actually okay, even though we were dog-tired from playing over 120 concerts the previous year, then going straight into the studio to record *Pornography*, and then back out on the road. It was a recipe for disaster, and one which is repeated again and again in the music business. When you're firing on all cylinders it's okay to keep going, especially when you're young and enthusiastic, but we really hadn't had much of a break in the three years since we'd signed with Fiction. No wonder we were in such a frazzled state! Add heavy drinking and drug use and we were a powder keg ready to explode.

Our set list included most of the songs on *Pornography*, making up a good third of the show. The album was released just as we went on the road, so a great deal of the show was unfamiliar to all but the real diehards. This was how we always operated, but *Pornography* was a very different record. It was confrontational compared to what had come before, and then there was the look. The stage set comprised screens that were remotely operated to come down over the drum kit, which was placed to the side of the stage. They also covered other areas of the stage to create different effects. It was stark, to say the least.

Mac would project washes on the screens, which he'd done before. That was the only continuity for us. There were other significant changes. For instance, during one song I would get off the drum riser and walk in the dark to the front of stage to play the keyboards during 'One Hundred Years' while the screen came down to shield the kit and create another space. The front of the amp and drum risers were coated in a mirror-like finish, which meant the audience would not only see themselves between Robert and Simon's legs, but also could be blinded by lights that were focused on the risers. The effect was similar to sitting in a pub or club with a mirrored bar. Strange, to say the least, and probably a little disconcerting for the audience, which was part of our intention. It was also a bit of an obstacle course for me, as I had to make sure I got off the drum riser in time to avoid being hit on the head by the rapidly descending screen support. I learnt the hard way.

A couple of times, I staggered to the front, having been hit with a resounding thump by the fast-falling screen. I then used the keys to hold me steady while I recovered from what felt like a mild concussion.

Our outfits were as stark and sharp as the monochromatic light show. White T-shirt and black trousers for Robert, a grey shirt with epaulets and grey trousers for me, with Simon favouring a slightly different look of leather jerkins and tight trousers with biker boots. The main difference was the make-up, though! Our hair was longer and more fierce-looking during the *Faith* tour, but *Pornography* was where it became a thing unto itself. We started to crimp our hair, backcomb it, douse it with hairspray and fix it in place with KMS gel. Our look was gradually evolving. But nobody could have predicted the bright red lipstick that now adorned Robert's face and eyes! The sheer shock of his appearance was tremendous to anybody that encountered him in the backstage area before the gig. It looked like his eyes were bleeding or someone had taken a knife to his face.

It was a pose, but a confrontational one. People responded with uneasy smiles when they met us backstage or after the gig. Simon and I had a sort of toned-down version of Robert's face. I figured that it was up to him to have the most extreme version in order to carry the very striking and aggressive songs we were playing. As Robert said, 'I wanted it to be the ultimate "fuck off" record.' I think on that front we succeeded, and if you missed the point, our look made sure you got the message.

For the first time we were booked into venues in Europe that were really too large for our present audience. At the Philipshalle in Dusseldorf only a handful of people turned up to see our large, stark stage show. Actually, it was probably several hundred, but that number of people in such a large hall meant only the first couple of rows were filled.

We walked out onto the stage and a pregnant silence filled the air, not the usual roar of the crowd to which we'd grown accustomed. The air filled with smoke, and dry ice billowed across the stage like cumulus clouds. The silence in the hall was almost overwhelming. After a couple of songs, Robert walked to the front of the stage, sat down with the mic, and sang the songs to the small crowd in a more intimate style. The tickets for that night said, 'Pornographic The Cure.' Quite!

The rest of the tour continued in similar fashion, and on most nights the atmosphere was morose and challenging. Perhaps that's understating it. Fans of The Cure know the *Pornography* tour ended up with the band in disarray.

By the time we rolled into Strasbourg on 27 May 1982, we had already played around thirty-three very intense gigs promoting *Pornography*. We were both tired and mentally drained. Which put immense strain on our relationships as a band.

I had struck up a friendship with Paul Bell, the singer of the opening act Zerra One. Later on we actually ended up living close to each other in north London, so we hung out off the road too. In fact, my friendship with Paul was to take me out of the eye of the storm brewing between Robert and Simon. After another fraught gig, we went out to a club in Strasbourg. I was actually having a reasonably good night, chatting with Paul and Grimmo, Zerra One's guitarist, and drunkenly dancing with a girl in a sailor costume, when it was proposed that we swap shirts. I had on a *Pornography* T-shirt and I immediately agreed, spending the rest of the evening dancing in my new white and blue sailor top.

'I don't know what's happening between Robert and Simon! They are fighting!' said one of the fans in the club.

I didn't really know what to do. The tension of the tour had been building, and I guess it had finally boiled over. The gigs were so intense I'm surprised it hadn't happened sooner.

I shimmied – or did a drunk impersonation of a shimmy – off the dance floor and flopped down beside Paul.

'What's yer man up to now?' he said in his broad Irish brogue.

I quickly relayed the scant details given to me by the fan.

Paul wanted to know what I was going to do. For once I made a really good decision. I was going to do absolutely nothing! I would carry on drinking, dancing and talking with Paul and the sailor girl, who by virtue of our shirt swap was now the porno girl, and keep well out of this. I had the feeling, correct or not, that my intervening would result in both parties taking out their frustrations on me.

We were only twenty-three years old – twenty-one in Simon's case. So we opted for that very English solution and just ignored everything, while keeping our feelings at bay with drinks and drugs. At least that's what I was going to do about it.

The music was loud and the room was steamy from all the dancing bodies. I was drunk and a little high from the gig and the perfume of the sailor girl. Dancing with her seemed like a much more agreeable way to spend the rest of the evening than adjudicating the fight between my two bandmates. So I stayed down in the belly of the club.

Some hours later, I made my way back to our hotel with Paul. The last thing I remember is hanging out of the rear window of our van, serenading people walking by the canals, and passing the beautiful old Gothic cathedral. I've seen the sights of many a city in the predawn hours, and Strasbourg was no exception.

The morning light shone through the curtains in my room and I recalled with horror the events of the previous evening. My drinking had taken on epic proportions and I was accustomed to the occasional blackout, but I had no trouble recalling what had happened. The previous night was somehow frozen in sharp relief.

The phone rang and I answered it, hearing the slightly deranged

voice of the tour manager informing me that earlier that morning
Robert had gone to the airport and caught a flight back to London.
*So this is how it ends*, I thought, *not with a bang but a whimper*. I
was slightly shocked, but not really surprised and, to tell the truth,
a little relieved. The whole year had been like a furious volcano of
emotions getting ready to erupt, a train about to go off the rails
and plunge into the ravine at any moment. Although it was not
really great news, I figured it could have been much worse. At
least no one was hurt.

Then another call came. This one told me that Simon had gone
home too. There I was on the edge of France by myself, the lone
representative of The Cure, with a gig to play in a couple of days.
What the fuck was I supposed to do?

I called Paul and arranged to meet him in the hotel café. We
were sitting discussing the night's events when the tour manager
came and informed me that next couple of gigs had been put
on hold, pending cancellation. I always hated cancelling gigs.
Everyone in The Cure did. Things were definitely getting out of
control. Suddenly an idea popped into my head, which until this
day I haven't really discussed.

'Paul, you can do a reasonable imitation of Robert, right?'

He nodded in agreement, albeit a little cautiously – and rightly
so, for my plan was most audacious.

'Why don't we dim the stage lights and put you in a wig and
have you sing, Paul?'

He blinked and looked at me uncomprehendingly.

'I mean, we have tapes of the gig, so we could run that mix in,
and Grimmo can stand in the shadows with a bass pretending to
be Simon. I'll just do what I normally do and it might just work.'

For a brief moment we looked at each other and then my lips curled slightly upwards in a smile. Paul smiled too.

'Yer a fookin idgit!'

Of course, it wouldn't work. We all got on the bus, as Robert had called and said he would be back for Montreux in two days' time. His father had convinced him to finish the tour. Alex Smith was old school, and believed, rightly, that if you say you'll do something, you are obliged to do it. The bus would roll on with just me and Zerra One – down the A5 to Lake Geneva at the foot of the Alps, where we would wait for the return of Robert and Simon.

The band reunited after a couple of days and everyone had cooled off. We had a few gigs left, and we played them perfunctorily. The last night was at the Ancienne Belgique, a famous Belgian theatre that normally I would have been very interested to be in. That night, however, it felt like death. It was the death of that version of The Cure. The glorious three-piece that had poured its heart out, and then some. The gig was of a certain manic intensity, but it was the finale that was really dreadful.

At the end of our performance it had become a habit to play a free-form song that we generally called 'Forever'. We had a basic format that we stuck to, but most evenings the lyrics and certain elements could evolve as the day dictated our mood. It was a sort of coda to the evening.

On this occasion we changed it around a little and swapped instruments. I played bass, Simon played guitar, and Robert played the drums. Our roadie, Gary Biddles, came on stage and started singing about Robert and me being wankers and only Simon was any good. So Robert threw the drumsticks at him, and eventually we all stopped and left the stage. The next day we all went back to England on the ferry. We didn't speak to one another on the journey home, but nothing needed to be said. It was the end of tour and possibly The Cure. Something would have to change for the band to continue, but at that moment things looked bleaker than they'd ever done before. As we got to London, I said goodbye to everyone and wondered if I'd ever see them again.

# 14

# IN FRANCE

After the disaster of the *Pornography* tour I did what I always did. I ran away. It's not hard to see why the tour turned out that way. We had been cooped up together for an awful long time on the road and in the studio the previous three years. We had played 377 gigs, approximately one every three days for over a thousand days. Although 1982 had been kinder in terms of the number of gigs we did, we were just plain exhausted.

I had met a French girl, and so it wasn't really a big leap to just up sticks and go live in France for a while. I usually crashed at my dad's house when I did come back to England, which was pretty depressing. He had not improved since mother's passing and now spent most of his time either asleep or drunk. It seemed to me a life destroyed. I would see him in passing and talk to him when I came home, but ours was not a loving relationship. I suspected his behaviour put mother in the ground before her time, so there was some resentment on my part.

I tried to be the dutiful son when I returned. I took him out to eat and got him a new TV when the one he was watching resembled an amorphous shifting coloured fishbowl, but I could not pretend we had any kind of bond. I was adrift, so I decided to shift my base to *la belle France*.

Before I knew it, I was living in Rue Cadet in Paris's 9th arrondissement. It was a market street busy with people buying food from the local shops. I stayed in Paris for a few weeks with the girl I was seeing, and from there we travelled across the whole of France down to Montpellier on the south coast, a beautiful city full of students and young people. The journey down on the train was quite an event, as we elected to take my girlfriend's cat with us to stay at a friend's house. We didn't have a suitable carrier so we had to take the cat on a leash all the way from Paris. It spent the whole journey hissing at everybody from the safety of the luggage rack above our heads while we made apologetic faces at our fellow passengers.

It wasn't the first time I luxuriated in being a stranger in a strange land. It felt very cleansing after all those days being with exactly the same people day in and day out. I felt like I could use the space to just clean out the accumulated stress and psychic tension of that last tour.

I spent many a day on the sandy beach at Palavas-les-Flots just outside the city, or at a café in the Place de la Comédie, clearing out the emotional flotsam that had built up from being on such a rigorous schedule. It was a liberating journey in a way that I've always found wonderful. I think I was always meant to travel the globe like my father and brothers before me. I had a kind of restlessness when I was a young man. I always found it stimulating to be around new ideas and new sensations. I lived for the new and unique. In it I found a kind of hopefulness to combat my inherently depressive side which was exaggerated by alcohol. Strange as it might seem, that year when I lived mostly in France I didn't drink like I did when I was with the band. I didn't intend to rid myself of that particular albatross – it just happened. Perhaps I was able to be the person I was supposed to be in France? I couldn't tell, and I didn't analyze it. I just felt a little freer.

That summer I went on a spiritual journey of sorts as The Cure effectively ceased. I needed to clear out the damage that had been done to my psyche. I hadn't heard from Robert and I knew Simon wasn't going to play in the band anymore, so I felt I should look for something else to do. I wasn't sure exactly what, so I went on a pilgrimage. It felt like the right thing to do.

We packed up our things in Montpellier, my French girl and I, left the cat with her parents who lived nearby, and headed for the Salvador Dalí Museum in Figueres, Spain. We stopped on the way at Perpignan to visit the train station, because Dalí had declared in 1963 that he 'always got his best ideas in the waiting room at the station so it must be the centre of the universe'. We figured it was worth a shot. We got a taxi to the border, walked across and picked up another cab on the other side in Catalonia and headed to Figueres. We stayed in town and visited the Dalí Museum there. Housed in the old municipal theatre, Dalí designed it to store all of his fantastic objects and paintings under an enormous geodesic dome designed by Emilio Perez Pinero. It was, to say the least, a mind-blowing experience for me. I was finally starting to feel better.

The next day we travelled to Roses, a beautiful fishing town on the Costa Brava. We took a crazy drive on tiny roads over the grassy, rocky hills to the Hotel Rocamar in Cadaqués. The manager of the hotel was very affable. He presumed that we spoke multiple languages like Dalí himself. Unfortunately, this was not the case, and though we struggled to communicate, we eventually managed to be understood in a combination of French and English (Franglais?). We stayed in this beautiful seaside fishing village with its white buildings topped with red tile roofs. Many artists have passed through or stayed in Cadaqués, including Dalí, who had a house nearby in Port Lligat. Picasso, Miró and Duchamp all spent time there at some point in their lives.

It was easy to see why. The air and the light especially had a wonderful quality, and the warm Mediterranean sunshine on the golden rocks made it a unique and beautiful place beside the sea. Looking at the scenery, it was very easy to believe we had stepped into a Dalí painting. I found the whole journey soul-renewing.

When I returned to England I found a flat in north London, near Abbey Road, and moved in. I figured I should change something, because I felt like it was the end of the line for The Cure.

# 15

# THE TOP

I kept myself busy with a couple of projects after I returned to London in 1983. I worked with the band And Also The Trees, producing their first full-length album. They were a band who had supported us on tour, and we all liked them very much as both people and musicians. It allowed me to give back a little of what had been given me, and I enjoyed working with the engineer David Motion at the anarchist band Crass's studios. It was a stress-free experience. I worked with a French band called Baroque Bordello, producing their three-track EP *Today*. I also had an abortive attempt to record something with my friend Paul Bell from Zerra One, while I waited for The Cure to regroup.

I felt certain that Robert would want to carry on, and knew we still had a strong bond that had just worn a little thin. Although the *Pornography* tour was so stressful, I held on to a glimmer of hope in the deep recesses of my being that The Cure were still viable. I knew that despite what had occurred, Robert and I were still friends.

I didn't hear from him for a month or so, which didn't really surprise me. Often when Robert felt threatened he would retreat into himself and escape with Mary. She was his point of connection with the world, his stability and true love.

Robert and Mary went off to the Lake District for a much-needed break. I didn't blame him for leaving. I felt the same way, but at that time I didn't really have anyone outside of The Cure since my mother had passed away. The Cure were my family, and the two people I had come to regard as my closest friends were at each other's throats. I felt like the poor child in the middle of a divorce who couldn't really escape from either of their parents' feelings. One distant and aloof, while the other was just angry.

I admit I tried to avoid the times, if I was visiting my father, when Simon might be in our local pub the King's Head. I think it took him a while to calm down after the tour, and he wasn't too happy about what happened next.

Robert called me: 'I'm thinking about going to the studio to record something, do you want to come, Lol?'

'Yes, but it will just be the two of us?' I wasn't sure how things really stood between him and Simon at this point.

'Yes, Lol. Just me and you.'

The first session as a two-piece was strange, but it felt right. Although I have always felt like a creative musician, I will be the first to tell you that I am not a virtuoso drummer or keyboardist. I have always tried to funnel my musical abilities into what was emotionally appropriate for the song or whatever I was doing. I also loved to write lyrics, and so for this session I came up with a few words but not much else. Robert had a few musical ideas already, and out of that session came what was to be 'Ariel'. I contributed a handful of lines inspired by my love for the poetry of Sylvia Plath, who is, to my mind, the greatest American poet.

It wasn't that satisfactory, and while we went home feeling better than when we started the engine room up again, we were a little unsure of the direction of the ship. However, Robert's next move showed why he was and will always be the captain of The Cure.

The 1980s were a great time for innovation with regard to electronic music. Pop music was starting to incorporate new types of keyboards and drum machines, with new ones coming out every month that helped refine and define the sound of that era.

I was very interested in that side of music. I feel it was probably in my genes, what with growing up with my boffin type uncles always messing about with radios, tape recorders and such. Robert and I discussed my involvement in that side of music, and now that we were a two-piece, we thought we should maybe get a different drummer to augment the sound.

I didn't object, as I never felt that I was wedded to just one role in The Cure. In my mind, I was a musical partner, and I would do whatever was necessary to make things happen. If that meant stepping into a new role and learning a totally new instrument, then so be it. I was not afraid of the challenge, and I felt that I had Robert's support. I therefore embarked upon a quick course in basic synthesis with a teacher recommended by the Musicians' Union, and started taking keyboard lessons. It was a new beginning for the band in more than one way. Robert told me that Parry had challenged him to see if he could write a pop hit. Although he was dismissive at first – after all, we had a strong hard-core audience – I sensed that something about the challenge – the gauntlet thrown down, so to speak – intrigued and irritated Robert enough to do something about it. On his own terms, of course. So a studio was booked.

Island Records had a studio housed in the old Royal Chiswick Laundry Works. We asked Steve Goulding, who played drums on 'Watching the Detectives' by Elvis Costello, to come and put the drum track down for 'Let's Go to Bed'. I admit it felt a little strange to have someone else play the drums on a Cure record, but I acquiesced for the greater good. I had my hands full anyway with a brand new New England Digital Synclavier. This was a very expensive (some versions were upwards of $200,000, an absolute fortune at the time) and cutting-edge precursor to the modern sampler found in every studio today. It's the sound of lots of famous recordings of the time, Michael Jackson's 'Thriller', for example. In many ways we were ahead of our time in terms of music production, and I like to think that my curiosity about all the new music technology to be found drove some of our better-sounding records. It's always about the song, of course, but sounds are exciting too. After a few days, a pop single was born. Now we just had to navigate what The Cure were to become.

It seemed almost in a blink of an eye that things had changed again. The brotherly bond that held The Cure together had been broken with Simon leaving, and it was a different beast that rolled forward. We were still very young, not yet twenty-five, and yet we had already seen a lot and done even more. We were growing up in public, which I think is always hard, no matter who you are. In the making of the new Cure rising from the ashes of the old, something had tilted a little, and Robert and I were aware that we would have to adapt. We were still those same English boys who found it hard to really communicate our feelings directly. We had more late-night conversations where, after drinking a great deal, our real thoughts and feelings would come out. It was clear that we needed to move forward despite what had happened. It felt almost inevitable that the band would change after the break with Simon. I used to wonder why people in bands seemed to do crazy, mysterious things from time to time, stuff that I couldn't relate to growing up in suburban south London. Now I was beginning to understand just how fraught and fragile the bonds that bring a band together can be.

The rise of MTV in the 1980s changed a lot of things for bands – for better or worse. We had released a few videos without much success until 'Let's Go to Bed'. We hadn't found someone we related to and trusted in terms of a visual representation of The Cure.

For instance, one of the previous videos we had done was for 'Charlotte Sometimes' with Mike Mansfield. I think Parry suggested him, as he had made a video with Adam and the Ants. I don't think we really saw the connection, but we also didn't really know much about the process of making a video either. It was all very new, and the form was still in its infancy.

It was decided to film 'Charlotte Sometimes' in Holloway Sanatorium in Virginia Water, Surrey. This abandoned mental institution was built by Victorian philanthropist Thomas Holloway. Holloway had made a vast fortune from patent medicines and decided to give something back to society. He built an institution where the middle-class insane could be treated and reside permanently. How quaint. The institution was the 'summit of high Victorian design' according to Sir Nikolaus Pevsner. Quite a sight to behold.

When we arrived at the recently shut down sanatorium for the shoot we were ushered into the grand entrance hall. This hall had very elaborate murals. Looking at them casually, I thought they might be depictions of angels and other heavenly beings. Perhaps the Victorians thought this might be soothing to the agitated mind. On closer inspection it turned out that the murals portrayed some frightening-looking demons, which was surprising to me, to say the least.

Much of video-making is tedious for the performers, as it takes a long time to light the set and get things ready to shoot, so we went exploring the abandoned institution. It was a very interesting place. It was quite progressive in its approach, rather like Netherne, which we were familiar with from our teen years, in that it had had a large art department for the inmates. There were many paintings and sculptures just lying around on the floor, as if everyone had left the place very quickly without stopping to collect their belongings.

A sign on the wall said, 'Visitors: Please do not offer any criticism in any way of the patients' artwork. Thank you for your cooperation.' The reason why was obvious, I suppose, but still, it felt strange to read this warning. I picked up a small green sculpture, its surface smooth to the touch. At first it looked like a blob of clay. On closer inspection I realized it was a dog drinking from a bowl. Its strange design, glazed in a lurid green, and slightly twisted features spoke very clearly to me of the tortured, fragile mind that created it, and I decided to take it home with me. It still sits on my bedside table today.

There were other clues to its previous use. I found an abandoned filing cabinet in an office full of old nurses' ward records from the 1950s. Most of the notes made quite horrific reading. Back then, although there was a progressive train of thought with the art therapy, there was also a regime of heavy medication for patients who became 'too agitated'. That's probably where the ghostly looks on the faces of the inmates that roamed around Horley on Saturdays when we were teens came from. I involuntarily shuddered at the thought.

The video itself, although filmed beautifully, failed to capture what was really needed with The Cure. We were not a one-dimensional band, which didn't come across in our early videos. We had yet to find a way to put across our complete and complex personalities. We needed someone who could illustrate both the absurdist side of the band as well as the serious side.

'The Cure are one of the stupidest bands you could ever work with yet they're the brightest, most intelligent. They're the noisiest but they can be the quietest – that's what I love about them.' Enter director Tim Pope.

Tim understood the conundrum that was at the heart of The Cure, and he was determined to find a way to present that to the world. At long fucking last.

We had a great rapport with Tim. The first video we did with him was for 'Let's Go to Bed', which was really quite an exercise in absurdist thought. Parry, Robert and myself had spent a long night trying to devise ideas for 'Let's Go to Bed'. We threw all the strange abstract ideas we thought of that night at Tim, and remarkably, he was able to make sense of it enough to make the first excellent video of The Cure.

In nearly every video we did with Tim over the next few years, and there are lots of them, he invariably made me do something strange and/or uncomfortable. 'Let's Go to Bed' was no exception, in fact it set the template for the future. He also liked to put little 'surprises' in the videos. In 'Let's Go to Bed', look closely and you might see there's some obscured nudity in it. I was dancing behind a screen to get a shadow thrown up on the background of the scene in a couple of shots. Well, it was looking a little too much like an amorphous blob, what with the extra large billowing set of overalls I was wearing. I don't recall whose idea it was but I have a sneaking suspicion it was Tim's that I dance naked behind the screen to make a more 'angular shadow'. So I disrobed and held on to my modesty amongst the crew with strategically placed duct tape. I have every sympathy for burlesque dancers after that particular shoot.

The video was really good and clever in a way that let people see both sides of The Cure, the funny and absurd. Contrary to popular belief we were not pale-faced Goths who sat in dark rooms with candles and cried all the time. Although we had some fans like that – two very sweet Japanese girls used to just stand and cry in front of us whenever they managed to come in contact with us. We named them Doom and Gloom. In the nicest way, you understand.

I think that the videos we did with Tim chronicle our growing up.

Although MTV started out in a little place in Hell's Kitchen in New York City, it was growing rapidly and there weren't enough videos of bands to fill the programming slots. I believe in the early days there were only six to eight new videos released each week, so that's pretty much what got played. As we soon found out, some heavy rotation on MTV, together with our rigorous touring, would start to accelerate the rise of the band.

\*

After 'Let's Go to Bed' we were asked to do 'The Oxford Road Show', a TV show on the BBC. The only problem was that we didn't really have a band. So we had to get some stand-ins. That's when we met Andy Anderson and asked him to drum for us, as I was going to be playing the keys from now on. For the gig we had Derek Thompson from one of our labelmate's bands, SPK, to play bass, as we had no bassist at this time either.

The gig turned out to be great fun. Watching the video clip I can see that we are invigorated again, especially Robert. I think that after all the toing and froing with the Banshees and the ceaseless touring, we had found a way forward. Robert was energized by the vitality and viability of The Cure once more.

We made two more singles in what I think of as our pop singles phase. 'The Walk' was an experiment that I really enjoyed, despite the interference of my drinking.

We hired Steve Nye to produce the record. It was the first time we had worked with a 'proper' producer, as opposed to doing production with an engineer we really liked. We picked Steve because we liked his work on *Tin Drum* by Japan. He was able to make electronic instruments sound more natural, and that's what we wanted.

There have been rumours over the years that we copied New Order's 'Blue Monday' with 'The Walk' or that at the very least it was our inspiration. I can put that particular accusation to bed. We recorded 'The Walk' before 'Blue Monday' was released in March 1983. Without the aid of a time machine we wouldn't have been able to hear 'Blue Monday' before we made 'The Walk'. The truth is that both bands were incorporating electronic instruments, synths, drum machines and sequencers into our arsenal at the same time, and some similarity could only be expected, as we were probably using the same equipment. There wasn't that much available to use back then.

A few years later, when Yamaha put out the quintessential 1980s synth, the DX7, it was a favourite hobby of ours to listen to records in the Top 10 and spot which preset synth sound from the DX7 was used on which record. It was that ubiquitous!

The picture of me and Robert on the sleeve of 'The Walk' is one of my favourites that Parched Art (Andy Vella and Porl Thompson) ever did. We took the photo one night in the back garden of Jam Studio and then they went to work in their magical way.

Although we had used Andy Anderson for a gig, he wasn't a full member yet, and with all of the electronic equipment we used he wasn't needed for 'The Walk'.

It was strange to be just a duo, having always been used to being in a band, but The Cure were always so much more than just something we did. It was and remains a way of life, a belief system. When we started we had to struggle so much against people's preconceived notions of what a band, and the music we were making, could be that it began to seep into every pore of our being. It had to. That was the only way we could succeed, or indeed survive.

When we started, we sprang from a strict Catholic upbringing. For some strange reason, or maybe not so strange, that seems to create artists and musicians of a certain intensity. Over the years I've had various conversations about the nature of faith with Robert, and I think we have both found the music and the process of making art is where we can perhaps get some answers. I know it has taken me on a journey that has allowed me to understand a little better the perennial questions that have kept surfacing and turning around and around in my head since we were teenagers. I think that for Robert, The Cure has always been a way to bring his focus back to those ideas, and in the working out of those ideas comes a sense of fulfilment for him. The fans grasped this, and that's why they are so loyal. They understood there was an inherent honesty in what we were doing.

I have several fond memories surrounding the making of 'The Walk', of Robert and I enjoying an open communication as artists. I came up with the first part of the vibratoed lead keyboard riff that introduces the vocals. I showed it to Robert and he finished it off. However, those moments of mutual inspiration were getting fewer and further between.

People always want to try and dissect the way bands make music. I certainly understand why that would be, but as Joe Strummer said, 'You can't mess with the chemistry!' In the end it comes down to many factors, not least the personalities that exist within the band. The feeling you create together is where the life of the art comes from.

The making of 'The Walk' was a slight lull before the storm. Steve Nye helped us to get the sound we were looking for. Apart from the guitar and Robert's vocals, everything was programmed into the Oberheim synthesizer system, an OB-8 synth and DSX sequencer. The drums were the relatively new DMX drum machine, which we also fed out into the studio room through a speaker and rerecorded, acoustically 'triggering' a regular snare drum.

This was similar to the technique to make the electronic instruments sound natural that Steve Nye had used before. I spent a lot of time trying to work the system with limited success. I could get a few sounds out of it, but it was hard to get what we wanted. Steve turned to me after a fruitless day of knob twiddling and said something that has always stuck with me.

'Lol, you know what that needs?'

'No?'

'RFM, mate.'

I asked him what RFM meant and he replied, 'Read the fuckin' manual!'

We eventually got it firing on all cylinders, except for one thing. On the very first note at the beginning of the song, we couldn't get the sequencer to turn off before starting the drums, so we just incorporated it in to the song! You would be surprised how many happy accidents make it onto records. Robert used to call me 'the X factor', as he was never quite sure what I might come up with – sometimes it was good, sometimes it was terrible.

My other memory of that session is twofold: one, the view from the upstairs room of the studio looking out over London in the early morning, just as the sun was rising and the mist was still enveloping the treetops. Magical! The other was the strange look on Steve Nye's face as I drunkenly kicked champagne bottles across the control room of the studio. Shit was getting real.

When we were making the video for 'The Walk' we were in a studio not far from RAK, where we knew Phil Thornalley still worked, so we looked him up during a break from filming and I asked if he wanted to come play with us at the Elephant Fayre, a festival in Cornwall on Lord Elliot's estate. We needed a bass player and drummer to play the songs live.

The Cure finally felt like a real band again. We did some

warm-up gigs for the festival in Bournemouth and Bath. In Bath we played at Moles, a really small club. There wasn't a stage, so we played on the floor, just like back at Laker's Hotel again. Robert told me he had to close his eyes while he sang, because there was a bloke about six inches in front of the mic singing along with him, which was a little off-putting. After the gig we were visited in our dressing room by none other than Lady Helen Windsor, a minor royal and great-granddaughter of King George V. Seems she was a mad Cure fan, too! Truth is stranger than fiction, truly.

The Elephant Fayre was a really wonderful festival in lots of ways. We stayed at a seaside hotel nearby, and I recall the high spirits the night after the gig as I celebrated with my girlfriend. We had Lisa, the artist who did the famous fish guitar sculpture of one of Robert's Jazzmaster guitars, staying with us in our suite, and I'm sure we freaked her out by laughing like loons at all sorts of things until the wee hours.

During the gig a symbolic act occurred, one that was to fore-shadow events to come. As I was walking off the stage, the lead of one of Robert's favourite guitars, his Vox Teardrop, got caught in my feet and unbeknownst to me I accidentally pulled it over and the neck snapped. We got it repaired and all was forgiven . . . for the moment.

Not too long afterwards we did a short tour of the USA with Andy and Phil, and that's where a further change took place.

People always ask me if there was point when I realized that The Cure were going to be as big as we became. I've generally answered in the negative, but one pivotal moment should have really given me a clue. We were in Los Angeles to play some gigs in August of 1983. That's when we went from being some English guys playing songs to becoming a part of the popular culture of the time.

After the gig, we were taken to a club in Hollywood. When we were ushered in, somebody told us there was some equipment from a previous band on stage which we could use if we wanted to play something. We played 'The Walk' or 'Let's Go to Bed', I don't recall which, but what really sticks in my mind is what happened when we walked out on stage. We were accustomed to being greeted by rows of earnest young men. Perhaps a few would have their girlfriends in tow as well, but our audience was decidedly male. That night at the club was a different story. The place exploded with girls screaming at us like we were The Beatles! It was amazing. I looked over to Robert and he simply smiled. I remember it was just so overwhelmingly beautifully brilliant, how we could feel the change in the air right there.

Just after that we all flew to Paris to record 'The Love Cats', the last of our trio of pop singles. It was recorded at Studio Des Dames in Paris, which was owned by the record label Polygram. We had a great time making that record. It felt like we were firing on all cylinders once more. I felt creative in a way I hadn't in a while and even managed to start writing some lyrics again. I also added another instrument to my list of ones I can't play, the vibes.

It was silly and irreverent and tremendous fun – apart from the night our hotel caught fire. We arrived back from the studio one night to see burning mattresses being thrown out of the fifth-floor window into the street. We never did figure out quite what was going on, but even that couldn't dampen the feeling that The Cure were back as we were always meant to be.

We filmed 'The Love Cats' video with Tim Pope back at the helm at an empty house in north London over the course of a rather deranged night. There were cat wranglers and all sorts. We had several different scenes that Tim wanted to film. One of them involved dressing me in a full-size catsuit and prowling up and down the predawn street in this get-up, hiding behind postboxes and street signs pretending to be a cat, albeit a six-foot cat. It was all a little surreal, to say the least. I actually terrified an old Rastafarian who was walking along the street at about 6 a.m. He was walking along the road minding his own business and suddenly out of nowhere I appeared dressed as a very large cat. He must have thought he was hallucinating, poor fellow.

This was Mark 2 of The Cure. This version was more expansive and less stripped down than the previous iteration, the *Pornography* Cure, as it were. I think that in order to break away from what we had been, it was necessary for us, and Robert in particular, to do something quite different.

I think it shocked some people, but I always knew that there was that side to Robert. You only had to listen to his personal tape collection, which always came out late at night in his room on tour, to know that he valued the odd heartfelt pop tune as much as the next person. Perhaps more so. I recently asked him which he liked doing more, singing or playing guitar, and he told me, 'singing, because you can really put yourself into its expression'. All the songs in his collection had that quality.

There was also a psychedelic side to Robert that he explored in depth on *The Top*, which to all intents and purpose is a psychedelic album, albeit a couple of decades after the original psychedelic era.

We decided to work at Martin Rushent's Genetic Studios in Streatley. It was wintertime, so it seemed like a pretty good place to record in the English countryside to the west of London. That's where we first met Dave Allen. He had been the engineer of the Rushent-produced Human League album 'Dare'. We liked him immediately. He was witty and sharp and very knowledge-able about recording both electronic sounds and conventional instruments. Right up our alley. We decided we would stay in the John Barleycorn pub down the street, which perhaps was not the sanest idea.

It was just myself and Robert for the sessions mostly. Andy came to do the drums he had played on the demos that we did in Eden Studios. We also really liked the way he played his leather trousers with his hands. Yes, that's the sound on 'The Caterpillar' that sounds like butterfly wings beating: Mr A.'s leather trousers.

We had all the rooms at the pub to stay in, three to be precise: me in one room, Robert in another, and Andy, and occasion-ally Porl when he came to the studio, in the last room. Most importantly, we had the key to the pub, because we often worked through the night and would arrive back about seven or eight in the morning. The landlord, being fairly used to bands and musi-cians, knew that we might want a couple of drinks after recording.

'Please help yourself to any drinks from the bar, just write down what you have on the notepad and we can add it to your bill.'

Consequently, we came home every night in the early hours when the pub was shut but we opened it back up again. Every country pub in England has regulars – usually old men who are there every day at opening time because it's their whole social life – and the John Barleycorn was no different. I think we completely amazed some of the regulars because when the pub doors opened we were still sitting there quaffing pints of best bitter with deranged looks on our faces. We tried to make the scenario a little normal by eating breakfast and then going straight to bed for seven or eight hours. The pub was owned by one of the members of the band Ten Years After, so they tolerated such behaviour.

It got more surreal as the album progressed. Some people think that *The Top* is more or less a Robert solo album. Yes and no. There are a couple of songs that I contributed to and am credited for, but for the most part it was Robert's album. I think after the stuff with Simon leaving and the fight in Strasbourg, he wanted to try something on his own, which led him down a slightly more psychedelic path. It seemed weird, but where else could we go after *Pornography*?

A great part of the reason for Robert announcing that this would be the last album or tour, as he has often done in our career, was him trying to invigorate himself and the rest of The Cure into making the best record possible. I've always admired that desire in him, although I didn't really like working through the night, because I find it depresses me after weeks of not seeing daylight. However, I was happy to go along with that plan as a way to reinvent the band. During the recording of *The Top*, what was being reborn was a different understanding of the group. I couldn't really complain that the creative responsibilities were becoming more one-sided, because I didn't feel well enough to take on more, yet I was confident that a better version of the band was emerging. At the end of the day, Robert was my friend, and I enjoyed collaborating with him even though it seemed like things were veering into that crazed area again.

One wintery day at Genetic Studios I was helping to carry out the newly repaired Vox Teardrop guitar when I slid on the ice and the Teardrop broke again on the hard ground. I felt awful, as I knew how much Robert liked that instrument. I think it was a sign that marked the beginning of the worst time for our friendship.

We had to have a slightly bigger band for the next tour because there were more keyboards and guitars than a four-piece band could play live, so Robert and I asked Porl to come and play with us again. That probably implies more of a plan than what actually happened. He was coming to the studio to show us the artwork for *The Top* when we asked him to play the sax on 'Give Me It'. At that point, it seemed inevitable that he would rejoin the band. He was able to fill in the bits that neither Robert nor I could do on stage with guitar and keys and add his own brilliance to it. To my mind, Porl was always the most versatile musician in The Cure.

I wasn't the only one in the band who had problems. At some point, everyone has done something to hinder The Cure, but that's what happens when you put extreme young men together. All kinds of dysfunction pops up.

Andy was the next casualty. We were in Nice on tour and staying at a very nice hotel, which meant security people roaming the corridors. Andy had been out and returned late at night. The fashion then was to carry your music with you in the form of a boom box on your shoulder, one which Andy subscribed to wholeheartedly. He walked into the hotel in his army fatigues with a boom box playing. The security guard thought Andy was an intruder.

'Are you staying here, sir?'

'Yes, I am, actually,' Andy replied, at which point the security guard maced him in the eyes, which was mightily unfriendly. Not unreasonably, he chased the guard down the corridor of the hotel. Andy mistakenly thought he saw the guard disappear behind a door. With his eyes streaming tears, he started kicking the door, swearing blue murder. Unfortunately, the mayor of Nice's daughter was staying at the hotel, behind the very same door that Andy was trying to demolish. Police were called, and Andy was hauled off to jail.

I awoke the next day knowing nothing of this until our tour manager called me.

'You hear about Andy?'

'No, I've not heard anything, why?'

'Well, he's in jail.' And the whole sorry story spilled out.

Andy and I were friends. Still are. So I elected to go with Parry to get him out of jail. I spent several hours talking with Andy on the beach, trying to dissuade him from putting a palm tree through the windows of the hotel. I sympathized with his point of view. He had been unfairly targeted. But we had a gig to play, and we couldn't afford to leave him here to answer any charges. After a brief talk with the mayor's aides, a solution was reached.

'If Mr Anderson leaves town today, no charges will be pressed.'

The cheek of it! What about *us* pressing charges? In the end, we had to act pragmatically, and Andy was smuggled out on the crew bus to the next town. However, it was a foreshadowing of the future. Later on in the tour, in Tokyo, Andy had another run-in at a hotel. The details are sketchy, but we had all been out to a club the previous night and when Andy got back some kind of altercation took place, and once again the police were called.

Robert and I had a short meeting in Parry's room and we decided that we couldn't really carry on with the situation like this. Andy's behaviour was getting worse, not better, and it was probably best that he leave the tour and go back home to London.

Robert stepped up to the plate and said, 'Okay, well, I better go tell him, I suppose.'

Robert generally loathed confrontations, but when push came to shove, he knew it had to come from him, otherwise Andy might not take it seriously enough. Off Robert went and told Andy he was out of the band and that he would be given a ticket back to London.

There was only one problem. We still had a three-week tour to do in America with no drummer! For a moment we wondered if I could play by making some adjustments to the set list. Perhaps we could play as a four-piece. In the end we opted to get a friend of Phil Thornalleys's in to drum for us: Vince Ely, who was the original drummer for The Psychedelic Furs.

We rehearsed for a couple of days, and we augmented the drum set-up by adding a couple of floor toms on the riser, so I could add some extra drum sounds along with Vince. Not quite The Glitter Band, but it sounded strong. Vince could only help us out for a while, as he had other commitments, so once again it was Phil to the rescue. Phil had been working with The Thompson Twins, and their drummer, Boris Bransby-Williams was on holiday in Los Angeles with his soon-to-be wife, Cynde. It was perfect timing. Boris came on board, and once again we had the extra tom set-up to bolster the drum sound. It became apparent that Boris was the right drummer for The Cure, and so when the tour was over we asked him if he'd get in touch with us and not go back to The Thompson Twins. It was a happy accident meeting him in the first place, but he fit right in. But what does that mean exactly?

I would say that to play in The Cure you have to have the same sense of humour. I think that's probably true of most bands. You spend so much time together that it helps to have similar views and feelings. You have to be able to laugh at the same things otherwise it can get very uncomfortable on those long journeys on the tour bus. I would say 99 per cent of band bust-ups are because of an inflexible position being held to the extreme by one party or another, and usually over the most ridiculous things. The movie *Spinal Tap* is funny precisely because it's so accurate.

Even though we had a secure set-up with me, Robert, Phil, Porl and Boris, we went through another change, one that would essentially bring the band to its old self but keep the expanded line-up.

We finished the tour in New York at the Beacon Theater. We now had a really strong international following. Suddenly many things were possible as long as we didn't bring the whole house of cards down on our heads.

We thought that Phil would want to continue with The Cure. We enjoyed playing with him, and he was a little different from us in that he was reasonably sober most of the time, which added a different dynamic to the band. While it might be true that we were hedonistic in our behaviour, at this point we were still interested in the world that Phil helped stimulate with his more sober outlook. He also had a burgeoning solo career, and I think it was a hard decision for him when I asked him if he would like to continue as the permanent bass player of The Cure.

He declined, and I don't really blame him as he had a lot on his plate. I think if he hadn't had the extra pressure of his own record deal to contend with he might have stayed, but that's just speculation on my part.

Back in Horley, Simon had a band with Gary Biddles who had worked for The Cure as a roadie for a while and was also friends with all of us. Gary called Robert around Christmas time and asked him to come for a drink with him and Simon. I think things had gone on for too long and both Robert and Simon regretted not talking to each other. In my mind Simon has always been The Cure's bassist, with due deference to the others who have filled that position. He's a good foil onstage for Robert's persona, and he has an absolute rock-solid rhythmic musical feel.

When Robert met him again after all that time apart he realized he had to get Simon back in The Cure, but knew he had to go about it slowly. Simon had his own band and Robert wanted him to know that he valued what he was doing, but wondered whether he might like playing with us again more.

It took a while, but after the first meeting at the pub they started to warm up to each other. We were doing some demos for the album that became *The Head on the Door* at a studio called F2 on Tottenham Court Road in London. We invited Simon to come and play on the demos, and that was the first time the new Cure played together: Robert, Simon, Boris, Porl and me.

It wasn't long before we had all the songs demoed and ready for the next phase of The Cure.

## 16

# THE HEAD ON THE DOOR

After a lot of trial and error, *The Head on the Door* signaled a shift to being a real band again. Robert has always preferred having a band comprised of friends – people he liked and felt comfortable with. It surprised me to discover that some bands are not based on that kind of algorithm. I am certain The Cure would never work without the type of emotional commitment and involvement of the musicians who were mainstays of The Cure. The music would not sound true. One reason I feel The Cure's fans have always been so loyal is because they understand that we are equally committed on the other side of the equation.

We recorded the majority of *The Head on the Door* at Angel Studios in Islington, London. As I said, my belief is that Simon Gallup was always meant to be the bass player in The Cure. Yes, Michael was the original player and definitely had a very beautiful style, but the bass-playing style of Simon is what people associate with The Cure.

It had been hard for us when Simon left after the *Pornography* tour. Although we had done quite a lot after Simon's departure, it left a rather large hole in the sound and, more importantly, there was a certain feeling that Simon's personality brought to The Cure. It always, always comes down to the chemistry, and that's something that can't be manufactured, no matter what anyone says.

While The Cure is most definitely Robert's band, it's also mine, as it is Simon's and maybe even a bit Porl's. There is a definite dynamic between us that created The Cure. It's one reason why Robert is not a solo artist. Yes, he writes a lot of the music and lyrics, but the musicians animate the songs with heart and soul. Without Simon, there was a definite emptiness.

That said, it made it difficult to face Simon's simmering resentment when I encountered him in the King's Head before his reconciliation with Robert. Mostly he was fine, but I could see he was hurt, and Simon is a very emotional man, a true Gemini. If he was feeling okay he might be pleasant, but if it was the other Simon, then watch out! I didn't really mind, though, as I knew both sides of his personality. It was hard for Robert to always have to sort out band problems, but on the other hand, if it's your band, that's what you do. He had a very English reserve when it came to talking about internal conflict, so if it could be ignored or glossed over that was the path he took, which was hardly the way to reach a resolution! I suppose that's a nice way of saying we lacked the maturity to deal with each other.

That made things difficult when the sessions started. I was not feeling great emotionally, and my drinking was causing more trouble than it alleviated, but I was still unaware of the seriousness of the problem.

I had started, with the best of intentions, to learn how to operate a couple of pieces of new gear. I had recently obtained a Yamaha

RX15 drum machine and a new E-mu Emulator II. I had these instruments at my house in London and was working on them, trying to figure stuff out. Unfortunately, alcohol, and now some drugs, had a different idea, and large swathes of time were lost to inebriation and the craziness that goes with it. And it got crazy.

One morning, having been up all night doing stuff that keeps you up all night, the doorbell rang. There on the doorstep were two of London's finest. I immediately assumed that I was done for and I must be guilty of something I couldn't remember from one of my many blackouts. I've always felt guilty of something. It's a throwback to my Catholic upbringing, all fire and brimstone and all that, and a terrible thing for a blackout drinker like me.

'We are asking local residents if we can use their premises for surveillance for the north London railway rapist. Can we come in?'

I looked around for the cameras, as I was certain this was a set-up and Jeremy Beadle or some other 'comedian' was going to pop out of the bushes. I had rehearsed that particular scenario in my paranoid head a few times, I can tell you!

'Oh, okay, I guess so,' I said with a thick, heavy mouth that wasn't working too well. Funnily enough, neither was the rest of my face, which seemed to be going in many directions at once. A sensation familiar to users of stimulants. I looked nervously at the detectives from the Metropolitan Police and tried to focus on what they were saying.

'Okay, you better come up.' I said, enunciating the syllables very carefully, hoping they wouldn't notice my gurning features.

I was certain the cuffs were going to come out at any moment, but they seemed relaxed and quite relieved that someone had agreed to their proposal. They told me I was the only person in my street that had actually let them into their house so far. Their plan, it seemed, was to use their binoculars to gather evidence about the rapist who apparently used to escape after his assaults down the side of the railway tracks that were directly opposite my window. In my somewhat befuddled state I took this all in, and then without further ado agreed to let them camp out in my flat and do their reconnaissance from my place. Normally, I wouldn't be letting Babylon anywhere near my domain, as I didn't really have a great deal of trust in the old Bill, but they were actually engaged in an important community project and I felt I should support that.

And so it was that for the next week or so two coppers turned up at my door every morning to survey from my window. They carried their equipment in two large plastic bags and shuffled nervously inside when ushered in every morning. I brought them tea and carried on with my day. You might ask whether the presence of police inside my house curtailed my bad behaviour?

Not at all! And that is the insanity of it. One might think that with the police about five feet away, I might be a little more circumspect, but I carried on as normal (normal for me) and every so often I popped my head in to say hello. As the day progressed and my intake assumed more monstrous proportions my behaviour must have seemed very strange, but the two good policemen didn't bat an eyelid. Every evening they bade me farewell until the morning with a cheery wave and not a single recrimination. It was all very strange, but strange was beginning to be the normal state of things in my life.

Down at Angel Studios we were getting to grips with a lot of new things, including a huge Scalextric train set that went all the way around the studio and regularly featured alcohol-filled cars ablaze in the darkness. A diversion of sorts from the serious business of making *The Head on the Door*.

The songs were all pretty much ready when we went to record them due to our intensive demoing. Sometimes when we recorded a demo it turned out so good that it would have been wise to just leave the song as it was, but did we do that? No chance.

Recording is a process of constant refinement and polishing things and, more often than not, undoing and unpolishing stuff that's too perfect and bland-sounding. I think this is why recording never gets any easier. The more you do it, the more things you can mess up. This is especially true if you've had some success, because you tend to want to refine things unreasonably past the point of perfection. What often happened with The Cure was that because we were able to record in more sophisticated studios, with more tracks and gear, the songs would fill up with a lot of layers that didn't need to be there, and ultimately might never be used.

I always likened it in my head to the making of a sculpture from a large block of stone. We had this large, monolithic slab of sound, and we had to carve the song from it. Even though much of the final song was already worked out by Robert, I had set up a keyboard in one of the recording booths and started to doodle along with the tracks on my headphones. When I found something I thought might work I'd play it to Robert, and if he thought it was cool I'd record it. Sometimes it would stay and sometimes not. For instance, in 'Six Different Ways' there's a strange vibratoed keyboard sound that I added. It worked, so it stayed.

A lot of the time, however, I was working through whatever booze we had on hand in the studio, which seriously impaired my creativity for this album. I would come in every morning with the best intentions of staying sober that night, but I was finding it harder and harder to hold on and to stay true to my word. My thirst for alcohol was running rampant and destroying all my attempts at control. I would try to restrict myself to a beer or two with dinner, but that was never enough. The cravings I felt for more were too strong to resist and I would find myself drunk by the evening. More nights than not, I was sent home in a taxi, too inebriated to function. *Well*, I told myself, *things will be better on the road.*

Before we started on *The Head on the Door* tour, we did a handful of gigs and festivals, including the largest we had ever done, in Athens, Greece. It was possibly the most dangerous, too.

It was the first time I thought we were in deep trouble as a band. I had been in riots before. Back when I was seventeen, Porl and I went to the infamous Notting Hill Carnival; the riot that ensued that day between the Rastafarians and the police, forever enshrined in the photo on the back of The Clash's first album, was pretty scary for a teen from the suburbs. 'Police and Thieves' was not just a Clash version of the Junior Murvin song to me. I had been there when it went down. However, it's one thing to be present at those historical flashpoints of societal change, and quite another to have it intrude into your everyday existence!

We had been asked to play the Rock in Athens '85 festival in Greece for European Youth Culture Year so it was a very prestigious and important festival. The Clash, Culture Club and Depeche Mode were also on the bill. Melina Mercouri, the famous actress turned politician who had helped bring Greece out of the era of the fascist military junta of the 1970s into a more liberal 1980s, was the minister of culture who had made the festival happen, and it was a priority for her personally.

It was apparent to me that it was a very important gig when we arrived at Athens airport and were met by the army and police on the tarmac, who then escorted us to our hotel without any of the normal formalities of entering another country. No passports or visas needed, sir. You are most welcome to Greece!

We got to Athens with a group of friends in tow, as we thought doing a few festivals around Europe might be a kind of holiday for us. The atmosphere was relaxed and festive while we camped out in the Athens Hilton. We had arrived a couple of days before the gig and decided we would like to see Depeche Mode and check out the festival site where they were playing the day before us. The venue was the Panathenaic Stadium, an old and venerable Olympic stadium in the shape of a horseshoe with an opening at one end. This was where they put the stage and erected fences to create another backstage area. The place held about 50,000 concertgoers.

That first night we went down to the site, the mood felt tense and there were a lot of police about. It turned out someone had counterfeited tickets, and now there were several thousand very angry fans unable to get into the stadium. We watched Depeche Mode from the side of the stage and they put on a great show. Depeche Mode and The Cure had a lot in common: we both originated in 'new towns', us in Crawley and them in Basildon, and both bands still have a large US following, which can't be said for some of our peers, like Echo and the Bunnymen, for instance. We have also over the years shared several crew members, including the infamous Bamonte brothers Daryl and Perry, both of whom had stints playing with the bands they worked for – Perry with The Cure and Daryl with Depeche Mode. Little did we know that we were going to get even better acquainted that night.

I don't remember quite when the first rock came sailing into the backstage area, but I certainly recall how scary it was. A brick-sized lump of pavement hurtled over the thin and flimsy corrugated sheeting that walled off the backstage area where there was the usual selection of small trailers and porta-potties. We got a small ladder and peeked very carefully over the parapet.

'Bloody hell, Lol,' Simon said to me. 'Why are they so mad, do you think?'

'Can't get in,' I said, and at that point we saw our first casualty: a policeman with a large cut on his forehead was being carried bodily above several people's heads like a newsreel shot from a war zone, which the stadium was rapidly resembling now. I looked further out across the street and could see people ripping out chunks of pavement to hurl at the police and security people from the festival. It didn't look good at all. Just then I saw the water cannon, a huge structure mounted on top of a heavy truck. The deluge of water was aimed squarely at the rock-throwers, who slid back along the road very violently.

I felt a tug on my trouser leg. It was Mick Kluczynski, our Scottish/Polish production manager.

'Lol, we're all getting out of here. 'It's getting too fuckin' wild!'

Just then a rock whizzed past my head and it was a sign, if ever there was one needed from the universe, that yes indeed it was time to get the hell out of there. I jumped down from the ladder and Mick shepherded us all to the ramp of an artic that was waiting at the backstage entrance. We all went up the ramp and into the cavernous trailer. The guys from Depeche Mode came in right behind us, fresh off the stage, with towels draped around their shoulders. We all knew each other but it was rather surreal for both bands to be sitting together in this empty, dimly-lit trailer. Ah, the glamour of rock and roll!

Mick appeared as the ramp was reinserted into the artic. 'Good luck!' he winked as he closed the doors on us.

And with that the two bands pulled out into the teeth of a riot going on at the back of the stadium. It sounded a little like clapping, but it was the sound of many hands banging the side of the truck. The furious crowd had seen the large gates open with what was to all intents and purposes an enemy transport coming onto the scene. Images of embassy sieges flashed in my mind, but most of all I thought of the Trojan Horse. A few bumps as we drove over the kerb and we all exchanged nervous glances. It was one of those moments when you wonder if this is where it all ends. A few more loud bangs on the side – rocks, perhaps? Finally we started picking up speed and putting the scene behind us. We took a circuitous route back to the hotel, which was only a half-mile away. There were no windows in the trailer so it was only the sounds of the boiling, dusty city outside that gave any clues as to our possible fate.

A few minutes after we departed, we pulled over, and after what seemed like an eternity the long doors of the trailer opened. Adjusting out eyes to the light, we saw Mick. He had run back through the rioting crowd and down the street strewn with rocks and was there to welcome us back to the Hilton personally! I never saw anyone intimidate Mick. Ye cannae mess with the Scots, man!

We descended the hastily lowered ramp at the back of the trailer. It was possibly the strangest entrance the Athens Hilton has ever seen before or since. Somewhat relieved at our narrow escape, we repaired to the bar where, much later, Nina Hagen would regale me loudly with Jimi Hendrix songs sung in German. I shook her wolf's head cod piece by way of greeting and ended up breakdancing on the bar floor well into the early hours. All this and we hadn't even played the gig yet! But we had survived.

The next day Melinda Mercouri herself turned up to say, 'Athens trembles' after looking out at the scene of devastation that followed the riot. The new version of The Clash played before us. Boy George sang behind a Perspex shield, as certain morons decided to throw stones at the Culture Club singer. I wore my blue silk wizard shirt all through the show with a Batman sticker on the back that, unbeknownst to me, Robert had slapped on as we mounted the steps to the stage.

Much of the second half of 1985 was spent preparing for, and performing with, *The Head on the Door* tour that went around much of Europe and North America. We played at Sylvia Plath's alma mater, Smith College in Northampton, a private independent liberal arts women's college. It was an exceptional gig, as I recall, and I was pleased to be at a place where one of my heroes had been a student.

We played at Radio City Music Hall within a week, which was another iconic landmark venue I had heard about, and now we were there. A magical place in New York lore, complete with the story of the lion that roams the theatre at night to deter intruders.

When we finished the final leg of the tour in Europe in December, we were now playing at a huge arena in each city – the Enormodome, as *Spinal Tap* has it.

We finished off the year in Paris playing first the modern arena of Bercy to a sold-out crowd of over 20,000 Parisians, and later that night to a more exclusive audience of the hotel staff at our Paris hotel. We made a typically pragmatic offer after learning that the staff holiday party was in progress in the hotel ballroom.

'We'll play three songs for the staff, and in return free champagne for us!'

It must have seemed like a bargain for the hotel at the time, but like many promoters of our early concerts, at the end of the night they probably wished that they hadn't made what turned out to be such a generous offer to us. And so we ended the year on a piece of our past.

Christmas came and went, and before I knew it we were back on the road again. Somewhere during that time I had moved from my rather compact flat in north London to a larger house up the street within staggering distance of my friend's bar.

The first gig that year was at the Albert Hall, another iconic venue. This concert was a benefit in aid of Greenpeace, as we played I wistfully thought how mother would have liked to have been there, in her grand box, proudly watching us.

Later that year we played the Nürburgring Festival in Germany. We nearly didn't make it in time, as our airport was about three hours' drive from the festival and we were scheduled to play just three hours after landing. In a couple of very fast Mercedes we literally drove up to the stage steps for our set. People probably thought we were being divas turning up at the last moment, but in fact it was just bad planning on our part.

Later that summer we played the Glastonbury Festival. We pulled up to the festival site in a large tour bus during a downpour. As I looked out the window I was met by the sight of about two hundred 'mud people' – festivalgoers covered from head to toe in brown mud. Quite impressive, I have to say, but it sharpened my resolve not to go out into the festival site proper and to stay in the drier and less swamp-like enclave backstage. However, we didn't even make it that far.

Our set was delayed somewhat by the fact that it was a World Cup year and we were all watching a TV on our tour bus. A particularly important quarter-final match was taking place that day, France vs. Brazil, which went into extra time with a dramatic penalty shootout at the end. So my apologies to The Cure fans present for our late arrival that day. I am reminded of the famous quote attributed to Liverpool manager Bill Shankly: 'Some people believe football is a matter of life and death. I'm very disappointed with that attitude. I can assure you it's much, much more important than that!'

The Glastonbury Festival is actually much, much more important than that to many people, and The Cure ended up playing a couple more times, but I imagine that the 1986 performance is the one a lot of fans remember. It was a great set, and despite our late start we did three encores, which is a lot for a festival. The rainstorm ceased the moment we walked on stage, which allowed the lightshow to sparkle amongst the night sky, with eerie, greenish-tinged water drops. Magical!

Later that year we had the beach party tour. We played at Jones

Beach in New York. When we arrived, I was nursing a huge hang-over, and I decided the best treatment for this was to go swimming at the beach. As I was idly floating about in the water I noticed several members from our opening act, 10,000 Maniacs, waving to me from the shore. Wanting to promote *entente cordiale* with our American compatriots, I gamely waved back. It finally dawned on me that they weren't waving but furiously motioning to me to come ashore quickly. Apparently they had information about a large jelly fish infestation in the waters around Jones Beach that I did not. It was kill or cure for my pounding hangover headache. I soon realized I was better off out of the water when Perry Bamonte proudly showed me a live jellyfish in a bucket that he had fished out of the water off the edge of the backstage area.

We played on that summer as I barely managed to keep my drinking under control, although I was determined to play as well as I possibly could every night. By that time we were completely professional in our approach as a band, which meant that every night we could rise up to a certain level no matter the circum-stances. Even if we were ill or suffering from sheer exhaustion, we put those feelings aside to make the gig the best we could. I think that tour included some of the most magical gigs we had ever done.

The year rolled on, and eventually we arrived in France at the city of Orange in Provence. We played at the Theatre Antique, an ancient Roman amphitheatre. We had decided that as we were playing to such a high level, we should document the gig, espe-cially in such a wonderfully evocative place. We asked Tim Pope to film it as we felt comfortable with him and knew that he could capture the essence of The Cure live. I think he did an admirable job and the whole film (because it was a real film, meant to be shown in cinemas) works on many levels to express that.

We filmed it in two days: the first day was the concert proper with an audience, and the second day we performed again to an empty place to get all the close-up shots and other interesting angles that aren't possible to get in a live gig situation. Before the gig on the first night, we filmed above the stage quite high in the air where a statue is ensconced in an alcove. We found out that the only way to stand directly next to the statue was via some very dodgy-looking wooden planks. This probably accounts for our slightly terrified expressions at the beginning of the film as we wave hello from the precarious perch. I think it was another one of Tim's tricks to make me feel as uncomfortable as possible and capture it on film. I bet there was a real floor that he had them take up before we got there just to get the right 'cinematic effect'.

The gig started with a surprise, as Robert had decided to cut off his trademarked spiky hairdo, and so for the whole concert he had a very striking crew cut. Fans probably remember the start of the concert with us walking onstage and Robert with a wig that Simon removes with a thespian flourish. It took a moment for the rapturous audience to realize that this strange short-haired man wearing make-up was Robert. It was a sublime piece of showmanship that added to the overall hallucinatory feel of the film. It reminds me of *Live at Pompeii*, but a little to the left of the Floyd.

The filming went well, and the audience was very wild and appreciative – perhaps being aware that the gig was being filmed for posterity helped. After the gig everything was left as it was for the filming of the close-ups the next day, and we retired to our hotel on the Mediterranean a little over an hour away. I went for a walk along the side of a small seawall. In the darkness I could see the ocean, as the wall was only about three feet high. I was full of joy and excited about the film and grateful for being in such a beautiful and historic place. I was practically skipping along the ocean walk. I jumped up onto the wall and, believing it was the same distance on the other side, jumped off it. In the darkness I didn't realize that it was a steep drop to the beach, maybe another three feet more, so I fell about six feet onto the sand. Surprised and slightly winded, I attempted to get up. That's when I felt the sharp pain in my ankle where I had twisted it violently. I managed to scramble up to the beach path and limp back to our hotel. I went up to my room to lie on the bed and massaged my ankle, which was rapidly swelling. This was ominous. We had to film the cut aways and close-ups for the gig the next day and it looked like my ankle might not be up for that. I called our promoter, Jules Frutos, a lovely man who had promoted many of The Cure's gigs in France.

'Hi, Jules, I had a small accident walking out by the beach and I think I've hurt my ankle badly.'

I heard Jules's sharp intake of breath on the other end of the line somewhere else in the hotel.

'Okay, Lol, I'm going to get a doctor to come look at you.'

'Yes, please. I think I may need him!'

About forty minutes passed before Jules and the attendant doctor arrived. I let them into my room and hobbled back to bed, where I lay wincing in pain from the now bulbous ankle. I hoped that he could fix me. I didn't want to be in a cast or crutches for our film.

The doctor examined my foot and pressed it in a few places, presumably to check if my bones were broken. With my schoolboy French I understood that he wanted me to flex my foot, and from there Jules translated the rest of his diagnosis.

'Okay, Lol, he says you're lucky it's not broken.'

I heaved a sigh of relief.

'But it is badly sprained.'

Some rapid-fire French between Jules and the doctor ensued that was hard for me to follow. Jules told the doctor I had to perform again on film the next day and needed to be able to walk. The doctor wanted me to rest for a few days to let the ankle heal, but that was impossible. In the end, he decided to give me a special shot and some cream to rub on my ankle that would make it easier to stand without too much pain.

The doctor prepared the shot and I removed my trousers so he could inject my leg. I felt the sudden pinch of the needle and then a warm flood of painkilling medicine. He next produced the tube of cream from his bag and gave it to Jules.

'The doctor says once every four hours with the cream on the ankle and don't walk for about eight hours, and the swelling should go down enough to do the gig tomorrow.'

The doctor wrapped a white bandage around my foot a few times, pulled it tightly and fixed it in place. I rested that night and the next day I found I could indeed put pressure on my foot and stand at the keys for the second night of filming. If you look closely at The Cure in Orange film, you might just see my ankle expand and contract and turn from black to the colour of the crepe bandage.

# 17

# KISS ME

We decided not to go back to the UK after the second night and just keep rolling along on our first band holiday. Although we had been together for months at a time, on the road it was work. I sometimes think people don't really understand that for the band it's their job. Robert remarked to me recently that one of the reasons things got so crazy with the partying was that people would come see us and afterwards we would hang out to talk and drink and party. Our friends could go to sleep the next day and recover, whereas we had to go on to the next town and the same thing would happen all over again. We really didn't have a good perspective on our lives and careers, and never knew if we'd ever be able to do the things we were doing again. We often said yes to everything, especially me, and made the most out of every opportunity, even though it led to some extreme behaviour.

So we really needed a holiday. We drove a couple of hours down to Le Mourillon by Toulon on the Côte d'Azur. We stayed at a small seaside hotel that served as our retreat from the rigours of the road before we departed for the real work of recording *Kiss Me, Kiss Me, Kiss Me*.

It was a blissful first night as we checked in at the hotel. I had a room with a balcony overlooking a small courtyard right in front of the Mediterranean, which beckoned invitingly. We had enough time to relax that Robert even had his own car brought from London to be able to drive around in.

I awoke the next day to the August sun streaming in through the curtains onto the old French shutters. I ordered up some coffee and croissants to enjoy on my small balcony overlooking the courtyard. I went over to the shutters and flung them open, dressed only in my boxers as it was warm and gorgeous outside.

As I opened the wooden shutters I absentmindedly scratched my stomach and as I glanced down into the courtyard I did a double take. The whole courtyard was full of Cure fans! There were probably fifty of them. They immediately saw me and shouted as one, '*Bonjour*, Lol!'

A little taken aback, I acted as nonchalantly as one can when caught almost naked in front of an audience of French fans. I waved and smiled, saying '*Bonjour*', and slowly backed away into the darkness of my room. We were obviously not going to be alone for our holiday.

We spent the next week in a strange kind of cat and mouse existence as we attempted to do all the normal things one wants to do on holiday but while being stalked by Cure fans. A walk down the beach took on a surreal quality as we became aware of people following us who miraculously vanished behind a sand dune as we glanced behind us. Very disconcerting.

A group dinner at a seaside restaurant was very strange as

more people than were in the restaurant turned up to peer at us through the windows. Robert's car, a white jeep, was the recipient of many messages of love and loyalty to its owner – some written in black sharpie on the actual vehicle!

We left after a few days of 'holiday' for our next destination on the Riviera: the town of Draguignan where we were to work at the studio of Jean Costa, a famous French musician who had worked with Johnny Hallyday (the French Elvis), among others. We spent a couple of weeks here refining the songs before heading off to record at Château Miraval.

We took the demos we had made at Boris's house earlier that year and refined them some more. The days had a rather blissful quality as we worked with good humour. All the local kids who were Cure fans would sit on the pavement outside the small studio in Jean's house and listen to us record. Every day we would work on our songs with Jean at the controls, and every evening when we finished Jean would declare 'Pastis time!' Out would come the bottle of the yellow, anise-flavoured aperitif so beloved in that part of France.

Jean's wife would bring us food to nibble on with our drinks. It was an idyllic time as we reconnected as friends again. It felt like we were back at the Smith house all those years ago when we would rehearse three times a week. I know it's what Robert has always wanted from The Cure: that beautiful feeling we had that last summer as teenagers when we were looking beyond ourselves into the new world of adulthood and excited by life. It felt as if anything might be possible. It just felt right again.

Sometimes after the pastis we would play a game of kick-about football with the kids who had come to listen to us. It was a welcome break from all the pressures of the music industry and the various forces pulling at the band. It felt almost as if we'd reclaimed some of our lost innocence. We were a successful group and bound for glory, whatever that meant. Our initial contract with Fiction Records was finishing, and now we would be offered much better terms. Record labels were lining up to hand us the keys to the kingdom. However, dark clouds were just around the corner.

I squinted into the sunlight and felt the taste of dirt in my mouth. Gritty and foreign. Turning slightly, I realized that my left side ached a great deal, like I'd been hit by a truck. Looking up, I saw a groove cut into the edge of the vineyard terrace about eight feet above me. I must have fallen down from there and thus came the realization that this was the cause of my current pain.

Pulling myself up to a sitting position, I could see that I wasn't far from the little collection of houses and outbuildings that comprised most of Château Miraval, the residential studio in the south of France where The Cure had been holed up for several months recording what was to be our next album *Kiss Me, Kiss Me, Kiss Me*.

The sharp pain in my side reminded me where I was and I looked back towards the buildings of Miraval. What time was it? I couldn't make out if it was late or early in the day, dawn or dusk. I couldn't recall how I got here. There was a blur of Chateau Miraval and the rosé wine of the same name . . . The studio and control room and various instruments and people's faces . . . Then running across the meadow at the side of the studio and a dim recollection of my girlfriend, Lydia. I was picking up stuff and hurling it at her. Oh my God, what had I done?

I had met Lydia, an American girl, about a year before at a dinner in Los Angeles, where Boris's girlfriend, Cynde, had introduced us. A few months later she visited London and I started seeing her. My relationship with my French girlfriend, Anne, was not going well, and if I'd been in a better frame of mind I would have perhaps realized that I should take a break from being involved with anyone, and focus on getting right with myself. But as my drinking worsened, I thought I needed someone to help organize my life, as I couldn't seem to do it on my own anymore.

I had always been able to run my own life ever since I left home. I managed my bills and the other responsibilities of adulthood by myself, but all of that was becoming overwhelming to me as I went deeper into the bottle. I co-opted Lydia to take care of my life, which was more than a little unfair. It was a lot to deal with for her, especially as she didn't come from a very stable background. The whole foundation of our relationship was rickety from the start.

I staggered to my feet and limped down the grass and dirt to the little roadway that led directly into the band's accommodation. Everything hurt. I looked at my feet and I only had one shoe on and a muddy sock on the other. I pushed open the door to my house on the site – a two-storey French peasant cottage – and looked tentatively inside. Nobody. I wheeled around to see if the police or such might be behind me, which they might be if my terrible memory from the previous evening was true, but I was all alone.

I climbed the stairs, stubbing my muddy foot. I did not call out but bit down on my sleeve. I opened the door of the bedroom and crept over to see Lydia sleeping in the bed. She shifted slightly in the covers. Alive, at least, then. I walked around to her side and saw no blood or anything on her face or head. Maybe I'd imagined it, thank God. Just then her eyes opened wide with the sense we all have that tells us someone else is in the room with us while we're sleeping. Her expression was halfway between pity and anger.

'You were a complete ass last night. I can't believe you were throwing stuff at me as we came home.'

'What happened?' I asked meekly.

'You ran out screaming into the night! I wasn't going to go looking for you out there. Did you just get home?'

It was all too much for me to process and I fell back into the small armchair in the room, pushing the clothes on it to one side as I did so. Slumped in the chair, I felt relief and shame all in the same moment. What the hell was wrong with me? We had only been together for less than a year and already I was trying to run her out of my life.

I suddenly remembered the sharp pain in my side as I tried to turn towards the bed. Wincing, I pulled my shirt up to see two large bruised areas. Must have been the fall I'd had as I went over the side of the vineyard terrace. I also had some scratches and a livid cut. Damn. I had come to Miraval feeling like it would be a good place to recover and reconnect with the rest of the band. Especially Robert, from whom I was feeling more and more estranged. Unfortunately, the pleasant feeling from Draguignan had evaporated with the return of my emotional problems.

I washed off the blood and mud in the tiny shower in the ancient bath in our little house in Miraval. Feeling less than stellar was my normal situation most days. The sick, unsteady feeling endured for a few hours until I could stand no more and had to take my 'medicine' to start to feel normal for a while. Then the madness took over once more.

I walked up the small winding path through bushes of Provence lavender, blue in the late morning sun, occasionally tripping on the small rocks and spluttering a little. I could smell the aroma of strong French coffee wafting from the main studio house of Miraval and was glad to sit down at the table and pour a cup of coffee from the silver percolator into my mug and mix it with steaming hot foamy milk. *Café au lait*, one of France's gifts to the world. Trembling, I raised it to my lips and drank a large stimulating draft of the strong brew. Looking up, I saw Boris and Porl coming across the grass towards me.

With that ever-mischievous smile, Boris asked me if I was okay. It was moments like this, lost in time and space, that made up my existence more and more. Fleeting moments of clarity surfaced very rarely, and I felt that I couldn't trust my senses to tell me what was going on. All too brief fragments gave me small glimpses, then blackness.

'I think I'm okay. Whatever that means nowadays.'

We sat and talked at the red-chequered tablecloth under the trees in the soft autumn sunlight and I felt almost human for a moment.

After our late breakfast, Porl and I went over to the small and deserted pool and sat by the side, dangling our legs in the blue water, the air filled with the fragrant smell of the Mediterranean foliage all around, and looked across the water at the long autumnal shadows flitting about on its surface.

'You know, Lol, if you wanted to go get some kind of help, nobody would mind.'

'*I* would mind,' I struck out defiantly. 'I still want to do something here!'

We had been at Miraval for what seemed like for ever, but it was only a couple of months. Isolated from the outside world with the band and a small studio staff, we were in a really wonderful place to be creative, and although I had taken an inward, self-destructive turn, I was sure I could pull myself out of it. My bandmates didn't see things that way.

'I don't think you're going to get better by yourself, Lol,' I heard Porl say through my own meandering thoughts.

'I don't know,' I said noncommittally. 'I think when I get home and go to a health farm I might feel better.'

I had been bandying the name of the health farm around vainly and weakly, expecting that, like holy water, to be splashed by its name would produce results. By now Porl's face had set into that half-smile I knew well from the last few years. It meant that he knew he and everybody else was in for another bout of madness with me at the helm. It didn't help that some of the others in the band were also struggling with their own demons at the same time, but mine were causing the most problems.

The Cure were nothing if not a lesson in group psychology – at its best and its worst. As the different tensions arose and pulled at us, something or someone had to break, and this time it was going to be me.

It was 4 a.m. and studio time was coming to an end.

'Doesn't Alain de Cadenet live up on the top of the valley?' Robert mused as we left the large studio control room.

'I think he does,' said Patrice, the assistant, 'not quite sure where, exactly.'

'Well let's go and find him and see if he wants to race us!'

So off we went – Boris, Robert, Simon and myself – in the white Russian jeep that Robert had had brought down from London. We were all very drunk and tired as we climbed into the vehicle. The dark deep Provence night had but a few stars flitting across the cloudy sky. Maybe they were meteors. That would have been more fitting, considering the destructive arc my life had taken.

The headlights barely illuminated the grassy track between the steps of the vineyard. It felt a little like driving down the rabbit hole in *Alice in Wonderland* with foliage on all sides, a green curtain across the hard rock walls of the vineyard steps. Then it happened as we spun around a corner of the dark green tube. We were lurching to the left and then I felt a sudden pain in my head as we stopped short. We had crashed into something and were now on top of it.

At that moment the atmosphere inside the vehicle changed dramatically. A second before all was jollity, laughter and lurching velocity, and now in an instant there was silence. I had bounced into the roof of the vehicle, which was what caused the sharp pain in my head and neck. Looking around me, I could see that Boris was rubbing his head where he had collided with the roof, too.

The car was still running, and Robert was trying without much success to get us off the rock we had inadvertently jumped onto from the grassy track. I could hear the sound of the engine revving higher and higher as he pushed the engine to its limits, and then I smelled the thick black acrid smoke from the clutch burning out.

'I suppose we better get out,' Robert said and started to open the door. At that moment, the jeep lurched to the left, and looking out of the window into the darkness, I saw nothing and instantly realized that we were on the crest of one of the vineyard's terraces! There was a drop of about eight feet to the left of us, as I well knew, having taken a tumble off of one during my most recent blackout. The reason we couldn't get off the terrace was that two of the Jeep's wheels were dangling in space with zero traction. I imagine it occurred to us all in very quick succession that a delicate balancing act was required if we were not to be killed here on a precipice in a vineyard in the dead of night. Shifting very slowly to the right, we opened the doors and fell out of the car onto the dirt and grass path. It was completely dark and quiet, but we were alive.

The next day we asked Mick if he would go and see what the area looked like where we crashed. I think we were all probably a little scared of what we might find up there! About an hour later he reported back in his Scottish brogue.

'Well lads, the car's fucked. I'll have to get a garage to come and pull it off the ledge with chains. You burnt the clutch out and it probably won't be able to be driven again by the looks of it. You were very lucky not to die, I reckon!'

Gallows humour was Mick's specialty. He'd seen lots of rock-star shenanigans in his time.

And so, yet again, we escaped death by a slim margin. God saves babies and drunks, right?

The autumn of 1986 saw a sea change in the way The Cure operated as a band. In the beginning Robert, Michael and I were partners in the band and the band's affairs. When Michael left it was just

Robert and myself. Over the years, as people came and went, different side deals were struck, and we were always willing to be generous and inclusive.

In 1986, the original contract that we'd signed with Fiction all those years ago had run its course, and because we had made a rather big success of the band, various labels we were connected to around the world were all anxious to see the relationship maintained.

There was a little bit of bargaining and such, but in the end we stuck with the devil we knew: Chris Parry. But there was a major change in the way the labels dealt with us. They now saw the band as just Robert, a view Parry encouraged, as I don't think he relished band meetings with both Robert and me at the table. It was much simpler for him to have to deal with one person.

I went from being a partner in The Cure to being an employee. In essence, I was being demoted. It's something I have had many years to think about, and the honest truth is that it really couldn't have gone any other way. I can't really blame Robert for wanting to free himself from a business partner who wasn't performing as he had in the past, but at the time I saw things very differently. I conveniently ignored my worsening health and increasing recklessness, to say nothing of my lessening creative input, and laid the blame at everyone else's feet except those I walked about on.

One morning at Miraval Studios a letter arrived from Fiction's offices that needed to be signed. As far as I recall, it was to help facilitate the new arrangements. I was not really surprised, but it still rankled, and I simmered in hot resentment. Of course that meant I decided to keep on drinking and numbing myself. This, rather than trying to think things through and work out how to actually resolve the main problem in my life, which stared at me from the mirror every morning.

Amidst this inner turmoil, the album sessions for our by now double album rolled on amid the beautiful hills of Provence. If I had been in a better state of mind I would have enjoyed it immensely. Instead, every day was a battle of wills to maintain my sanity and equilibrium. I was losing badly but unwilling to concede defeat.

The autumn days grew shorter and the hills surrounding us glowed with a sad feeling of finality in the wan sun. There was nothing left for me but a sense of impending doom. I left the studio and went back to England to fume over my misfortune and wallow in self-pity.

# PART 3

# (WHAT IT'S LIKE NOW)

# 18

# BROKEN

In 1987 we toured in South America for the first time. We found that Cure fans in Europe, North America and Australia were more or less the same. In Japan they tended to be more reserved and polite. In South America all reserve was thrown out of the window and it was a joyous and riotous occasion. However, there were a couple of gigs in Argentina that were more riotous than joyful.

We arrived in Argentina in March of 1987, not that long after General Galtieri and his minions had been wrenched from power. Soon after the Falklands War the infamous, self-appointed president was arrested and his death squad, Intelligence Battalion 601, disbanded.

We were one of the first bands of our generation to come to the new Argentina after the end of that bloody dictatorship. Even after a couple of years of democracy, the country was still a tumult of emotions and distinctly unsettled. It felt like anything could happen and probably would.

Galtieri, you might recall, was the Argentine military leader who sent conscripted teenagers to face British Royal Marines and

missiles in the battle over the Falklands. We were in Germany
when that particular episode of British history started, and were
unaware of the nature of the war until we saw a newspaper in
a service station on the road to Berlin. Upon reading about the
Falklands War, I felt that I had made the right choice to leave
Hellermann's for a life with The Cure. Once I'd learnt that the
various things we manufactured at Hellermann's ended up in
those aforementioned missiles, I wanted no part of it.

After we arrived at the airport in Buenos Aires, we were driven
through the melancholy streets of the capital. We were escorted
to our hotel by several cars full of 'bodyguards'. We were told
that they were probably previously employed as henchmen by the
military junta. We shuddered to think what they might have done
in their previous role. They drove around in unmarked cars with
their revolvers placed on the dashboard. This had the advantage
of making the public aware of just who was in the vehicle and
still in charge.

The city of Buenos Aries was like nothing I had ever seen
before, a little like Werner Herzog's film *Fitzcarraldo*. The Paris
of South America indeed. European grandeur in the jungle. Long
stretches looked sad, dark and derelict, which wasn't surprising.
The 'people of the port' had been through a lot in the preceding
years of the fascist dictatorship.

The next morning I looked through jet-lagged eyes out of the
window of my hotel room to see several hundred people gathered
in front of the building. One of them spied me looking at them,
so they all turned their heads as one, like a shoal of herring, to
look my way.

'Lol!'

'Welcome to Argentina!'

'We love you! We love The Cure!'

They smiled and waved, and I sensed even through the fog of jet lag that something extraordinary was going on here. Music really is the international language. All the places I've been in the world are divided by language, ideology, religion, etc., but music unites us all. It's quite spectacular, really. I realized in that moment music's extraordinary power to heal, to help in a very real sense. I was really looking forward to the concerts.

We had two gigs arranged at FCO Stadium, a large football stadium that held almost 25,000 people. In forty-eight hours we would play to about 50,000 Argentinian Cure fans. These were fans that had never seen us play, and after living under the boot of fascism needed something good in their lives to celebrate.

The day of the first show we went down fairly early to see how things were progressing at the stadium. I walked out into the centre of the grass pitch and looked at the stage. Something didn't seem quite right. I wasn't sure immediately what it was, but walking closer to the stage it became apparent: the wooden barrier between the stage and the audience was so high that in order to see the band at all the crowd would have to stand a good fifty feet back from the stage. I couldn't imagine that this would be something the fans would be okay with. I knew they liked to get as close to the band as possible.

I voiced my concerns to Mick. 'Why is the barrier in front of the stage so fucking big? Won't that just piss the fans off?' I asked.

'Definitely!' Mick explained that unfortunately the powers that be said the barrier had to be that big as they had TV cameramen in the pit in front of the stage and they wanted to protect them from the audience. They expected it to be pretty wild. People hadn't had a reason to celebrate for quite some time.

'Well,' I said, 'I'd lay even money that it will be down in a matter of minutes once we start to play.'

'You know, Lol, I wouldnae be surprised,' he said, with that Scottish/Polish grin that lit up his whole face. I loved Mick's understatement. He was not one to be troubled by anything in the concert business. He had seen it all.

Mick had started out promoting monthly blues concerts in the Shetland Isles in the late 1960s, which meant constantly dealing with running fights between fishermen and oil workers drunk on whisky. Before that he'd worked for the local Scottish health authority bringing insane crofters into hospital who had gone mad alone up in the Highlands. Apparently the police would escort Mick up to these lonely shepherds' farms and open the door of the farmhouse while Mick, armed with a syringe full of some heavy-duty sedative, would run full tilt at the mad crofter, plunge the needle in, and then help drag the sedated shepherd out to an ambulance. Obviously he was destined for the crazy world of rock and roll.

Somehow, after winning a card game with Marc Bolan, he ended up working for Pink Floyd and their company Brit Row, which was how we came into contact with Mick. Rumour had it he'd single-handedly given the Mafia a run for their money in Los Angeles when he was working for Pink Floyd in the early 1970s. Some Mafioso thug had waved a gun in Mick's face in the parking lot of the Forum in Inglewood, insisting that the Floyd's crew would do as he said, 'or else'. Mick responded in a very Scottish manner with a 'Glasgow kiss', sending the thug running back to mommy with a broken nose. Gun or no gun, you couldn't intimidate Mick Kluczynski. He was from Scotland. Obviously nobody had told the Mafia what happened the last time the Romans tried to run roughshod over the Scots. Hell, Hadrian even built a wall to protect himself from the wild Highland men in woad!

Before the first show, one of the team dressing rooms served as our backstage. For a relatively poor nation, Argentina lavished money and attention on their football stars, so there were a series of sumptuous warm-up rooms and the best masseur I have ever met. The team physiotherapist was a small and wiry man but blessed with healing hands. I walked out onto the stage later that night almost floating after his ministrations.

Just then Mick came in with an update. 'Getting a little out of hand out there, boys.'

'Why, Mick?' asked Simon.

'They just had a scuffle with the security not letting people come onto the pitch from the stands. They had some dogs but it seems to have calmed down. You'll be fine, nae problem.'

I did not share Mick's certainty, and I would unfortunately be proved right. The audience was anxious and their adrenalin was pumping. The night air was pungent with the smell of weed and the humid heat of the South American jungle when we walked out onto the stage. A roar went up and, as Boris launched into the powerful drum roll that starts 'Shake Dog Shake', the place erupted. All the pent-up energy repressed for so many years was unleashed. By the third song, 'Play for Today', it was obvious that the promoter had made a really bad decision in erecting an enormous barrier in front of the stage. First I saw flaming yellow wads of rolled-up newspaper sailing over the top of the barrier, with some landing directly on the TV cameramen and their equipment in the pit. Every time this happened a security guy would come running out with a fire extinguisher, trying to douse the onslaught with little bursts of white powder. They couldn't keep up with the torches, and the TV men sensibly beat a hasty retreat. They lasted two songs longer than I thought they would.

Then it happened. A small crack appeared in the top of the barrier right in front of where I was standing. Like a medieval siege I caught a glimpse of the marauding faces through the expanding fissure in the wooden panels. I felt my heart pound the way it did as a small child the moment I fell off my bike and before I hit the pavement, that split second when I knew just what was coming but I couldn't do a thing to stop it.

A piece of the barrier disappeared into the crowd and the hole enlarged. I could now see many more faces, smiling but angry at the same time. They were happy to have broken through but still incensed that they were being blocked from seeing the band they'd paid to see. A piece of wood about the size of my arm flew over the top of the remaining barrier, braining the security guy standing underneath. His compatriots picked it up and threw it back at the crowd. Bad idea.

The crowd tore more pieces from the barrier and a sizeable hole appeared in the structure. Bodies flew like arrows over the top of the barrier to land in the pit. Security fled for their lives, leaving nothing between us and the rabid fans. I had the awful realization that we might actually get hurt here. Bits of the barrier were being hurled forward into the now deserted pit, but a few well-propelled chunks landed on the stage. Suddenly, the barrier disappeared under the onslaught of the crowd like a machine munching it up into tiny pieces.

I looked over to my right at Robert. He had a steely, determined look on his face. He wasn't going to back down or give in because of the violence. We had come to play to the Argentinians and that was exactly what we were going to do, his expression told me.

The audience had reached the lip of the stage, pushing the last of the barrier out of the way. The surging crowd that seemed on the verge of boiling over held back and did what they came to do: they danced to the music. I felt so relieved to be looking at a calmer sea of faces again. I sensed from Robert's demeanour his determination to win them over now that the barrier was completely gone. I could see faces smiling up at me out of the crowd. Their fearful power to scare and terrify dissipated in the hot and humid air as we charmed them with our music.

However, we were not out of the woods yet (even though they were out of wood to throw). We had one more show to play, and it, too, proved to be a day to remember.

The next day was even hotter and more humid then the one before. We arrived at the stadium and tried not to think about the violence of the previous day. It was so hot our crew had covered all the keyboards and other sensitive electronics with foil space blankets to protect them from the scorching effects of the South American sun. We soundchecked with cool white towels draped over our heads to protect us from the piercing rays. It was going to be an intense day.

An hour before the gig, we were sitting calmly in the basement of the stadium next to the warm-up rooms. It seemed like a good idea to use the facilities, so Boris and myself were doing just that.

Through the walls of the subterranean locker room came a strange howling sound with a sort of roaring behind it. I asked one of the crew what was happening up in the stadium.

'The police have dogs out and are chasing a bunch of fans off the field into the stands.'

'Well, that's stupid,' I said. They would be spilling out onto the pitch as soon as the music started, so why stop them? Just creates more conflict. I supposed a lot of the junta's henchmen had been assimilated into the police force or private security and had little training, patience, or desire to deal with concertgoers, much less hard-core Cure fans.

Boris and I moved to the next room, which was closer to the stage entrance area. The sound was louder here and quite frightening. I turned my mind to the songs we were going to play and hoped that everything would be okay.

Eventually the appointed hour arrived and we trooped out onto the stage. Looking out onto the crowd, I thought of Christians being thrown to the lions in the Roman Coliseum.

We started with the same song as we had the night before, 'Shake Dog Shake', and things seemed calmer. Maybe things would be okay. Then I noticed something hovering slightly in front of me and just out of reach. It looked like a small drone in the mould of a Harrier Jump Jet, but of course it wasn't a Harrier or a drone. It was an insect, a huge fucking prehistoric insect, and it proceeded to land on the keyboard surface right in front of me. I looked at its fiery red eyes and bright green body and felt that kind of primeval terror Stone Age man must have felt the first time it laid eyes on this damn thing. I stared at it intently, willing it to go away. No chance. It enjoyed tormenting me. I couldn't swipe it away with my hands because I was playing a song and I was scared that it might actually take a chunk out of my hand. It lifted off the keyboard just in time for me to see the shower of sparks flying through the darkness behind the spotlights on the stage. It took me a few moments to realize that they were coins that had been hurled on stage. All manner of other stuff came flying at us. Small felt toys are okay, but anything with a hard edge presents a hazard. Once, someone lovingly tossed Robert a small metal cross. Unfortunately, it landed down the side of his boot and worked its way down to his foot, where it proceeded to cut and scrape his flesh – a fact he only noticed after the gig.

I heard a shout to my right and looked over at Porl. He had been struck by something much harder and larger than a coin. It turned out to be a huge wood and metal cross, and there was blood pouring from a gash on his forehead. As Porl was ushered offstage to get medical help for his wound, Robert went up to the microphone and in no uncertain terms told the idiots in the audience that they would have to stop throwing things or we wouldn't play anymore. It took a great deal of courage to do that. In my experience, most audiences are really happy to have you there to play, but there's always a handful of morons who think it's a good idea to try and start trouble. They throw things, start fights with a few people, and they almost always sit about three rows back, because they think we can't see them because of the stage lights. Wrong, morons! We can see you and you can't hide your intentions. Robert looked straight at these guys in row three and told them what's what. I don't know if they understood Robert's south London English, but I'm sure the message got across because they slunk back into the crowd.

Porl came back with a large bandage on his head and we went on with the show. The dogs were back, too, as were the security guards. I could see them on the periphery of my vision at the edge of the stadium. I had a bad premonition, and as we continued, an uneasy calm descended on the crowd.

Just before the second encore, we were all standing at the entrance to the dressing rooms, anxiously deciding if we should go back on again. We had never been to Argentina before, and The Cure have never been a band to short-change anybody. I don't know if it's the old Catholic guilt or just a sense of responsibility to our fans, but The Cure, and Robert in particular, always wanted (and still wants, as far as I am aware) to play as many songs as he can and give the fans the best show possible. It is something that we were known for, and Robert wanted us to go back on despite the dangerous atmosphere.

We all concurred and out we went, but halfway through '10:15 Saturday Night' Robert turned around and motioned for us to stop playing. I think he had had enough of things being thrown at him, and I have to say it was scary. He basically told the people doing it that they were idiots spoiling everything for everybody else who wanted to see the gig. A great cheer went up from the audience. The Cure generates great loyalty from their fans because they know that the band is on *their* side and a part of *their* lives. As a result people are very committed to The Cure. They wanted the show to go on. I sensed that and so did Robert. Turning around, he motioned to Boris to count us all back in, and off we went to finish the encore. As I walked off the stage, I felt the heavy weight from all the coins that had been thrown at me in the front pockets of my grey/blue suit.

The next day, the headline on the local paper read, 'Three Die at Rock Show!' That was about as far as I could get with my schoolboy Spanish. I was flabbergasted and went looking for our interpreter.

'Please tell me this is not what I think!'

He quickly scanned the story. It turned out that a man in a hot dog stand outside the stadium had had a heart attack when his stand was attacked by a mob, and that two of the police dogs had also died. All very sad and regrettable, but not quite as dramatic as the headline had me believe. We left Argentina with heavy hearts. I think for some years afterwards, Argentinian fans believed that we harboured some misgivings about playing there, and that there was some ill will because of those two gigs. I know that was not the case. The Cure have never been afraid to go to the front lines, as it were, if it meant we would be able to play our songs to people who really wanted to hear them. I always believed that we felt we were sincerely wanted in Buenos Aires, and it was just the release of a lot of emotional repression and ill treatment by the military junta that caused the insanity of those two gigs. It had nothing to do with us or our fans, but what we represented was perhaps too dangerous to the status quo for those in power, so they tried to sow unrest and discontent. The power of The Cure has always amazed me.

My drinking worsened during the South American tour of Argentina and Brazil. The Brazilians have a white rum called cachaca that's made from sugar cane. We had lots of it to drink and, combined with the heat and humidity, it was absolutely lethal. I found it very disorientating and there are many missed moments in time from that tour. Once I thought that I might actually be hallucinating, which was disconcerting, to say the least!

We had been taken out to a rooftop nightclub by the local Brazilian promoter after the second of our sold-out gigs in Rio. It all seemed fairly normal, but normal to me was completely crazed. Reality had started to take a back seat to the wild hallucinations going on in my life on a daily basis. Drinking, drugs and anxiety about my position in the band compromised my mental state. It was fast becoming a Catch-22 situation for my fractured psyche: the more I thought about what was going on, the less I was able to come to terms with fixing it, which would lead to more anxiety and more self-medicating. I was caught a vicious circle with no end in sight. Despite my best intentions, I couldn't get off the crazy roundabout of violent emotional twists and turns, and what made things worse was the knowledge that I was doing it to myself.

My relationship with the rest of the band was deteriorating because all they saw was someone who wasn't pulling his weight. Not only had I been given an equal share in the band while providing very little creative input, my drunken antics were getting old.

Back in the nightclub, I was certain that I had seen a very well-known figure in British cultural history: none other than Ronnie Biggs, the Great Train Robber. An older man in a white suit had passed me by and I was sure – no, I was certain – it was Ronnie Biggs. I grabbed Simon to give him the news.

'Hey, Si! Did you see who that was?'

'No, Lol. Who?'

'Ronnie Bloody Biggs!' I said, clutching my umpteenth glass of sugar cane rum. I could tell Simon didn't believe me.

'No, really! It was!'

'Really? You sure, Lol?'

'I'm going to go find him and say hello.'

I had a habit when drunk of introducing myself to any random celebrity that happened to be passing by. Both Sir Clive Sinclair (inventor of the ZX80 home computer and the C5, an electric vehicle) and the singer Nina Hagen were victims of my drunken bonhomie. Sir Clive seemed bemused by this apparition in front of him at the Virgin Records party in the old Biba shop in London.

'Siiir Clive Sinclair! I love computers too!'

Nina took it in better stead when I introduced myself to her in Athens.

I went looking for the older, white-suited gentlemen that I had seen, the one that I was sure was the Great Train Robber.

I ran up and down the rooftop terrace, and at one point I caught sight of an older gentleman descending the stairs out of the club. I swear he turned and looked directly at me and smiled that notorious Biggs grin before disappearing in a throng of people. I was sure it was him, but I couldn't catch up in time and he disappeared.

The mystery will never be solved. I've talked to people who were there and they can't recall seeing him, and Ronnie himself passed away in 2013. So we will never know.

Back in London, things were not getting any better for me. I just carried on like I always did, except I was no longer in control. I used to go to a club at the Camden Palace on a Thursday night with friends. But after one night we got so drunk we got in an accident and wrenched the door off my friend's car as we reversed down a street, and hit a post in front of the bar. It seemed unwise to go back after that.

Instead I resolved to stick to my friend Pete's wine bar down the street in Queen's Park. A pleasant lunch followed by a few too many drinks ended up with me lying comatose on the street. I have a vague memory of being picked up by a couple of burly coppers and being dumped in the back of their van.

I woke up and the light bulb on the ceiling seemed to be swaying a little – or was that me? I squinted at the brightness above my head and steadied myself with what looked to be a concrete bench. I sat upright, and as my eyes adjusted to the greenish-yellow glow of the room, I realized exactly where I was. A police cell.

Suddenly the little spyhole in the door opened and I heard a voice.

'Oh, awake now, are we?'

I glanced at the source of the sound and saw the unmistakable uniform of a Metropolitan Police officer. I heard the sound of the door being unlocked, and then a bucket and mop was pushed into the room.

'Clean up that mess and then you're out of here.'

I looked over to the corner of the room at the stainless steel toilet. Apparently I had used it when I arrived, but my aim was off and I got nowhere near the intended target. I rose unsteadily to my feet. The smell of alcohol mingled with the disinfectant in the bucket, and I retched. This time I made it to the correct place in time.

I cleaned up my mess as asked and then banged on the door.

'I'm done, officer!' I slurred, still a little drunk. I tried to look at my watch, then saw it was no longer on my wrist. Hmmm . . . I wonder what happened to that? I didn't have time to think about it as the iron door of the cell swung open and the policeman was framed in the doorway.

'Okay, come out here now and sit in the chair by the wall.'

I did as bidden, shivering a little in the hallway of the police station. I realized my jacket was also missing. I sat on the hard plastic chair, shifting on the uncomfortable surface.

My ears adjusted to the sound of radio static and people moving about the station as I wondered what had brought me here. I remembered talking with my friend Pete, bidding him goodbye, and then walking towards home. Did I fall and bang my head?

I reached up and noticed a little lump forming on the right side of my head. I looked at my fingers. No blood.

'Okay, sir, here are your possessions and jacket.'

So they had taken them before putting me in the cell. I looked up and saw a policeman at a desk across the hall. He motioned to me to come over and sit opposite him.

'Sign here.' He pushed a sheet of paper towards me.

I focused and read something about a warning and acceptance of my possessions. I signed the paper.

'Am I being charged with anything?' I croaked.

It seemed the right thing to ask at this juncture. I had seen it in a lot of movies.

'No, sir, we are just giving you a warning this time.' He glanced at another policeman sitting in a cubicle across the hall. 'You're very lucky. Go home.'

And with that I gathered up my belongings and pushed open the door. I didn't need to be told twice. At 4 a.m. I made my way out of the station and up the hill back to my house. Meanwhile, my girlfriend Lydia had finally worked out where I might be and called the station, only to be told that I'd just been let out. She drove down to meet me, but for some reason we missed each other. On returning she found me face down on the living room carpet. As she got closer she could hear me muttering, 'Bastards, bastards . . .' As to whom I was referring to I have no idea. The voices in my head, maybe?

I still think that the 'Kissing' tour that started the second half of 1987 was the best production we ever had as a band. In terms of visual presentation of The Cure, I don't believe there's been a better gig while I was in the group. I loved the white kabuki curtains that hung over the front of the stage.

As anybody who saw that show will tell you it brought the audience to a fever pitch before they had even seen us!

The curtains surrounded the whole stage so the audience couldn't see what was going on. When they entered the arena, the first thing they saw was a gigantic white rectangle. As the show started we screened the film *Eyemou* on the white curtains. This was a film of Robert's lips and eye. We would creep onto the stage behind the curtains and assemble into our positions for the show. By the time we started up with 'The Kiss' we could feel the excitement building in the arena as the audience realized that we were actually on stage and playing – but they couldn't see us yet.

The best moment, in fact the absolute climactic crescendo, came when Robert sang the opening lines 'Kiss me, kiss me, kiss me' and the kabuki curtains dropped into the pit in front of the stage in the space of a second and all at once there we were: The Cure!

People went nuts. It was pretty wonderful to experience that every night of the tour. Then we went straight into 'Torture', during which we had lights roam over the audience like gigantic green tubular searchlights. These were very special and had not been widely used before. The Cure have always been at the forefront of new types of lighting equipment, thanks mostly to our lighting specialist, Mac. Robert always took a keen interest in the visual displays we used during our performances.

We played over sixty gigs for that tour, and they were some of my favourites despite my problems. Even when it went wrong, the kabuki was great entertainment. On a couple of nights I looked out from the stage into the pit to see Mick swinging like Tarzan, pulling down the recalcitrant curtain that had got stuck in the lighting truss up in the rafters.

I remember playing at the Santa Barbara Bowl and how from the top tier of the bowl you could look out and see the Pacific Ocean. It looked idyllic and reminded me of the first time I had come to California six years before, happier and healthier, just me, Simon and Robert. Now the band had doubled in size, and so had my problems.

It's strange now looking back at our gigs at some of the most prestigious venues in the world: Paris Bercy, New York's Madison Square Garden, Los Angeles Forum, Rotterdam Ahoy and the Philipshalle in Dusseldorf. All grand and great concert halls. The finest the world has to offer. Playing these places meant that we had most certainly arrived.

One would think that this would have made me really happy. It was the fulfilment of a boyhood dream to play Madison Square Garden. I used to read about it when I was marking up newspapers in Horley as a teen. There was always a review from 'Madison

Square Garden in New York' and I would let my mind wander and fantasize about playing there. Now it was a reality. I was just twenty-eight years old. I had done so much and been to so many places over the course of the last decade. But happiness cannot be manufactured, nor can it be pursued as a goal. Rather, it is a by-product of our other life experiences. It didn't matter how many people came to the gigs or how many records we sold. Deep inside I was desperately empty, and my loneliness was a vast hole that my addiction couldn't fill. All it had done was isolate me from those I loved, especially Robert. Most importantly, I no longer knew who I was or what I really wanted. On the outside it might have seemed to a casual observer that I had it all. Fame and fortune and everything that goes along with it, but I was an empty shell of a man and nothing I could put in that huge gaping hole would fill it. No amount of fame or adoration would subdue my misery, and no amount of alcohol or drugs could numb me.

The tour ended in London at Wembley Arena – another iconic place I had dreamt of playing as a boy. We finished the 'Kissing' tour with three nights there. As it was the end of a long tour, we thought we might have an end-of-tour party. My friend owned a restaurant where we could relax and enjoy a drink and have something to eat with friends and family. I don't remember a bit of it. In pictures from that party my eyes are just pinpoints. I look like a man whose soul has been zapped. It's terrible and sad to look at.

We ended the last gig of the year on 9 December 1987 with a cover of a song we all loved and remembered from our teenage years, 'Merry Christmas Everybody' by Slade. But there was no cheer in my heart. As the cannons blasted fake snow at the ecstatic audience, I sneered, 'Merry bloody Christmas!'

It was to be the last gig I'd play with The Cure for nearly a quarter of a century.

# 19

# DISINTEGRATE

The teacup was shaking uncontrollably. Or maybe it was me. I was shivering like I had just been dunked in the Thames in December. I put the thin porcelain cup down into the saucer with the blue swallow pattern and the hot tea splashed over the sides.

'Are you okay, Mr Tolhurst?' the psychiatrist asked. 'Do you want to stop for a moment?'

The nurse and the psychiatrist looked at me with kind but inquisitive eyes as I continued to spill my tea all over the place.

I was holding one shaking hand with the other to try and quell the small tsunamis of liquid, but to no avail. I let go of the cup and I put my shaking hands back in my lap. I noticed the doctor write something in his notepad and then he cleared his throat:

'I'm going to give you a set of numbers to remember, okay?'

I nodded in confirmation, hoping to look nonchalant.

'Okay, 1337. Just remember those numbers. We'll come back to them later.' He smiled a sort of fatherly smile, but I was probably only a few years younger than him, so I didn't take him that seriously. My eyes darted around the room, which was a pale primrose colour. They say that yellow is the best colour for healing and recovery, which is probably why a lot of hospitals have yellow walls.

I'd already correctly answered several questions concerning the current prime minister, the president of the United States, and my age. These were the sort of questions they asked of brain-damaged patients, and I supposed they were trying to see just how much harm I had done to myself.

Meanwhile, I kept repeating the number in my head like a mantra while the doctor gave instructions to the nurse.

' . . . milligrams of Librium and a vitamin shot daily.'

He turned to me and explained that the shaking was caused by delirium tremens. He needn't have bothered. I knew what the DTs were and that they came with a vengeance when I hadn't had a drink for a while. The doctor closed his notebook and put it back in his little black bag. He motioned to the young woman.

'The nurse will answer any other questions you may have and see that you're comfortable. I'll see you tomorrow. Good day, Mr Tolhurst.'

With that he turned to leave, but at the last moment he swivelled slowly round in what must have been a well practised move, part of his medical repertoire.

'So those numbers I gave you a while back . . . ?'

I opened my mouth and in a small little boy's voice I barely recognized as my own I said, 'Er, one, three, three . . . seven!'

I beamed triumphantly, but my joy was short-lived, as I saw the sadness reflected in the young doctor's eyes as he looked at my face. The nurse also left and she closed the door behind her with a swish. I was finally alone for the first time since my arrival at the detox unit for the chemically dependent in the Lister Hospital on Chelsea Bridge Road, London. It was 1988.

The gigs at Wembley were a dim memory as we assembled at Boris's house in the Devon countryside to record demos for what would become the album *Disintegration*. We had a session to play our home demos, and we all sat around and gave each other's songs marks out of ten. Then, later on that year before Robert and Mary's wedding, we had a longer session at Boris's house to record the demos we'd selected for the album.

In between these two sessions I decided I should try to do something about my drinking problem. My neighbour, an Australian lady, had a suggestion.

'Lol, I have a doctor I see sometimes. Perhaps he can help you?'

By this time I was quite terrified when I woke up each day. If I started to drink, I couldn't tell what was going to happen and how the day would turn out. I had absolutely no control over myself.

I made an appointment to see the doctor, Campbell was his name, and he had some very nice offices in Harley Street, which, of course, is the premier address if you're a doctor in England.

'So, Mr Tolhurst, how might I help you?' Dr Campbell asked after a few perfunctory medical questions. I described in detail the events of the last few years and how erratic my behaviour had become while under the influence of alcohol.

'Well,' he said, looking up from his notes, 'You have all the symptoms of an alcoholic. You are right inside the bottle and we need to get you out.'

Alcoholic? I knew I had a drinking problem, but I wasn't an alcoholic. I had heard of such things, of course, but I didn't really see how they applied to me. My father, now there was an alcoholic.

The doctor patiently explained to me what he meant and then dropped the bomb on me.

'You need to go to detox first and then we can see about rehab.'

'Er, when?' I asked nervously.

'How about this afternoon?'

That hit me hard. I was in denial about the seriousness of my condition, but now I had to face up to the reality of what I was being told. With great reluctance, I agreed to go over to the Lister Hospital.

After I'd been given a vitamin shot, the nurse left and I was in my room at the Lister all by myself. They had given me some Librium earlier, which helped calm me down somewhat, but the effect of the shot was to make my head feel as if it was fizzing inside. When I finally relaxed, I slept.

The next day I was awakened at an early hour by a nurse who informed that some people from AA were coming to see me. I wasn't sure what that meant so I nodded noncommittally.

The two chaps who came to my room looked normal and were friendly enough, but what they had to say shocked me.

They explained how as an alcoholic I had a two-fold disease that meant I would never be able to drink again if I wished to have a happy life. If I did, I would end up in jail, an institution, or dead. They also explained that alcoholism was a cunning malady that pretended it wasn't what it was, even as it led me to insanity.

I thanked them for telling me what was wrong with me, and

armed with this information I felt all I had to do was be careful and watch myself for certain signs. If they had recovered, then so could I, and I would be able to control my problem. With pure willpower I could conquer my drinking.

Rather than take the good doctor's advice and go into rehab, I decided to discharge myself from the Lister after about a week. I felt better, I told myself, now that the fog had lifted and I had the valuable advice the AA people had given me. I would be fine.

That proved to be a bad move.

A really, really bad move.

I stayed sober for a couple of weeks after I got out of the Lister, but I really wasn't happy about it. I decided to go see my friend Pete at his bar at the end of the street. What was the point of living within walking distance of my friend if I didn't pay him a visit from time to time?

Pete welcomed me back and gave me the beer I asked for. I hadn't really told anyone what I was doing, although I had said to Robert and Porl I was thinking of 'going somewhere to get healthy before we get back into the studio'.

They had heard that before. I had gone to a health farm where, at 140 pounds, I puzzled the staff.

'So why are you here, exactly? Your weight is fine.'

I never owned up to the real reason. I just told them that I wanted 'a rest' and I got it. It didn't really help that much since the place had a bar! They only served organic wine, mind you, but it was a bar nonetheless. I dutifully exercised every morning with a crippling hangover.

The beer tasted good and I didn't really feel any different. So I had another, then another, and then I saw the abyss open up in front of me and I knew I wasn't coming back for a while.

We reconvened at Boris's house in Devon during the late summer for the second *Disintegration* demo session.

'Boris?' Robert asked with a mischievous gleam in his eye. 'How far away is this from here?' He pointed to an advert in the local paper for a pool table for sale.

'Not far,' Boris replied.

'Could we go get it and put it in the hallway?'

'Sure,' said Boris. 'I have a trailer. Let's go.'

We got the pool table that day and put it in Boris's house. With the beer cellar next door in the old house, it was beginning to look suspiciously like a pub.

Oscar Wilde said, 'Life imitates art far more than art imitates life.' The making of *Disintegration* was to prove this. As the songs got darker and more intense, so did my life.

We moved into Outside Studios at Hook End Manor, which was once the house of the Bishop of Reading and was more recently owned by David Gilmour of Pink Floyd. A beautiful place for me to finally fall apart.

We had developed a penchant for recording in residential places outside of the mainstream. This worked, as we were seldom interrupted, and when the recording was finally done Robert could take the tapes to mix somewhere else.

It was a wonderful idea, recording in the countryside. Unfortunately, I couldn't appreciate it. My world was getting really small. I spent a great deal of time alone inside my head while *Disintegration* was being recorded. Slowly coming apart both physically and psychically. Living in a tiny place in my mind.

We would start our days in the middle of the afternoon and, as it was later in the year, there wasn't much daylight. During the winter in England it tends to get dark about 4 p.m. We would work in the studio until about 8 p.m. and then we would break for dinner, a vast and long affair over which much was talked about and much was drunk. Then we would work until nearly dawn and retire for the night once it was almost day again.

We did this for six days a week for quite a few weeks, with one day to do as we wanted. The trouble with that was by the time we woke up on our day off, it was not really possible to do much else, as the sun was going down again and it would soon be dark out in the heart of the countryside. The nearest town was Reading, which was not that lively. So we were left to ourselves in Hook End Manor, which meant playing snooker or watching TV.

Outside the studio, the grass and wet brown leaves of the English countryside seemed much darker to me than before. My days were mostly spent in the back of the studio area in a little lounge off the main control room, slumped on slightly worn-out couches of various hues. We'd come such a long way, yet something inside of me couldn't break free of the mental fog that permeated my very being. I had an idea or two from our demos that made it onto the record, but the hardest thing for me was to get out of that morass of self-pity that had enveloped me. In my heart I really wanted to contribute to the band I loved, but my spirits were so low there wasn't much I could do. So I idly sat outside the control room waiting for inspiration to come.

One day Porl's kind and concerned face interrupted my brooding.

'Bloody hell, Lol, it's really sad seeing you sit here. You know nobody would mind if you went back to the hospital to sort yourself out.'

'Yeah, I will go back,' I said, 'but not until the album is done.' I was in denial about what was wrong with me and believed I could still control what was going on by contributing to The Cure, the group that had been my whole life, but I was starting to resent people intruding in my personal life. It was still my life, wasn't it?

The long autumn dragged on into the dark end of the album. There was a fire one night at the studio's living quarters. Robert's room had caught fire. Half of the fire brigade were volunteers who were in the pub when the alarm was raised. The part-time firemen rushed from the pub onto the truck and over to the burning studio. We all helped them in with their equipment and emergency lights, as all the power had shut down when the fire started. Great clouds of black smoke enveloped the old house as we stood outside in the late-night drizzle waiting for the all-clear to go back in after the firemen had extinguished the blaze.

The whole house smelled of charred wood the next day. Robert's original room, now a black, burnt mess, was right next to mine with a connecting door. I had felt safe there, like a small child protected from the world, but Robert was now forced to relocate to another room on the other side of the house. Now nobody was next door, and the smell of charred wood permeated my clothes, my hair, everything.

The house felt cold, as all the windows were left open all day and night to rid the air of the smell. I shivered at night in my bed. Every breath I took was tinged with ruin.

The sessions dragged on as the icy winter approached. Now we hardly saw any daylight, as we had started going into the early hours to finish the recording. At dawn one cold morning with the wind whipping through the draughty old manor house, Robert came across me in the kitchen. I had a bottle of whisky in my hand and took a slug. We had been up all night. He looked at me sadly.

'You're fucking insane! You don't even like whiskey. Each time you take a shot you grimace!'

He shook his head, and whereas before there would have been a grin on his face at his friend's crazy behaviour, now there was that look of sadness and concern. It was as if he could sense the end approaching.

The session wound down and I went back to my new house in Devon in the middle of Dartmoor, a rock star mansion if ever there was one. I had decided after the fiasco of the last tour that what I really needed was to relocate. That would sort out all my problems, I thought. I figured I wouldn't have to deal with a city full of people that didn't understand me if I was out in the countryside. I bought a house right inside the desolate and wild Dartmoor National Park, 220 miles from London. Lonely, miserable, and in glorious solitude, I carried on doing what I had to do, seeking oblivion again and again.

One day, just before Christmas, I got a call from the Fiction office. It was Ita, the de facto manager of the label.

'Robert wants you to come and hear the album mixes with everyone at RAK in London.'

'Okay, I'll be there.'

I booked my usual hotel and later that week I got on the train. I had never learnt to drive because I'd always been driven about from place to place. It was also a convenient excuse for never having to sober up. On the train I looked out of the window during the two-and-a-half-hour journey to London. A single silver birch tree reminded me of the cold but emotional beauty of what we had made during the early days of The Cure, and sadness engulfed me.

I arrived at the studio and came into the control room. Robert was at the desk, pushing up faders, and we all listened to the final mixes of *Disintegration*. I slumped on the couch at the back of the studio and listened to the music. It was, and is, quite a wonderful album, but I felt very removed from it. This was unbearably painful for me who had lived and breathed The Cure since the very beginning. Unfortunately, this was the last time I was to be involved with my childhood friends and bandmates in an artistic fashion for a very long time.

As the night wore on, I visited the small fridge in the studio that was full of beer, gradually getting more intoxicated. Sometime during the playback, I got up from my seat at the back of the studio and announced to all and sundry that what we were listening to was not really a Cure album.

'Half is good, but half is shit!' I roared. 'I mean some songs sound like The Cure but some don't,' I fell back into my seat with a thump.

Honestly, I don't really know what I meant. I think I felt so bad that I hadn't been able to pull it together enough to contribute to the album that I lashed out against it. I'd kept my mouth shut all through the recording process, and now I was going to speak my mind? My timing couldn't have been worse.

A long, uncomfortable silence ensued while we sat and listened to the rest of the tracks. When it was over, everyone avoided me. When I couldn't stand it anymore, I ran out into the night, a tearful mess of incoherence.

The next day I awoke with an impending sense of doom that I couldn't shake off as I tried to piece together the events of the previous night. I had made a terrible mess of what I wanted to say. It wasn't so much a matter of whether I was right or wrong. We had always been able to express our views without them being taken personally. This time I didn't think that Robert would be able to brush off my drunken dismissal of an album he'd poured his heart and soul into. I'd finally reached the breaking point.

A simple white envelope with Robert's handwriting on the front arrived in the post. I didn't need to open it. I knew what was inside. It had been three weeks since that disastrous night at RAK Studios in London, when I fled drunk and crazed into the long dark night.

I'd spent that Christmas holiday waiting for the news to come. Christmas was no longer the fun time I remembered from living in Horley, when I'd spend Christmas Eve at the King's Head with Robert, Simon, Gary and all my friends from home. I'd retreated to a sprawling home on the edge of Dartmoor National Park. The wild and stormy moors were literally right outside my front door. It was a beautiful place, untamed and utterly real. It was the perfect place to quietly break down.

I opened the letter that had been crisply folded in three parts and started to read:

'This has been one of the hardest letters to write for me . . . Either

*I felt it was too hard or too soft . . . Everybody in the band says if*
*you come on the next tour they won't be coming. So you should*
*not come on the tour I am planning . . . . Please don't build a wall*
*between us but don't try to change my mind as this decision is not*
*changeable . . .'*

The words swam before my eyes as I took in their meaning:
the end of the biggest era of my life, the loss of my second family.
I went to the kitchen to inform Lydia what had happened. She
stood, looking a little stunned, in our lovely Smallbone kitchen that
she'd wanted so badly. It didn't really seem to matter much now.

My faithful dog Yarda nuzzled my palm and I thought to
myself, 'I must get out, clear my head. I feel claustrophobic and
trapped here.'

I put on my jacket and grabbed the dog leash and announced
to Lydia that I'd be back and slid through the door. I saw Lydia
traipsing behind me, but I just wanted to be alone with my
thoughts. After a few minutes of walking back and forth in the
garden in total silence, I said to Lydia 'You know, I'm going to
walk up to the Cleave with the dog.'

Something about my dog's loyal muteness was comforting and I
think she sensed that I needed a long walk up the craggy hillside.
Yarda forged ahead down the muddy, stony path into the dense
woods that lead up into Lustleigh Cleave, a large rift full of trees
more like America's Pacific Northwest than the south-west of England. It is a place of beautiful tranquillity and space surrounded
by large, strange outcroppings of granite stones Untouched by
human habitation for centuries. Totally timeless.

The dog and I sat on one of the larger rocks overlooking the
valley. It was late afternoon and the winter sun was wan and dim

through cloud cover. A light mist hung in the valley, and I could feel the slightly sun-warmed rock beneath me. The air, however, was rapidly turning crisp with the setting sun as I stared across the Cleave.

I thought I should feel something, anything, but I didn't. I just numbly stared into the middle distance. I lay down next to the dog and looked up at the grey sky above as the fog drifted across the moors. A hawk glided high in the sky above, searching for prey.

Then I felt it. A solitary teardrop rolled down my cheek, hot and salty. As if on cue, the heavens opened and the Dartmoor rain started to fall cold and wet. I would have stayed there and let myself be washed away into the granite if I could, but I couldn't. I had to find my way back, if only for the dog's sake, who was anxious and shivering now. We walked back to my house and my life – or whatever was left of it.

I did what most alcoholics do in this situation: I took a hostage. I got married to Lydia. The wedding itself was an orgy of grandiose excess. I invited everybody I knew from around the world, and I put them up at my expense in and around my country house in Dartmoor. The Cure, my other family, were on tour the day we got married, so they weren't there, another reminder of my diminished life. Remarkably, I managed to stay almost sober the day of the wedding, but when I look at the pictures taken that day I see a man whistling in the dark, hoping that this change in his life will be for the better.

That summer I spent all my time at the local pub. I had only been married for a few months and things were not going well. I was either passed out at home or attempting to out-Oliver Oliver

Reed at the pub. One day I took my small nieces for a ride on my mower, and I managed to turn the machine over with them on-board, throwing the girls out onto the ground. Miraculously, they were unhurt, but it gave me the horrors to think what might have been a most terrible outcome.

That summer dragged on and I went to see Michael in his house in Sussex. I behaved as drunks do, horribly and shamefully, in the home of one of my oldest friends. The next day I was mortified by my actions, which I only dimly recalled. I was burning bridges left and right.

The following day I returned to Dartmoor on the train and I had an epiphany of sorts. I had always loved travelling by train. It made a mundane journey from A to B so much more exciting, and being able to drink was just the icing on the cake.

That day, however, felt like a waking nightmare as I bounced from carriage to carriage clutching the small bottles I had brought from the little bar on the train. I couldn't buy enough to drink and carry them back in one go, so I had to make several trips with my little spirits. As I stumbled along, I fell on top of people who at first were laughing at my antics, then gave me shoves and scowls as I lurched violently down the aisle.

I got into the carriage with my bounty and caught sight of my reflection in the train window. Empty and disintegrated, I barely resembled the young man I had been. The man who had a passion for life and beauty and art, and a bond that he shared with his friends. Here was the sad mess I had become. A despicable old drunk on a train.

Eventually I made it home. Miserable and done in. The next day I called up Dr Campbell and asked him if I could come and see him again. I told him this time I intended to go all the way to rehab.

'I'm done,' I told him. 'I need your help.'

A day or so later the arrangements were made and I was on the train to London once more. This time, my eventual destination was the Priory rehab facility in Roehampton, just on the edge of London's Richmond Park. First, however, I had to go to through detox at the Lister. The night before I was to be admitted, I stayed at my friend Martin's house. I had a change of heart, but the next day he convinced me to go and not bolt back home.

After completing detox, I arrived at the Priory and discovered that I didn't have a room in the chemical dependence unit and would have to spend my first night on the other side of the hospital, where people had very different kinds of problems.

I was not really sure what that meant and I felt a little uneasy as they put me in a room with bars on the windows. I settled down and unpacked my belongings. Late that night I realized I was housed in the part of the hospital where people were more than a little disturbed, because some of them screamed at irregular intervals all through the night.

I went out to the nurse's station and discovered that they had a smoking lounge down the hall, so I went over and had a smoke. A young woman, perhaps about twenty-five years old came in, and I had a sense of déjà vu, a vision of a day many years ago in Hyde Park with Michael. I was about twelve years old and we were getting a Coke while watching our first concert. Like the girl at the soft drink stand that night long ago, this woman wanted me to give her something.

'Do you have a ciggy?' she asked.

I gave her one and lit it for her with my Zippo. After the smoke break I went back to my room and firmly locked the door, placing a chair underneath the handle. I didn't want any midnight visitors, thank you.

The next morning I was informed that my room was ready and I could move over into the dependence unit.

I imagine I ran to it.

For the next six weeks, I learnt all about what had been wrong with me for a very long time, and how I could recover from 'a seemingly hopeless state of mind and body'. Each day I felt a little stronger, and I believed I was where I belonged. It felt as if the people understood exactly what I had been going through. In a strange, ironic twist, one of the counsellors who took a shine to me and helped me see the light was an old Catholic priest named Tom. He was a fearsome Glaswegian who knew how to prick someone's pomposity with a word or two, especially mine. We became friends, and he opened my eyes to a new way of existing in the world I could barely have imagined before. I emerged from the Priory a month and a half later renewed, reborn, and in much better health than I had been for years.

## 20

# THE ROYAL COURTS

After I'd been sober for a year or so, I started to think about making music. My health was better than it had been in years, and the old feelings were back, the overpowering urge to create, to make music again.

The difference this time was that I had been through the machinations of the music business and I was a little gun-shy about re-entering the fray. As the saying goes, 'Fool me once, shame on; you fool me twice, shame on me.'

Although I was no longer with The Cure, I wondered if I was still connected to Chris Parry and Fiction Records in any way. The last thing I wanted to do was to start making music again and have some unforeseen contractual obligation prohibit me from making a new album or going on tour. If I was to be cast out of The Cure, I wanted to be free of everything.

Even though I was sober and had not had a drink or used any mind-altering substances for over a year, and had no desire to do so, I had not really started on the 'treatment' of my disease, which is the most important part of recovering from alcoholism. To do so I had to undergo an intense analysis of the root causes of my problems. My drinking was a symptom of much deeper issues that had spurred me to seek solace in the bottle in the first place. I hadn't begun the hard work of resolving the issues in my life and removing all the emotional baggage I had been carrying around for so long. In other words, I had a lot of soul searching to do.

A friend of mine, Chris Youdell, recommended a firm of lawyers to me. In his last band the singer had used their services and found them very useful.

'What I really want to find out,' I asked the lawyer, 'is if I am contractually obligated under the terms of my 1979 or 1986 contract to Chris Parry, Fiction Records or The Cure.'

I was sitting in a stuffy, overheated smoke-filled office in an anonymous white square in the middle of London.

'Did you know that when your contract was renewed in 1986,' the lawyer's voice broke through the fog, 'you went from being a partner in the band to a contract performer in Smith music?'

'What was that?' I asked, although I had understood perfectly.

'I think we can send a letter asking that they explain this to us, don't you feel?'

The lawyer's voice was probing and insistent. I wasn't sure what the words meant, but when he implied that I had been wronged, I found what I'd really been after.

I wanted the relief I thought it would bring, and so I set in motion the terrible events of the next few years. Looking out of the steamed-up windows into the grey overcast sky, revenge slipped slowly into the comfortable fog of the room. Everything from the dull brown tones of the furniture and the crackling fireplace had been designed to impart that paternalistic assurance that they would fix whatever needed to be fixed. Lawyers are the new high priests of certainty in an unreasonable world.

Unfortunately, that fearful attitude that I have come to recognize as the precursor to the worst excesses of the human condition had reared its ugly little head. My warped thinking, while pretending to lead me somewhere good, was actually my undoing. In the recesses of my mind I knew what I was really looking for . . . revenge. Big, stinking, loud, dark revenge. I had been wronged, and now I was coming to get mine, you bastards!

I didn't know at that point that there are but two major players in music lawsuits in London, and I would have ended up with one or the other representing me. Growing up, I'd heard the phrase 'never go to law' repeated over and over again, but the wisdom of those four words would not become salient to me until it was too late. Looking back, it's easy to see how I was seduced by their oily assurances, but I don't excuse my actions. They obviously had their own commercial concerns, whereas I was lashing out at those who'd hurt me. I was unable to see that I was in fact the architect of my own demise.

It took around four years from that first letter to the point where Robert and I both walked into the Royal Courts of Justice. Those four years were a tedious procession of letters crossing London from my lawyer's office to Robert's, with bills following soon afterwards. Please let us see this document. What about this one? A mountain of paperwork. This paper chase culminated in several weeks of meetings in London to describe and prepare for what would happen if we went to court.

I had not had any contact or communications from Robert,

or anyone else involved on the other side, until one night about a month before the court date had been set. The phone rang in my Devon home around dinner time, which seemed unusual. The phone never rang at dinner time.

'Hello, Lol, my old friend.'

It was Parry on the line. I asked him what he wanted.

'I wanted to talk to you about the court case. It doesn't seem necessary. Perhaps we could stop this now and go our own ways and forget about it all?'

I immediately became suspicious. 'Oh?' I asked.

'We could all just stop, pay up our own lawyers, and leave it at that,' Parry said.

Looking back, this seems like a perfectly reasonable suggestion, but at the time it felt like he was asking me to admit defeat, to capitulate just as the final battle was taking shape.

'Well,' I said, choosing my words carefully. 'I'm not sure I see it that way. You'd have to talk to my lawyers about that.'

I could hear the frustrated sucking in of air at the other end of the phone. Finally the exasperated sound of Parry's voice returned.

'Well, okay, but I think it's a very foolish thing you're doing here, Lol.'

'Yes, Bill, I guess we'll see, won't we?'

And with that I said goodbye.

It didn't take me very long after that to firm up in my mind what had to happen next. Although I had spent a lot of time with Parry, especially when he was going through a tough time with his marriage and subsequent divorce. I felt that he had edged me out of the discussions about the future of The Cure and our new contracts. Although in hindsight I can see that I was rapidly becoming a liability both to the band and his label, back then I couldn't see the role my behaviour played in the fiasco. Selfish and self-centred in the extreme, I viewed the world through my own myopic lens. I had been wronged and I would set things right – at all costs.

I still had time to stop the process. I so wish that I had.

A couple of days after I talked to Parry, my friend Chris Mason called me. He tried to convince me that not only had I made a disastrous decision, but it would be like a knife through the heart of the bond Robert and I shared. He was more concerned about that, about my friendship with Robert. He was right, of course.

'Forget about all the stupid shit, Lol. It's about you and Robert and your bond. Don't break that.'

That's when I pressed the self-destruct button.


The Royal Courts have presided over the Strand since the 1870s. Built in the Victorian Gothic style, they reminded me of *Gormenghast*, the irony of which was not lost on me.

I walked there from my barrister's rooms in the Temple Inn not far from the court. You have to have a barrister to represent you in the high court. Your lawyer can't stand up and present your case. I think it was originally designed so that any man, rich or poor, would have good representation in court. Of course, the expense is still built in, and although you don't directly pay counsel, you pay your lawyers to pay them! The antiquated bureaucracy of England never fails to amaze me.

I met my barrister on a typical grey London day at his 'rooms' as they are called in the Inner Temple. It was a very Dickensian scene, with young men running around with sheaves of papers on small trolleys for all the cases going to court that day. The streets were all cobblestone, adding to the antiquated effect, and beetle-like men in flamboyant coats policed the area.

On the door of the building before me, my barrister's name had been written in flamboyant cursive script on the inside of the door. When they were working in their offices, the door opened outwards so one could see the names. It was all very secretive and strange. Upstairs in my barrister's rooms, Mr Garnet was waiting for me. He was a very soft-spoken, well-cultured, middle-aged man and I liked him immediately. I had a lot of trepidation about how the whole affair might turn out, but the English legal system was designed to lull you, in soporific fashion, into believing that even if the odds were against you, you'd receive a fair trial.

Although there are jury trials for criminal cases in the UK, it is rare for a jury to be appointed for a civil trial, which is what my case was. I was to be heard by a lone judge. Trials involving judges and pop stars are enshrined in English popular history, ever since the famous Rolling Stones drugs trial at which the judge declared that the charges should not be too harsh, 'Lest we break a butterfly upon a wheel', a poetic way of saying he was going to give Jagger a break.

Since then it has become de rigueur for trial judges to make jokes about the circumstances of the musicians lives they sit in judgment upon, to indicate that they are not completely out of the loop. My judge was no exception, and he made a few witty remarks during trial.

All this obfuscated what was really going on: making money for the legal system. I was given all kinds of percentages and figures about the likelihood of victory for my cause but in the end I came to the conclusion that the odds were really fifty-fifty. However, it wasn't up to me. It was up the judge, and based on what the judge decided, one party would win and one would lose.

I arrived dressed in a new suit. I had brought two for the trial, thinking, in a rather old-fashioned way, that you should get dressed up when appearing at the high court. I think it was probably just another indication of my rather sad state of mind at the time.

Although I had been to rehab at the Priory and I was clean and sober, I had not done the hard work of bringing about a complete change in the way I thought about the world, which, in turn, would bring peace and serenity and long-term recovery to my life. Instead I pointed fingers and laid the blame at the feet of others. I was primed to take as much destructive action as possible by taking my friends and 'band family' to court.

For three weeks we sat in the court. I spent three days on the witness stand, which was the saddest part of the entire process. Robert and I had been friends since childhood, yet there we were facing off in court. It didn't seem right to me, but I had spent so much time getting to this stage that I was on autopilot. The legal process is set up to roll along until it becomes an unstoppable juggernaut destroying everything in its path before it finally comes to a stop.

It felt completely horrid sitting a few feet away from my best friends and having to avoid them in the corridor or the lift. Our gaze never met once during those three weeks. I was running on resentment straight down a hole of my own making.

Eventually, the awful days of the trial ended, and the judge decided that he would reserve judgment. This meant we would have to wait for the final verdict. I didn't really need to know.

I had already reached a verdict in my heart. I wished I'd never started this terrible process.

It was an interminable wait for the judge's verdict, and when it came in the autumn of 1994, it was not really a surprise to me that I had lost. My lawyers wanted to know if I wanted to appeal, but in my heart I knew that I had gone about things the wrong way. I had looked outward for a solution and struck out at those I felt had wronged me, when I should have looked inward.

# 21

# DESPAIR IN THE DESERT

After losing the court case, I fell down the rabbit hole. I didn't have much experience of life outside of The Cure. It had defined my whole existence thus far and, truth be told, the band was more of a family to me than my actual one.

I had been married a little while and some other awful stuff had happened. We had lost a child, a daughter, due to complications during her birth. The day of her birth our original doctor who was going to deliver her was not available and a stand-in took over. Unfortunately, he was fresh out of medical school and didn't have that much experience yet. Consequently, when an unusual situation occurred during birth, the wrong decisions were made, and our daughter suffered a severe loss of oxygen for several minutes – enough to ensure that she would only live for about two weeks.

It was the most horrible two weeks of my life. I sat in the neonatal intensive care unit praying for a miracle that would somehow give us our daughter's life back. It wasn't to be. When we had exhausted every test and explored every option, we took her home to Dartmoor, where she passed away after a couple of days. After losing Camille India, it felt like nothing would ever be right again. It would have been easy to fall into the morass of misery and pity, but within a few months Lydia became pregnant again. We had been given another chance and had a beautiful son we named Gray.

Unfortunately, that spelled the end of the marriage. Something was not right. I wasn't sure if it ever was. To be fair, I had married Lydia at my lowest point, and I was not thinking very clearly when I met her. I hadn't wanted a relationship with another person so much as someone to manage my life for me, which was then spiralling out of control. I dumped my emotional baggage on her and abdicated all responsibility. Lydia came from a pretty dysfunctional background herself, so our union was recipe for disaster.

After the trial and the death of my daughter, we decided to leave England and relocate to southern California. I had always been happy there. I had fond memories of being there as young single man with The Cure, so I thought it would help to go someplace where I'd felt contented.

Two weeks after Lydia left with Gray in November 1994, I found myself on a plane to Los Angeles. I'd stayed behind to tie up some loose ends, but I soon discovered that running away to another country was not enough to keep us married. The day I landed in Los Angeles and arrived at our new apartment in West Hollywood, Lydia informed me she wanted a divorce. She wouldn't let me stay with her and Gray, so I left and went to see my friend Gary who lived close by.

For the next six months I rattled around various friends' houses in Hollywood (thank you, Gary, Beth, Chris and Tara) while I tried to put my life back in some kind of order. I was now separated, and like most men in my situation I had occasional visits with my son, which were the highlight of my existence.

One of the universal truths of alcoholism is that in order to be recovered you have to reach the bottom, the point at which you feel you can fall no further. In 1995 I had most certainly reached bottom.

I had no band, no wife, no place to live of my own and only about 25 per cent of my income to live on. The judge had ordered that I allocate 75 per cent to pay off my trial costs and legal fees. I was really quite depressed, and while I was technically clean and sober, I was fucking miserable.

Everything that had gone before had to be destroyed if I was to rebuild my life and become a stronger and better person. I was to spend the next few years reinventing myself and renewing the part of me that had been burnt out by the events of the last decade.

On reflection, I could easily have ended up in the stupid club, as I like to call it, of musicians and artists who die too young as a result of drugs, drinking or other misadventures. It's plain to me now why that happens. You are thrust into a world that resembles normal existence in name only. This usually happens at a young age when the brain is still developing, but because you have no experience of dealing with the world, the pitfalls become more dangerous. It suits the music business, because it's easier for the money men to control you when you're in this unreal world. I'm immensely lucky that I made it out in one piece and with most of my marbles intact.

It took me a long time to realize that the other world I'd lived in for so long wasn't coming back. It was a slow process of learning how to deal with the messy, problematic stuff of life and not the hollow glamour world of rock and roll. I had to get to grips with the fact I wasn't special, that we are all the same people in the end, and that we are all on a journey to discover something. Peace and compassion for my fellow humans was the way forward. To get there I had to go all the way back to the reasons I started making music in the first place. It seems obvious now, but sometimes you lose sight of the forest for the trees.

My old ideas and thought processes had to be burned up in the cauldron of experience to find out who I was, what I believed in and, most importantly, what I was going to do about it. I learnt that I had to stop fighting everyone and everything if I was ever going to find any kind of peace. At first this was a hard lesson to learn. I had to embrace the truth right in front of my face. I needed to let go. Absolutely.

I studied a lot in those years, I read constantly. I talked to as many people I could. One of the things I loved about California was that in the early part of last century it had been the place where various utopian communities had started, and that always intrigued me. My hard punk roots might have spat on that, but I always maintained that under the hardness of the punk movement was a search for meaning out of no meaning, kind of like a Zen koan. Whatever it was, I hoped to find it in California.

On 1 May 1995 I was so fed up with everything that I asked my friend Keith, 'Where's a place with nothing, no buildings, no people, nothing! I need to get out of here or I'll just go mad!'

He thought for a moment and a smile slowly crept across his face. 'Death Valley! Ever been there?'

'Nope.'

'Well there's nothing, I mean absolutely nothing, out there. No people, no buildings, no telephone poles even. You might as well be on another planet.'

Why not, I thought. I could do no worse.

So I left Los Angeles. I drove out the next day through the dust bowls of Lancaster and Palmdale, forgotten places full of forgotten people, places where you can't remember your name. I spent the night in Mojave in a seedy 1970s motel listening to the sound of artic trucks racing through the desert night and my own thoughts rattling around in the orange plastic hotel room after a dinner of chicken fried steak (snake?). The threadbare carpet on the floor matched the sandpaper-like towels for luxury. The ancient AC unit humming in the window groaned to itself in the desert dust. It was the sort of place that, unless you had no choice, you wouldn't want to spend more than a few hours in by yourself, because it would make you even more depressed.

I poked my head outside the door and spied a soda machine and icemaker across the parking lot. I decided to get a Coke and watch some crap on the TV covered in a brown wood veneer. The hot, dry air outside reminded me of the first time I came to California in 1981, a magical time I'd never forgotten. The people and places, and especially the weather, made a lasting impression on me. I'd found nothing like it in Europe in my admittedly small experience of the world thus far. Although I had been to New York it felt more like a movie, like London on steroids, and was grimy and dirty and smelled like urine. With a few notable exceptions, most of the people seemed slightly deranged, whereas the Californians I had met were much more to my liking. But that utopia-like feeling was long gone by the time I arrived. Everything had fallen apart since that golden moment in time. I had no band, no wife, one dead child and another whose presence has been denied me, no money, and no future to speak of.

I was sober, but my life was still shit. I was 5,000 miles from home, and it never felt further away than it did that night in the Mojave Desert. What had I got to lose that I hadn't lost already?

I put the coins in the machine slot, pushed the plastic bar, and listened for the thud of the plastic bottle of brown foaming sugar water to tell me my drink was served. I filled the little scratched plastic ice bucket with ice from the hissing machine next to the soda dispenser and turned to go back to the room. Balancing the ice bucket and Coke in one hand, I slid the key into the lock and turned it to open the door and leave behind the hot desert night, returning to the smell of cleaning fluids and tobacco smoke.

Sitting on the orange nylon bedspread, I watched as the TV showed another evangelist telling me how I was going to hell unless I sent him money. I didn't need him to tell me that; I already knew what hell was like. Eventually I turned the TV off with the sticky plastic remote, washed my hands and face in the chipped sink, got between the prickly nylon sheets and went to bed, but sleep didn't come. Tossing and turning and feeling utterly dehydrated, I slept fitfully. My head was a mess of emotions I couldn't even put a name to. I just knew I had to keep going and find something other than this horrible mess my life had become.

The next day came peeking fierce and bright through the peeling, rubber-backed curtains, throwing shapes on the scuffed walls of my room. I put the coffee maker on and showered in the bathroom and dried with the thin scratchy towel the hotel had provided. I put my clothes on and took a glug of the tasteless brew that had bubbled out into the styrofoam cup. It tasted like the dusty desert itself. Perhaps I could get a better cup of joe along the road somewhere.

I ventured out into the glaring brightness and put on my shades out of necessity rather than vanity. I slid behind the wheel of my rented car and gunned the engine a couple of times, satisfied that it was all working. I pulled out onto the blacktop and pointed the car into another day. I had done one thing right for myself since I'd arrived in California: I had learnt to drive and passed my test. I had the freedom to go where I wanted. At least that felt good.

The scorching sun was already rising up and splintering the day with its sharp rays as I cruised along the highway towards my destination: Death Valley. The heat shimmered in the distance on the one road that crosses the desert floor. At 282 feet below sea level, it is the lowest, hottest and driest place in North America, and a good facsimile of hell, as the record temperature in the aptly named Furnace Creek was a mind-melting 134 degrees. The hottest place on earth.

I felt I'd either burn up or explode. A strange phenomenon occurred: as I drove across the dusty floor I felt my mind let go of all the pain and resentments of the last few months and a smidgen of light squeezed back into my soul. I allowed myself to luxuriate in this freedom, the pressure easing as the miles sped by. I put the car in cruise mode and folded my feet underneath me on the seat. There were no other cars at all that I could see, and with just a flick of the wheel I could steer the car and imagine I was sitting on a magic carpet as I rode through the desert. I wound the window down a little to feel the scorching air, and it seemed like I was being purified in this crucible. I listened to the rubber of the car tyres peeling along the highway and, with the turning of the wheels, a minimalistic mantra was set in motion. I allowed myself to be taken into its new heart. Why not, I thought?

Suddenly, the car made a loud sound and I realized very quickly that I had left the road some way back and that now I was careening across the desert floor in between the Joshua trees and the scrub. I put my feet down, and applied the brake gingerly, and I stopped right there with dust flying up all around my car. Thankfully, nothing was broken, and the road was but a few feet away.

I steered the car slowly back onto the highway. There was no need to look left or right as there was no one around for miles, but reflexively I did it anyway. You never know. And in that instant I realized that I had never really known anything. At that moment in time, I felt as if I had no past and no future, only the present moment with the hot desert sun and the scorched highway stretched out before me, beckoning me onward to an unknown destination.

That second day I made it into Death Valley proper and drove all the way down below sea level to the desert floor. To say that there is nothing in Death Valley is not quite correct. It had plenty of beautiful things to look at, none of which were made by man, apart from the road I drove on, a two-lane blacktop that dropped off into sandy desert dust at the edges.

Lost in thought, I drove a few more hours and arrived at the Furnace Creek Inn. It was quite a sight after travelling through the park's desolation. I pulled up and went in to get a drink and ask about a room for the night.

'All sold out today, sir,' the clerk said.

I found this hard to believe, considering where we were, but in this oasis was a surprisingly green golf course, so I accepted it must be so. When I spied the Harley-Davidson motorcycles lined up outside, I smiled a little. Hell's Angels were staying at a luxury resort? America was full of contradictions.

I enquired at the hotel desk if there was anything else nearby.

'Stovepipe Wells.'

'Where is that?'

'It's about half an hour back down the road, but you gotta get there soon as they give out rooms on a first-come first-served basis at dusk.'

I jumped back in my car and headed back the way I'd come. I recalled passing through Stovepipe Wells about twenty-five miles back: a collection of small buildings clustered around the highway being the only indication that something else other than me was out there.

I got to Stovepipe Wells in about half an hour and drove into the lot by the sign that said 'Room Registration'. The sun was hanging a little lower in the sky, but it was still in the upper 90s outside, the air a dry crackle. A few other desert-weary travellers were waiting on the bench by the door, including an old man. The only available space to sit was next to him on the bench. So I sat down beside him and we introduced ourselves. The door opened for the registration, and we all lined up like in a soup line in the Great Depression. It was a timeless place where my thoughts floated in and out, a jumble of images and feelings.

I signed in and got my key and went to my room, which had a small fridge that never really got cold, no TV or phone. I went for a walk to check out what one did for dinner in Stovepipe Wells. I was completely alone out there, and I could feel my head begin to clear from the everyday tumult and chaos of Los Angeles and my disintegrating marriage and life. The desert seemed to be working its ancient magic on me.

I noticed they had a dining room, and it was really the only choice, so I walked up the steps and into the room. It was a rustic and wooden beamed place serving hearty country cuisine. I ate a solitary dinner.

Afterwards on the bench outside I encountered the old guy that I had met at registration, and this was where everything changed for ever for me.

The old man and I started talking. It turned out he was from San Francisco and his wife had recently died, so he'd come out to the desert to explore somewhere he had never been before. He didn't want to end his days just 'rotting at home'. He asked me where I was from, with my accent and all, and I gave him the long and the short of it, telling it all and holding nothing back. Calmly, he listened without saying a word, just smiling and nodding at the appropriate times. Eventually my torrent of resentments and self-loathing stopped, and then the strangest thing happened. He stood up, shook my hand and placed his hand on my head very briefly, and said, 'It's going to be all right, son. I have a long drive tomorrow. So if you'll excuse me, I'm hitting the hay. Good night.'

I looked at the clock on the wall outside when he was gone and realized we had spent an hour together with me doing most of the talking. I felt light-headed and strange, almost drunk, but I hadn't had a drop to drink. Carefully measuring my steps, I went for a walk. I walked to the edge of the grounds as if I was walking on a tightrope. In the hot evening air I removed all of my clothes except for my shorts so I could feel the dry wind on my flesh. It felt better without clothes. I looked up and saw the whole sky, all of the moon and stars in a flash of eternity above me, around me, part of me. I stumbled half-naked back to my room and collapsed on the bed. I slept fitfully that night in a fevered sweat, tossing and turning throughout the hours, zoning in on the tick of the clock or fragments of songs or thoughts in my head, tapping the bed in rhythmic cadences and mantras. I eventually crashed out, and some hours later I woke to see the first glow of the sun's rays coming through the blinds.

My mouth was dry and swollen. I felt drained, like the comedown from an acid trip. What had happened to me? I tried to piece together the previous evening's events, but they seemed strangely out of focus. I couldn't even bring to mind the face of the man I had spent an hour talking to the night before. Weird. But there was something else. A lightness and excitement I hadn't felt for many years. I opened the door to the room and immediately a blinding light filled the doorframe. Gradually my eyes grew accustomed to it and I sensed things had changed.

I gathered my things together and walked across to the dining room, where I breakfasted on eggs and coffee and got ready to drive back along the 190, as I had promised myself I would go to see Zabriskie Point.

The day before I had not thought about going there I had been so miserable and helpless but I felt much better, as if the Kundalini had shot up my spine and out the top of my head. An hour later, passing through Furnace Creek again, I stopped to use the pay telephone and call my friend Tara back in Los Angeles, whom I was staying with. She had been very worried that I was going to die in the desert when I took off three days ago. But I wasn't dead. In fact, I had to tell her how alive I now felt.

I made it to Zabriskie Point that day and looked out over its vast, moon-like landscape. Maybe philosopher Michel Foucault had the same experience as me in the desert and it wasn't acid, but the place, that gave him that tremendous trip? I could feel a change taking place. I was no longer a melancholic drifter. I felt alive again, and all the beauty of nature that surrounded me in Death Valley helped heal me.

I called Tara again later that day. 'I think I'm ready to come home,' I said into the receiver. 'I'm feeling much better.'

I could hear her hopeful sigh at the other end of the line.

I got into the car and headed back to Los Angeles. As I turned onto the 15 and civilization I felt very strongly that I had found a type of freedom from my old self. I could feel the difference. It was palpable.

The next day I met Cindy.

I hadn't thought of being with anyone else since my separation from Lydia. I had been a lonely ghost, wandering the boulevards and avenues of the City of Angels. Occasionally I was able to spend time with my son, Gray, who was now living with his mother in Venice Beach in a house on the canals. It was never enough, so some nights I would walk the canal paths hoping to get a glimpse of him playing in the garden, but mostly I wandered alone. I sat on the roof of a friend's condo and read books, and walked. I walked for miles around the west side of Los Angeles. In the morning and afternoons, most of the side streets were empty of people. It suited me to not have to interact with anybody. Occasionally dogs sprung out of their boredom to snap and growl at me, but mostly

I walked unmolested, wrapped in my own thoughts as I carefully negotiated the neighbourhood sidewalks, great slabs of smashed pavement seemingly flung on the street like broken tombstones.

Some evenings when I sensed I should give Tara a break I would force myself to go to a bar or café to observe people and try to be part of the human race again. It didn't work, and I ended up more resentful than ever seeing the happy smiling faces of people. Seeing young couples obviously in love was especially irritating.

So I was a little apprehensive the day after I had returned from the desert when Tara said, 'My friend Cindy will be coming over this afternoon. You should meet her. I think you have a lot in common.'

Cindy turned up that afternoon and we talked, and within a week we met up and went on a date. A date! My first in years and years. Then the most amazing thing happened: we fell in love.

I often think about that time and how it came to pass, and I feel sure that one of the reasons that our relationship and marriage was destined to work was the fact that Cindy met Lol the man as opposed to Lol the guy in The Cure.

I had been stripped of all of the accoutrements of rock and roll-dom, so to speak, and the person she met and fell in love was the real me. That's not to say that you can't be a real person and be in a band, but it tends to make people approach you in a different way than they would with others, and that changes the relationship and what both parties expect out of the situation.

I know that this is one reason why Robert and Mary's relationship has lasted so long, because she knew him way before he was Robert Smith the rock superstar. She knew him when he was just Robert Smith the boy in our class at school.

I didn't have anything to wow or impress Cindy with when she met me other than the person she saw before her, so she got the real me, and that's who she fell in love with. She also was at a point in her life where authenticity was very important to her, and she wasn't going to settle for something facile or fake.

With the love that I had found, I started to turn things in my life around. First I needed to find a place to live, as I had been living with my friends Chris and Tara during the week, and with my other friends Gary and Beth on weekends. I needed to give them a break. I had been their house guest for about half a year and they needed their lives back.

Just before I met Cindy, I had put a deposit down on a small place in Brentwood that I was due to move into in about a month, but meeting her had changed those plans, and we moved in together almost immediately to our own place on the west side of Los Angeles. It felt like a happy and creative place and a good atmosphere in which to bring up my son Gray in order to minimize the disruption he had already faced in his young life. I was determined that he would have the most consistent childhood I could provide. I had seen a number of my friends, especially musician friends, have terrible marriages and child-rearing arrangements, and I didn't want to put my child through that. It was not his fault his mother and I couldn't make our marriage work. He deserved the best upbringing I could give him. I had very strong feelings about this.

Of course, when you get divorced, there are two sides to be considered, and Lydia felt that she wanted to leave Los Angeles and move to a small town in Idaho called Hailey.

I was none too keen on this as I most certainly wanted to keep

Gray here in Los Angeles near me. I felt it was important that his father be available to him, unlike mine had been.

Unfortunately, my lawyer informed me that 'If she has a job to go to and a support system in Idaho, the judge will let her take Gray with her. You can pay me a lot more money just to find out that he's going anyway.'

I'd already been through the wringer once with the court system and wasn't in a hurry to do it again. My lawyer suggested I ask for a six-month review of Gray's situation, and if he was suffering in any way, we could petition the court again. It wasn't ideal, but then again, nothing in a divorce ever is.

The next few years were difficult ones for Cindy and me because the court case and my divorce had left me without much in the bank, and so we struggled to keep our heads above water. I had to sell a few things just to keep a roof over our heads and food on the table. Although it sounds like a cliché, they were some of the happiest years for us as a newly-married couple, as every hurdle that we overcame seemed so much more amazing than if we had been in a better financial position. We also learnt to value each other for who we were as people, not what we had done in our lives. I think it made our marriage that much stronger.

The years from 1996 to 1999 were filled mostly with the mundane and beautiful parade of events that pass for 'normal' life, and I became accustomed to my new permanent home in Los Angeles. In 1999, at age 8, Gray returned to Los Angeles from Idaho, and I became a stay-at-home dad. I took our son to school and generally did all of the things that he needed a parent to do. I am grateful beyond words that I was given the time and situation to do that, because today I have a strong relationship with my son, unlike the one I had with his grandfather. We spent his boyhood years together, and that was a blessing I know was not given to a lot of working musicians.

Of course, that meant I was no longer a working musician. Sometimes little projects would come my way but up until his teen years I tried not to go out of town or on the road. I had seen the damage it had caused in other families. Unlike my father, I was involved in our son's life and always available to be a chaperone for school trips and things like that. I am so grateful that it worked out that way. Maybe that's what was given to me in the Mojave Desert: the ability to break the chain of family dysfunction and be a true father. The real measure of a man.

## 22

# HOUSE BY THE SEA

My first abortive attempt at a new musical career was with the short-lived band Presence. I formed it soon after I left The Cure with Gary Biddles, who had worked for The Cure and with Simon in his time away from the band. Michael was also involved in the beginning. I listen to the songs now and I hear a band out of time. I think if we had recorded those records a few years later we might have had a better chance of the band staying together. I believe the biggest impediment to us succeeding was the baggage that came with me. If it had been a new band that nobody knew, I think we might have got a different reaction. We were either too much like The Cure (surprise, surprise) or not enough. We couldn't win.

Truth be told, by the time we had our second album deal with Island in 1993, I was burnt out on the whole idea of being in a band. Although I enjoyed making both the Presence albums, *Inside* and *Closer*, in London and Los Angeles respectively, I didn't feel the way I'd felt when I'd been in The Cure. We lacked the sheer joy, excitement and passion that The Cure had. In The Cure, even the bad times were good. It certainly got crazy at the end, but at least I felt like I was alive. I can't say with sincerity that that was the case in my new band. I have much admiration for the various parties involved, but I think it was probably doomed from the start.

I had some money, as it was before the court case, so I funded the first album, and out of that we got a deal with Smash Records based in Chicago through Chris Blackwell's Island Records. The second album, which Smash declined to release, was made at Sound City Studios in Van Nuys, California, with John Porter of The Smiths fame producing. Sound City is now a very famous piece of music history, following Dave Grohl's documentary about the studio. Back then it was really pretty worn out and old, but it still had an undeniably special sound.

We tried to keep the band going after we made the album, but I got the call from Smash shortly after, saying they had decided not to put it out in the foreseeable future. I hunkered down, and for a while lived a very quiet life bringing up my son.

Eventually I knew I had to do something creative again. I could not exist without it. My son was getting older and more stable and secure in his life, so he needed me a little less. As with many parents, although I found it hard to let go, I knew there would come a time when he would have to fly on his own, and I had to allow that to happen. It's a natural process.

I was trying various ideas and sounds and had spent a lot of time trying to educate myself about the new electronic music. I have always had a great love for all kinds of experimental music, especially the early synthesizer pioneers like Morton Subotnick, and I loved Don Buchla's electronic machines. So I wondered: could I try and make something that was an offshoot of that?

There had been a less avant-garde vein of that running through The Cure with songs like 'The Walk', with that recording we had made a record that was mostly electronic except for vocals and a little guitar.

So I started to make music again. I took it slowly at first, and then as I grew in confidence, I finally made it back to the studio. That's the other thing that had been zapped by my alcoholism. I'd lost confidence in my own abilities as a creative musician. With Presence, I was able to hide behind the other musicians. Alone in the crowd. Now I felt strong enough to express myself with my own voice. Goodness knows I'd had enough experiences in the last few years to write about.

I had a new manager, Jay Frank, and a new lease of life. One day I was in the garden at my house. I was trying to think about a singer for the songs I had. Cindy was walking around the house, singing like she always did. She's a much more demonstrative person than me. I was sitting outside in the Californian sun and suddenly like a bolt out of the blue it hit me. Cindy should be the singer, and right there and then Levinhurst was born. The name was a portmanteau of both our last names.

I had spent most of 2002 writing the songs that would become *Perfect Life*, the first album with a new friend, Dayton Borders. Jay found us a great engineer in Meghan Gohil, a wonderful man and good friend. We put most of the album together at Meghan's studio in Hollywood, and Cindy would come to sing on the finished tracks that Dayton and I had made.

It was great to be finally working with my own agenda in place and a newfound confidence, born in part from finding out that my wife had a wonderful singing voice.

I wrote most of the lyrics for *Perfect Life* in a few sessions. I wanted to express how much things had changed for me in a positive way after coming to California and Los Angeles. That's why it's called *Perfect Life*. I had learnt one of the most important lessons in my journey: that for life to be perfect you have to be willing to accept life on its own terms and be in the moment rather than casting a look backwards or forwards. You just have to live, and that's what I was finally understanding. It had taken living in a place known for its excesses for me to understand that. For every yin there's a yang. I think that's very true of Los Angeles. There's a dark underbelly of broken dreams, but it's a wonderful place of hope as well.

We took *Perfect Life* on the road for a bit around the USA. With Presence, I had played a few gigs in America and in the UK, but it felt like I was on the road for the first time since I had left The Cure. It had only taken me fifteen years! We played up and down the West Coast and then further afield, getting all the way to New York, my first time back there since I had put together a DJ set as Orpheus. That was a few years back and had been a fun experiment, but didn't really go anywhere.

*Perfect Life* garnered some great reviews, including this one from Joanne Greene in the *All Music Guide*: 'Shimmering with delicate atmospheres, filled with supple and subtle effects, *Perfect Life* is indeed nigh-on perfect.' I have to admit that felt good to read after years in the wilderness.

*Perfect Life* made enough waves to get noticed by Rob Gordon at What Are Records, and together with Jay I made the trip to Boulder, Colorado, and met with Gordon. I had previously talked to him at an event at the South by Southwest music conference and we got on immediately. It took a couple more years, but the relationship we forged with Rob Gordon that day led to one of my favourite albums I've been involved with since *Pornography*.

*House by the Sea* was the first time I had done something that was completely and utterly me. I made most of the songs from the various bits of electronica that I had developed over the years and were lying about in the house, which of course is the *House by the Sea* of the title.

Both Robert and I have lived in houses close to the sea. For me it's the healing nature of the water. In England, the waves crashing upon the shore create a melancholic atmosphere. In California, it's both different and the same. I am especially fond of the humid air that hangs at night as a cool fog over coastal areas. It is at once gloomy and mysterious, but lovely too, like grey velvet. It is this feeling I tried to get with *House by the Sea*. More than that, though, it's an exploration of a father and a husband adrift creatively. It helped me focus my energy and purpose back to what it should be. It's not easy to sustain a musical career over several decades, but I feel blessed to have been able to do just that. It's been a design for living that has given me untold freedom, and I still live in a house by the sea. I always want to.

# 23

# THE PALACE

I suppose my newfound vigour was inspired in part due to the events of the winter of 2000. Back then, The Cure embarked on a short tour of the US in support of their new album *Bloodflowers*. The Los Angeles show was held at the Palace in Hollywood, an older theatre I knew well.

A few months earlier, I had written Robert a long letter. It was an admission of guilt with respect to our break-up and consequent legal troubles, and I expressed my willingness to make things right again between us. We were, after all, friends before the band, and I reasoned we could be friends after it, too. Despite all the pain and destruction, I wanted to believe there was still a beating heart of true friendship.

I outlined in my letter what I had discovered these last few years in California and explained that I had a progressive and deadly disease that would certainly kill me if I didn't take action to treat it. However, I had found a solution, and part of the solution was to make amends to people I had harmed. In other words, to right the wrongs that I had done to others.

I had made many of the amends on my list and had discovered that it was a wonderful process to go through – liberating and redemptive in a way that I had never experienced before. It had, in fact, given me a new life. I resolved to do the hardest one of all as soon as I could, which of course was Robert. In my letter I explained that when I next saw him I would like to talk and make peace personally. I had found that this was the best and most meaningful way to do it, both for myself and the person I was making amends to. Words in a letter can be powerful, but face-to-face is always preferable.

Robert had replied to my letter and asked that I come and meet him when The Cure played the Palace on 19 February 2000. Cindy and I left for the Palace that evening without having made any arrangements with Robert. We simply arrived at the venue just as the audience was about to enter, without a contact number or any kind of pass to get in. I hadn't really thought about that, as I had never needed to worry about getting into a Cure gig before!

However, arriving at the backstage entrance, I realized that I needed to convince whoever was guarding the door of my credentials. I didn't see any of the old Cure crew working the gig and quickly realized that getting through to Robert was going to be a humbling and difficult experience. I smiled as I stood at the backstage gate. It seemed that I should come correct size to our first meeting, so I swallowed my pride and knocked at the gate.

'Yeah? What do you want?' a suspicious security guard asked.

I told him who I was and who I had come to see. He scuttled off to find someone from The Cure's party to verify my claims. They duly appeared, but it was someone I had never worked with before so they didn't recognize me. They were rightly sceptical of my bona fides. It's surprising how many people turned up at Cure gigs claiming to be our brothers/cousins/long-lost uncles or even, in extreme cases, us, in order to gain entrance to the hallowed backstage areas of a Cure gig!

So with a scowl born of seeing off many impersonators, they went to tell Robert and see if this was genuine. Meanwhile, some fans that had been lining up noticed me standing there.

'Hey, Lol!' they said and some even produced stuff me to sign. As I started chatting with them, the switch flipped, and I felt like a teenager in Crawley again, the first time someone told me how much they liked what we played and what a difference it made to their lives. I relaxed and chatted with the people who had given me my whole life. The Cure's loyal fans will always be special to me in a way I am eternally thankful for.

Suddenly at the backstage gate the unknown crew member was back, panting because he had run directly from Robert, and hastily undoing the locked iron gate.

'Wow, I'm sorry, Lol. I didn't realize it was you, mate!' while flashing his credentials to the rather bemused security guard and the now fairly large group of assorted fans that had come to wish me well and say hello.

'See you, Lol!'

'Yes, you will!' I said and gave the nearest one a hug. Thank you, Cure fans, you are the best.

We ascended the stairs to the dressing room and in it I saw Robert for the first time since we had looked across the courtroom floor. Without a word needed, we hugged, and then he turned and said to everyone else in the room, 'Would everyone mind leaving us for a moment?'

Everyone began filing out, and then it was just us. Together again after so many years.

The single light bulb in the room hung from a wire with no shade, reminding me of the start of all this madness. As soon as the room was empty, I said, 'I have to make my amends to you, Robert, and I'd like to do that now, if you don't mind.'

'Okay,' he said.

I proceeded to pour out my part in what had happened to me and how sorry I was that I had hurt him and The Cure, and if there was a way to make recompense for my actions I would gladly do whatever he deemed necessary. The smell of Lysol wafted up from the freshly scrubbed bathroom and I felt my friend's hand on my shoulder.

'Hey, slow down, it's okay. We have time for all of this.'

I looked up in midstream to see Robert's smiling face and realized I had already been forgiven. The prodigal son could finally return home.

I watched the Palace gig from the floor of the theatre.

The last time I'd been there was a few years before, when I was at a Cure convention I had been invited to. It seemed weird at the time, like trespassing on another life, and I wasn't sure it was the right thing to do. I liked talking to fans, and for that it was worth it, but my heart was uncertain, and I had not yet learnt how to balance all of my emotions about The Cure, and Robert in particular, in a way that an audience might enjoy.

At the start of the second encore I heard Robert call out, 'This is for Lol! This is "The Figurehead!"'

It felt good to know I was back in the good graces of the band

I loved and had always loved, despite all the chaos and pain I'd caused.

After the gig I talked to everyone in the dressing room and we renewed our bonds. Simon was just the same as always. Simon is one of the most authentic people I know. I've known him since we were teens, and he is always true to himself and his beliefs, which is no mean feat in a business that is full of posers and pretenders. He's the genuine article. It was good to reacquaint myself with him after the debacle in the courtroom, where for three weeks we sat just yards apart from each other but never talking. Absurd is the only word that comes close to describing how strange that was.

The dressing room was clearing out, and Robert asked me if I'd like to come out with them all. They were going to a club for a drink, and he wanted to know if Cindy and I would ride with them.

I got into the band van. It was the simplest thing, but like Neil Armstrong's small step on the moon, it was a gigantic moment for me. I was coming back to the people I knew and loved, and it felt right.

In the club it was interesting to watch people's faces as they came up to talk to the band, especially those who knew the story about the court case. I would watch their eyes dart from Robert's face to mine and back again, looking for clues as to why we were here sitting in a club in Hollywood side by side and not at each other's throats. It's one reason I don't go out of my way to meet my heroes: I'm afraid of being disappointed by the reality of their ordinary selves.

I don't blame people for wanting to know the smallest details about the people who make the music they feel passionately about, but I don't really want to see the cracks, either. I'd prefer to keep my illusions, thank you. People have all kinds of ideas about The Cure that don't match up to reality. I'm sure that night in the club after the Palace gig must have confused some, but they shouldn't have worried, as it was all for the good. It marked the beginning of a new phase in my friendship with Robert.

Later that night Robert and I were deep in conversation in his hotel on the Sunset strip.

'You know,' he said, 'the saddest thing was when we drove out of the Royal Courts after the judge gave his verdict. We drove right past you sitting on the kerb. I don't think you saw us and you looked so sad and dejected,' Robert said.

'Yeah,' I replied. 'I think that's when it finally hit me that the only winners were the lawyers.'

'When I told my dad about the case he said, "Well, have you been paying Laurence?" I said, "Of course!" I just couldn't understand why you went through with it!'

'You know, I didn't really understand it myself,' I said, and I still didn't, but I'd managed to climb out of the hole of anger and destruction that I had dug for myself, and that was the only thing that mattered now.

Robert and I talked for hours. Laying the foundation for forgiveness and healing. When I left the hotel I drove home across Los Angeles down to my house by the sea just as the sun was coming up. I felt like a huge weight had been removed from my shoulders. In due course this would fully manifest, and an even more wondrous and healing event would come to pass.

# 24

# REFLECTIONS

The door of the studio swung open and suddenly it seemed as if the last twenty years had gone by in a blink. It was May 2011. I was back in Cure land. There was Simon hunched over his bass in skinny black jeans and boots, just like the first time I saw him play in his first band, Lockjaw, thirty-five years ago. Hair slicked back in the best rock and roll tradition. He had hardly changed in all those years, still totally youthful-looking even though he was in his fifties. After a quick scan around the rest of the room I saw Robert's bird's-nest hair, with some salt and pepper stubble and greyish sideburns adding gravitas to the overall impression of an Afghan clan chieftain with the various layers of sweaters and shirts he had on.

I greeted Robert and, with his guitar still around his neck, he embraced me.

'Welcome back, Lol! Good flight?'

I nodded in the affirmative. I had in fact just got off a flight from Los Angeles to London and been chauffeured down to the south coast town of Brighton where The Cure were rehearsing for the two gigs at the Sydney Opera House that ultimately would become the 'Reflections' tour. I was a little jet-lagged, but far too excited to worry about that. I had been thinking about this moment pretty much non-stop for the last few months, ever since Robert replied to my idea that we celebrate the thirtieth anniversary of *Faith* by suggesting that we play the first three Cure albums back to back in Australia. It felt like the perfect way to reconcile the past was to go back to where we first came from musically and celebrate these albums.

When I got to Brighton I had no idea what to expect. I think there was some trepidation on everyone's part that maybe things had gone so far for so long that it might be impossible to put us all back together again. Could we all be on the same stage and expect the old magic to happen?

As it was, no one needed to have worried. It was so natural for us to play music together that it was as if no time had passed at all. We were laughing and joking in a matter of minutes. The teasing started the first time we did a proper stage rehearsal, with us all set up like we would be on stage rather than in circle facing each other like we were in the rehearsal studio.

'Si, I think I've been staring at your arse for most of my life on stage!' Simon was always slightly to the right and front of me.

'That's right, Lol!' He beamed his toothy grin and pulled his bass slightly to one side so I could see that he had cut out a picture from a cycling magazine of his latest cycling hero and pasted it on the back of his bass. The more things changed, the more they stayed the same.

The rehearsals went well, and after a week or so I think we all had the songs locked in. Then it was off to Southampton to rehearse with all the lights and paraphernalia of a live gig in the Gaumont, a big old theatre from the Victorian era about seventy miles along the south coast.

Being back in England and playing all the old Cure songs was very emotional for me as I revisited my teenage years along the Brighton seafront. After rehearsals, everyone else went back to their homes, but I had no home in England anymore so I stayed in a hotel on the shore. In the morning I loved to go for a walk along the famous Brighton seafront and its pebble beach. It holds so many memories for me, as we would often come down to Brighton from Crawley, it being about the same distance as London but much easier to get to. It only took thirty minutes to drive here and a little longer on the train, so we loved to visit as much as possible. Just a straight shot down the A23, through the magical stone pylons at the entrance to greater Brighton, and finally around the Brighton Pavilion, that strange, Indian-inspired royal residence that together with the winding lanes and stony beach give Brighton an eccentric edge that appealed so much to us in our formative years. We saw a lot of bands here, and sometimes we went to the smaller clubs, like the New Regent, that hosted bands like Sham 69, U2 and XTC in a small pub.

In the dusk the lights from the old Georgian hotels spilled out onto Marine Parade – warm yellows and fluorescent blues. A flood of images from my youth came to me in the chilly spring air, and a few tears too as I waxed nostalgic. There was a tattered poster advertising a one-man show featuring Suggs from Madness on the old ironwork balustrade that lined the sea wall, and I realized just how long I'd been gone.

I have always been a restless type. I ran away to Paris and I ran away to California after The Cure ended for me. Robert was never one to travel much outside of touring, and he's pretty much lived within twenty-five miles of his parents' house his whole life. We are like chalk and cheese. Unlike me, Robert always had a reason to go home; whereas I didn't have a home to go to after my mother died. I loved to be on the road touring. Just to get on the bus and go to the next gig, the next town, the next country, was all I ever wanted.

I walked along the parade, looking across the grey sea to the horizon blurred by the leaden sky. A slight salt mist chilled my face as I recalled the pier on which I had enjoyed the innocent fun of teenage summers. The smell of fish and chips wafted out from the shop next to the sweetshop selling sticks of Brighton rock, with the word 'Brighton' running from end to end. I had a picture in my mind of being here as a small boy with my grandmother, her woolly lavender embrace comforting me as we looked out to sea.

At first I wasn't sure of what I was seeing in the early evening gloom. It looked like washed-out Japanese calligraphy on the canvas of the sky. I walked down the shallow steps to the beach path and onto the stone-filled beach. As I got a little closer I could make what looked like a huge black dinosaur skeleton in the water. Finally, I realized it was the West Pier, which had closed in 1975 and was later partially destroyed by fire. The charcoal limbs of the supports were all that remained of the old structure. I vaguely recalled hearing about the mysterious fire that had engulfed the pier several years ago, but to have it here in front of me was shocking. I felt the pull of yesterday, uncomplicated and pure, coming through the years as I stood on the beach. I wondered how it would all turn out as I wandered along the seafront. Was it too late to make it all work again? Had we drifted too far apart? Had we changed too much? The lapping of the water reminded me that change was constant and always with us.

The tears wouldn't stop. It was all too much for me. As my salty tears streamed down my cheeks I found that I could not staunch the flood of emotions that filled me to overflowing, pumping in waves threatening to overcome me as I stared at the small screen on the wall in front of me.

I was deep in the heart of the Sydney Opera House, that iconic bit of 1970s late modern architecture that instantly identifies Sydney, Australia, to the rest of the world. Tearfully I continued to stare at the flickering TV screen above my head. I was waiting in the labyrinthine basement of the Opera House, about to take the stage with my oldest friends for the first time in almost a quarter of a century. I was alone in our dressing room, not that the presence of others would have been enough to stop the tears and the raw, gut-wrenching surge of feelings coursing through my body. My God, real feelings! I never thought I'd experience those again!

I was fifty-two years old and I had known both happiness and tragedy in my life, but nothing had prepared me for the brutal assault my emotions were going through now. A mixture of joy and grief for all that we had experienced together.

On the flat screen television above me were my old bandmates, Robert and Simon, two men I had known since childhood, as well as Roger O'Donnell (a mid-term addition to the band) and Jason Cooper, the 'new boy'. He was unknown to me before this month, but soon proved himself to be a wonderful addition to this remarkable collection of musicians. The Cure, the Imaginary Boys, virtual inventors of alternative rock music, the founders of a worldwide brethren of difference, and as Robert Plant would graciously have it, 'the last great English rock band.'

After over twenty years in the wilderness and self-imposed exile on the edge of the Mojave Desert in California, I was back. The prodigal son had returned once more to the bosom of his family. This was the culmination of a set of improbable circumstances and, I suppose, fate. I don't question these things anymore. I have seen enough of life to know anything is possible, and that the truth is always going to be stranger than fiction. I barely took note of the empty room as I travelled through the past and present in a dizzying hallucinatory vision of all that had brought me to this moment. How did I get here? To understand the present I drifted back into the past.

I imagine that many of us have in our mind's eye a perfect time, a perfect place in our lives when we were supremely happy and fulfilled and felt intensely alive. Sometimes if we are lucky we get that more than once. I have been that lucky and blessed several times in my life. I have also known the pain and dark despair that goes along with not living life on life's terms.

The first few years of The Cure were such an extremely beautiful time in so many ways I never considered that I would be on any other path. It seemed to me to be fated to be that way for ever. We were young men barely out of our boyhood and yet felt as if the universe had decided we should be the ones and I was more than happy to go along with that decision. To travel the world with my best friends doing what we wanted was a dream come true. However, I don't really think any of us had the wisdom to see how things might turn out down the line. If we had the knowledge of what would ultimately happen, would it have made a difference? Would we have changed anything? Probably not. We were being pulled with inexorable force towards greatness or oblivion. Or maybe both.

'Band exiting stage right at the end of this song!'

My reverie was interrupted by the crackle of the film crew's walkie-talkies. They were here to record the momentous undertaking that was 'Reflections', a gigantic concert showcasing our first three albums played back-to-back-to-back in their entirety for the first time ever. The film director's commands cut through my musings and informed me that my compatriots were indeed about to join me in the dressing room during the intermission between album sets, having just completed the whole of *Seventeen Seconds*, our second album, to rapturous applause from the Sydney audience.

Hastily, I dried my tear-stained face as I greeted them with warm hugs and back slaps for a job most definitely well done. I hoped they were unaware of the maelstrom that had been going on in me for the last hour or so but as I greeted them a kindly but concerned look crossed Simon's face, and I knew that he understood.

'All right, Lol? You're up next!'

Simon had had his own emotional upheavals with the band, so it shouldn't have come as a surprise that he would be so perceptive, just like a brother would be.

I only had a few more moments to prepare for the final segment of the show. Now it was my turn, after nearly a quarter of a century, to tread the boards, to trip the light fantastic with my boyhood friends once more. I gently inserted my in-ear monitors, effectively isolating myself from any external noise and focusing my attention on what I needed to hear of the music we were about to perform. I flipped the switch on the radio pack on my belt to activate my own personal monitor sound feed, and as we walked up the stairs to the stage, I could hear the restless Australian audience, anxious to hear *Faith*, the final album of this triple-album show.

As we momentarily paused in the wings of the huge Opera House stage, I pulled one monitor slightly out so I could hear the rest of the band talking as we stood waiting for the house lights to be extinguished. We all wished each other the best of luck, and as I put the monitor back in my ear, the lights dimmed, and for a tiny moment just before the roar of the expectant crowd, there was complete and utter silence in the darkness, like standing on a dark midnight beach hearing the ebb and flow of the waves in the blackness. Then the adrenalin surged forth and . . . show time!

I strode out onto the Opera House stage to my appointed position: stage left behind my bank of percussion and keys. Looking into the sea of faces, I was instantly overflowing with the pure joy I always felt performing on stage as part of The Cure. It was a totally wondrous feeling that took my breath away as I stood on the wooden stage. I had almost forgotten what it felt like. In my ears I could hear the first loping, almost languorous, bass notes of Simon's introduction to the opening song 'Holy Hour'.

I raised the percussion mallet high over my head and brought it down hard to strike the first opening ringing bell-note of the song. It took everything I had to stay upright with the insanely powerful emotional forces racing through me. Ye Gods! I felt like Thor with his hammer! In that instant, as the immeasurable power astounded me, the final vestiges of pain and spiritual baggage I'd been carrying around with me jettisoned away from me like shooting stars into the vast cavernous Opera House. I finally felt like I was completely and utterly free. It was an absolutely transcendent moment.

The rest of the gig was a wondrous blur of sound and light. As I looked into the audience I saw many familiar faces smiling back at me, many older like myself, but still utterly familiar from the recesses of my memories. I always felt completely at ease on the stage with The Cure. It felt as comfortable as sitting in my own home, which I suppose it was, really. Yes, I was finally home again.

Like Einstein, I believe time is relative to what's happening to you and how fast you are travelling. To me, this three-and-a-half hour show passed in an instant. I was transported effortlessly to another dimension of existence where I was entirely in the moment. I was completely present, like a surfer on the crest of a wave, entranced by the music and performing it as a single experience. I knew that the audience could feel this remarkable power because I could see it in their faces from the stage. It was a beautiful feedback loop of love from me to them and back again. Love for my brothers on stage and, finally, a love for myself that cascaded off the stage and spread outwards into the dark Antipodean night and on and on across the endless universe.

# 25

# GHOSTS

For a lot of people, and in popular culture in particular, Los Angeles is the place where people either go to be discovered or destroyed. For me it has been neither. I've found a vitality and strength that I don't think I could have mustered if I'd stayed in jolly old England. The English are far too mean and unforgiving for my sensitive nature. I recognize that that's a valid reason for staying there, to be forged in the fire of English antipathy, but it's not for me. I've had enough of that in my life, I think.

I moved here not just for a change of scenery but to change my entire outlook. That's why I came to California and I think that I did it in a very profound way.

After the 'Reflections' tour, there was a long period of personal reflection for me. It had been wonderful to be out on the road with The Cure again and it felt absolutely marvellous to be on stage playing the old songs. I felt that I had renewed my friendships with Robert, Simon and Roger. I had also got to know Jason for the first time. I had repaired the damage that had been done to my relationships with everybody, but now it was time to move on with my life.

Looking at my transgressions over the last few years, I have come to realize that much can be learnt by acknowledging your sins and then rectifying your wrongs. It's a truism that you end up much repaired by the process. It enabled me to move forward, and in doing so go back and do something that I loved. More than the experience, I was grateful for the self-knowledge and peace that it brought.

While I had suggested to Robert that we do something to celebrate the thirtieth anniversary of *Faith* in 2011, it was his idea to do all three albums – *Three Imaginary Boys*, *Seventeen Seconds* and *Faith* – together. Together we had made it happen, just like the old days.

Returning home, I realized that a fuse had been lit and I needed to do something creative again. It was not enough for me to ride off into the sunset. I felt a kind of restlessness that needed to be addressed. Whatever happens after this life, our time here is limited. There had been several deaths of people involved with The Cure: Malcolm Ross, our tour manager, Mick Kluczynski our production manager, and Billy Mackenzie; but the hardest one to take for me was the death of Gary Biddles, our friend from Horley who had moved to California around the same time as I did. When he worked for the band he was the sort of person who kept everyone's spirits up on the road. He could be a charming, lovable man, but that still didn't stop the end coming for him too soon.

He'd been struggling with alcohol for as long as I could remember. He'd just finished the longest stretch of sobriety he'd had in a decade – almost six months – when he fell off the wagon again. With alcoholics it's like that sometimes. I think that his newly clean body couldn't take the strain of all the alcohol he put into his system and it shut down for good.

His long, painful journey was over, though everyone who knew him wished it hadn't turned out quite like this.

'Bloody hell, Gary,' I had told him years before. 'I don't want to go to your funeral!'

Yet there I was. I wrote a eulogy for him, a tribute to his better moments, for despite all the pain and sorrow, we had had some great times together over the years.

As I stood in the chapel full of people that knew and loved him, a tear fell down my cheek as I bade him farewell. In my Californian exile, he was a link to where I'd come from and where I'd been, my touchstone to the past, and a sad reminder of where I might have gone but for the grace of the universe.

The day after Gary's funeral was a beautiful warm spring desert day, the type that has always filled me with hope and joy since I experienced it the first time back in 1980. It seemed like a positive sign. Without my friend, without all the trappings of success, but with a new-found love of life and a determination to accept the circumstances no matter how they presented themselves, I was hopeful for a better day.

After the sadness of Gary's passing, I searched for something good to come out of it. I tried to figure out exactly what it was, but I didn't know what form it would take. I had already done another album as Levinhurst, this time with the addition of another Imaginary Boy, Michael Dempsey.

It had been a great experience to work together again as older men and find that we still enjoyed the same things and had come together to create again. But there was still a void, something lacking, that I couldn't quite put my finger on.

My son, now grown up, had moved to San Francisco to study and continue his life. In the preceding years, his mother, Lydia, had fallen prey to her own drinking problems and, just before her fiftieth birthday, her liver shut down. My son was like me: motherless at a young age. Of course, he still had his stepmom, Cindy, who loved him very much, as he did her, but it was a sign that he would have to grow up fairly quickly as life moved along apace.

My friend Rob Steen called me from New York and asked me if I wanted to meet a friend who was coming to Los Angeles, a book publisher.

I discussed it with Cindy that night. 'It seems like divine timing,' she said. 'You've always wanted to write a book.'

I thought it over and then I thought some more and I finally realized that it was a way forward, a new path for me to follow. I knew there was something I needed to write, not just a story of the band, but a story of redemption.

# 26

# STANDING ON A BEACH

'In the middle of winter I at last discovered that there
was within me an invincible summer.'

–Albert Camus, 'Return to Tipasa'

The hurricane had come and was almost gone. Hurricane Flossie
had been downgraded to a tropical storm and they were letting
people fly from island to island again. Cindy and I had been to
Lahaina in Maui where we got caught in a downpour. It was so
strong that it felt like we'd taken a swim in the ocean with all of
our clothes on. I had to change into dry clothes in the back of
my car.

Cindy and I were in Maui for a short vacation. We had planned
to fly over to see The Cure in Honolulu – their first time ever
in Hawaii. I had written to Robert to tell him that we would be
coming if the storm allowed. He emailed with words to the effect
that I should not worry about the storm and come see them
anyway. I really wanted to see Robert and the rest of the band. I

hadn't seen them all since the 'Reflections' tour had ended over a year before. So Cindy called the airline to get tickets over to Honolulu and booked a hotel for us to stay in on the night of the gig.

We drove to the airport in Maui and got on the plane to Honolulu. Outside the window the dark remnants of Flossie were scudding about the sky. It was just a short thirty-minute flight to Honolulu and then a quick cab ride to our hotel to check in.

Standing on the balcony of my hotel, looking out over Waikiki beach in the sultry night air, my phone beeped. It was a text from The Cure's tour manager, Nick, with directions and where to get passes to see everyone afterwards.

We showered and got a cab to the gig. The concert was sublime in a way all Cure gigs were, regardless of whether or not I was involved. The Hawaiians, who had never seen The Cure, really loved the show. Afterwards Cindy and I made our way to the dressing room. Robert and I embraced and we had much to discuss, including Gary's tragic passing. We had too much to say to each other.

He invited us back to his hotel on the seafront in Waikiki so that we could continue talking. We stayed up all night and eventually we made our way down to the beach to watch the sun come up. It was near dawn, and The Cure and many members of the crew and entourage were gathered on the beach. The predawn glow heralded the rising sun. Like a black blanket, the sea kept rolling forward, always forward, and gently crashed on the soft sand.

I have always loved Hawaii from the very first time I visited in the early 1990s. Something about the soft warm balmy air and the vibrant colours entranced me and never let me go. I get that beautiful feeling every time I go there and I was happy to be there with my oldest friend.

Robert and I stood on the soft sand slightly apart from the others. He had just come out of the water after a late-night dip. He had his arms around my shoulders and talked quietly into my ear.

'We are older men now, and now that we are older men . . .' his voice trailed off.

I looked up into his face and in that way that old friends have I understood his meaning. Like another late night a million miles away in our youth at Milton Mount Gardens, we understood each other. It was a different day and all that had gone before was quietly fading from our memories. The raw emotions that forced us apart were forgotten, all the hurt and the pain had evaporated, and all that was left was Robert and me in the predawn hour, two Imaginary Boys, standing on a beach.

I returned home to Los Angeles after that night on the beach in Hawaii. The sadness was gone, replaced with gratitude that things had worked out at last. I felt we had gone through so much in getting to this point that now was definitely the time to do something about it.

So I wrote to Robert and said as much. 'I have no talents other than being in The Cure and writing. I can't paint or do anything else creatively but I do have a story to tell.' I remembered when we started we had decided that the means of expressing ourselves was not as important as the actual doing of it. I told him it would be the story of the Imaginary Boys and what happened, and my memories of the memories of why and where. I would try to make some sense of it all. I started on a journey into unknown territory without a map.

*

In the autumn of 2015 I returned to England to finish my research for this book. Now many years absent from her shores, a different reality had shifted my perception of the place where I was born and raised. The place where the Imaginary Boys had started. As Cindy and I travelled around the country, meeting friends and family, I felt a slight unease with just *being* there. I couldn't quite put my finger on it but I felt really weird. As if everything I was experiencing was a little out of focus.

It was great to see old friends, of course, people like Chris Mason our old promotions man at Polydor, with whom I'd recently become reacquainted, and Dave Allen, the producer of several Cure records. People that I hadn't seen in nearly twenty-five years.

The streets of London looked the same, yet different. It was somewhere that I felt should be totally familiar to me but now felt very alien. I wondered if maybe it was me that had changed, or whether the experiences I'd had after I left had wrought some kind of shift in my perceptions.

Cindy and I caught the train down to Crawley. It was much as I recalled it from my youth. When we got there the autumn leaves were blowing around in the car park of the train station, a vortex of browns and yellows mingling in with the dirt of the streets, the same streets that inspired the Imaginary Boys to leave this godforsaken place for good.

I thought after all this time I would have a better understanding of what exactly it was that drove us out and away from this town as young men. Why had we wanted to change our world with such fervour?

I went to see my brother Roger, who still lives in Crawley. We spent many hours talking about the family, about the town, about what it meant for him to live here now as an old man.

Walking around the place it seemed like the stripping away of hope was still a daily occurrence here. Cindy and I passed a pub, one of the many I used to visit in my teens. The same type of people we used to encounter all those years ago, still there. They looked vacant, bored and miserable, same as always. It's a hard thing to describe but I know it when I see it. Apathy and hostility all rolled into one. Living in desperation on this cold little slab of rock on the edge of the Atlantic Ocean. That's my hometown in a nutshell.

The next day we flew out of Gatwick Airport back to Los Angeles. We had checked in and been through all the usual formalities. I was sitting with Cindy in the departure lounge waiting to board, lost in my thoughts about the past, the present, and what to make of it all.

Cindy looked up from her magazine reading, nudging me in the ribs. 'Hey, isn't that? . . .' Then I heard a familiar voice.

'Hello, Lol!' I turned to look at the figure approaching me. It was Porl Thomson! I hadn't seen him in nearly ten years. What was he doing here, I wondered.

He sat down, and after our mutual shock subsided, we started to chat about his plans. He explained that he was moving to California to live in the desert and paint. He had decided only the day before to make the journey and had just got a ticket!

I was amazed. The fact that, unbeknownst to either of us, we had booked the same flight, at the same time, from the same airport, having not seen each other for a decade. Synchronicity or what?

We boarded the plane and, as we took off into the autumn

sky, I had the strong realization that none of this, the book, the journey back from destruction was about me or even Robert. It was about the thing that we had been given that had changed so many people's lives and had once again changed me. The Cure. I understood that no matter what happened now, no matter where I went on this planet or what I might be doing, the dream of a band we had so long ago, the key to our escape out of our boring humdrum lives, was always going to be in me, a part of me. I understood at last that by recapturing that long-ago feeling, I could banish despair. I could forgive everybody everything, including myself. I could finally be cured.

# ACKNOWLEDGEMENTS

TRUE LOVE:

My wife Cindy, whose selfless belief and hope is the engine that gave this book life. You are so wonderful to me.

My son Gray, for his assistance in helping me realize this, his father's story. I am so proud of you and your life's path.

My live-in niece, Cailey, whom I love as my own daughter.

The other two Imaginary Boys, Robert and Michael: I'm truly blessed to have trod the boards and tripped the light fantastic with you both.

Simon Gallup and Pearl (Porl) Thompson: true friends.

My mates: Roger O'Donnell, Jason Cooper, Boris Bransby-Williams, Andy Anderson, Matthieu Hartley, and Phil Thornalley. There in the trenches with me when it counted.

THANKFUL:

Peter McGuigan at Foundry Literary + Media – for your vision, guidance and enthusiasm.

Ben Schafer at Da Capo – for your faith, edits and hiking.

Caspian Dennis at Abner Stein – for your sterling UK agency.

Richard Milner at Quercus – for your encouragement and editing.

Jim Ruland, my writing mentor – for your constructive guidance and help in refining my work into a voice worth hearing.

Rob Steen – for starting the ball rolling.

Deirdre Smerillo – for crossing the t's and dotting the i's

Pat Carpenter at Quercus – for UK art direction.

Sara DeNobrega and Mary Mallison – financial controls.

Marion Gibb – royalty.

Pearl Thompson – for the Mojave portrait, logo and star art.

Brennan Wheeler – for art scans and artistic directions.

Pamela Des Barres – for encouraging my writing ambitions.

Max Bean and John Lopez at Scout Idea Ranch – for providing the writing room and a year I won't forget.

Allison Van Etten – for caffeine and camaraderie.


WITH LOVE:

Martin Judd and Steve Forrester – for your enduring friendship and love.

Chris Mason – for heart and help along the way.

Tom, Adam, Brennan, George, K.C., Jeff, Joel and Kevin – for sharing your wisdom, strength and hope with me.

My family worldwide – for being there with your loving care.


Richard and Jill Smith

John and Margaret Taw

Frankie Bell

Richard and Anne Carroll

Lydie Goubard

Richard Bellia

HONORABLE MENTIONS:

Chris Parry – for helping us become The Cure.

Ita Martin – for your part in that also.

Gerald Greene and Martin Hopewell – true gents.

David M. Allen – my erudite friend.

Mike Hedges – first lord of sonics.

Angus 'Mac' MacPhail – truly light fantastic.

Tim Pope – visionary direction.

Sue Berry – for encouragement and questions.

Doug Dearth – for many a good idea.

Duff McKagan – for words of wisdom.

Mike Ferrucci – for sharing your knowledge.

Meghan Gohil – for invaluable assistance, sonically and otherwise.

Stefan Goldby – digital direction. It's all about the chemistry!

Jay Frank – for your help and friendship over the years.

Marjy Taylor – putting the show on the road.

G. Wilson – Guru of Fit.

Craig Parker and COF – getting the word out.

In the course of writing this book, I consulted several sources
that I want to thank here:

    www.cure-concerts.de (The Cure Concerts Guide)

    *Ten Imaginary Years* (Zomba Books)

    www.allmusic.com (All Music Guide)

    www.facebook.com/picturesofyouus/– Autumn Jade

In memoriam: Gary Biddles; Mick Kluczynski; Malcolm Ross;
Billy Mackenzie; David 'Sandy' Sandels; Brian Adsett.

# INDEX

**Lol Tolhurst** is a musician, performer and writer. He is best known as a founding member of the band that virtually invented alternative music, The Cure. Formed in 1976, The Cure is one of the most influential, successful and critically acclaimed bands of its generation.

As The Cure's drummer Lol toured the globe many times over, supporting the ground-breaking albums *Three Imaginary Boys*, *Seventeen Seconds*, *Faith* and *Pornography*, among others. He took on keyboard duties in the mid-eighties until his departure from the band in 1989, at the time of their master-work *Disintegration*.

In the early nineties Lol relocated to Southern California where he continues to write, record and tour with his own band Levinhurst. More recently, 2011 saw a momentous reunion tour with his former band mates and Lol performed with The Cure for the first time in over twenty years.